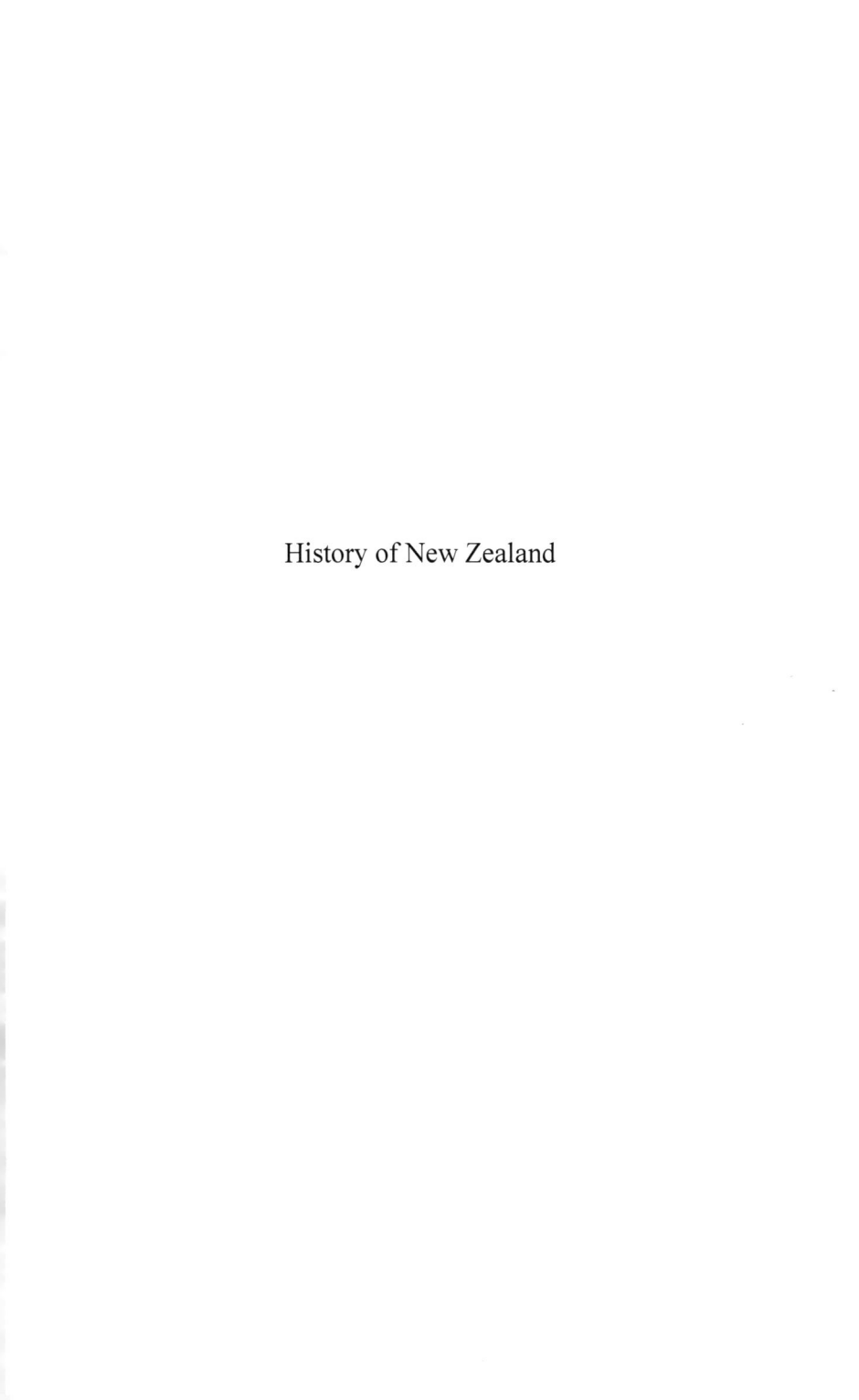

History of New Zealand

History of New Zealand

the Land of the Long White Cloud

William P. Reeves
John W. Gregory
David P. Gooding

History and Civilization Collection

LM Publishers

Part I
New Zealand and its General History[1]

Chapter I

New Zealand is an Island country of the southwestern Pacific Ocean. Unlike Australia, its geological structure is unusually varied, and owing to its instability, it includes, for its size, an unusually complete series of marine sedimentary rocks. It has, moreover, been a volcanic area of long-continued activity. The physical geography of New Zealand is closely connected with its geological structure, and is dominated by two intersecting lines of mountains and earth movements. The Southern Alps, the backbone of the South Island, rest on a foundation of coarse gneisses and schists, that are quite unrepresented in the North Island. The continuation of this line of old rocks is occupied by the basins of the Wanganui river and Taupo. E. Suess therefore suggested that the northern continuation of the Alps had foundered, and its summits been buried beneath the Pliocene marine rocks of the Wanganui basin and the volcanic rocks of the Taupo area.

The oldest rocks are Archean, represented by the band of gneisses and schists exposed along the western foot of the Southern Alps. To the south of the district in southern Westland, where the Alps have passed out to sea, the Archeans become more extensive; for they spread eastward and underlie the whole of the dissected tableland of Otago. It has been suggested that the jasperoids and diabases of the Tarawera Mountains on the North Island may be of Upper

---

[1] Based on the work of William P. Reeves and John Walter Gregory.

Archean age, from their resemblance to the Heathcotian rocks of Australia. No Cambrian rocks have as yet been discovered, but the Ordovician system is represented by the Aorere beds in the north-western part of the South Island. Here they contain numerous graptolites, including *Tetragraptus*, *Dichograptus* and *Didymograptus*. The Silurian system is represented by the Baton river beds to the west of the Aorere beds, occurring in the basin of the Motueka river, which flows into Tasman Bay. The Devonian system is well exposed in the Reefton mining field. The Carboniferous system includes either the whole or a large part of the Maitai beds. The Maitai beds include a thick mass of slates and sandstones, which form the bulk of the Southern Alps, whence branches extend southeastward to the coast. The beds take their name from the Maitai river near Nelson; they are largely developed in the mountains of the Tararua-Ruahine-Raukumara chain, on the eastern side of the North Island; they occur in the Kaikoura Mountains, and an outlier forms Mount Torlesse, near the eastern edge of the Southern Alps, west of Christchurch. The Maitai beds have generally been considered to be Carboniferous from the presence of species of *Productus* found in the Permo-Carboniferous of New South Wales. But Professor Park has obtained Jurassic fossils in the Maitai series; so that it will probably be ultimately divided between the Carboniferous and Jurassic. The two systems should, however, be separable by an unconformity, unless the Maitai series also includes representatives of the Kaihiku series (the New Zealand Permian), and of the Wairoa series, which is Triassic.

New Zealand includes representatives of all the three Mesozoic systems. The Hokanui group comprises the Triassic Wairoa and Otapira beds, and the Jurassic Mataura beds. The Wairoa series includes marine limestones characterized by *Monotis salinaria*, and the Otapira series is characterized by *Spiriferina spatulata*. The Mataura beds are largely of estuarine formation; they contain oil shales and gas springs.

The Cretaceous system includes the Waipara series, a belt of chalky limestones with some phosphate beds at Clarendon in eastern Otago. Their fossils include belemnites, ammonites, scaphites and marine saurians, such as *Cimoliosaurus*. These Cretaceous limestones are inter bedded with glauconitic greensands, as at Moeraki Point in eastern Otago. The second type, of Cretaceous is a terrestrial formation, and is important as it contains the rich coal seams of Greymouth, Westport and Seddonville, which yield a high quality of steam coal. Cretaceous coals have long been worked in the North Island, north of Auckland, on the shores of the Bay of Islands, where the age of the coal is shown by its occurrence under the Whangarei or Waimio limestone.

The Cainozoic system is represented by Oligocene, Miocene, Pliocene and Pleistocene beds. The best-known Oligocene rocks are the limestones of Oamaru and the brown-coal measures of Waikato. The Oamaru limestones have been largely used for building stones; they are a pure white limestone, largely made up of foraminifera, bryozoa and shell fragments, and contain the teeth of sharks (*e.g. Carcharodon*) and of toothed whales such as *Squalodon serratus*. In southern Otago the Oligocene beds are brown coals and lignites with oil shales, which, at Orepuki, contain 47% of oil and gas, with 8% of water. The Miocene Pareora beds occur to the height of 3000 or 4000 ft. above sea-level, in both the North and South Islands. Some of its fossils also occur in the Oamaru series, but the two series are unconformable. In Westland the Miocene includes the Moutere gravels, which rest on the summit of Mount Greenland, 4900 ft. above sea-level.

Marine beds of the Pliocene are best developed in the Wanganui basin. They consist of fine clays with nodular calcareous concretions rich in fossils. The Pleistocene system in the South Island includes glacial deposits, which prove a great extension of the New Zealand glaciers, especially along the western coast. The glaciers must have reached the sea at Cascade Point in southern Westland. On the eastern side of the Alps the glaciers appear to have been confined to the mountain valleys. The Pleistocene swamp deposits are rich in the bones of the moa and other gigantic extinct birds, which lived on until they were exterminated by the Maori. The Cainozoic volcanic history of New Zealand begins in the Oligocene, when the high volcanic domes of Dunedin and Banks Peninsula were built up. The Dunedin lavas including tephrites and kenytes correspond to the dacite eruptions in the volcanic history of Victoria. The building up of these domes of lavas of intermediate chemical type was followed by the eruption of sheets of andesites and rhyolites in the Thames Goldfield and the Taupo volcanic district. The volcanic activity of the Taupo district lasted into the Pleistocene, and the last eruptions contributed many of its chief geographical features.

Chapter II

The date of man's arrival in New Zealand is uncertain. All that can be safely asserted is that by the 14th century A.D. Polynesian canoe-men had reached its northern shores in successive voyages. By 1642 they had spread to South Island, for there Abel Jansen Tasman found them when, in the course of his circuitous voyage from Java in the "Heemskirk," he chanced upon the archipelago, coasted along much of its western side, though without venturing to land, and gave it the name it still bears. One hundred and thirty-seven years later, Cook, in the barque "Endeavour," gained a much fuller knowledge of the coasts, which he circumnavigated, visited again and again, and mapped out with fair accuracy. He annexed the country, but the British government disavowed the act. After him came other navigators, French, Spanish, Russian and American; and, as the 18th century neared its end, came sealers, whalers and trading-schooners in quest of flax and timber.

English missionaries, headed by Samuel Marsden, landed in 1814, to make for many years but slow progress. They were hindered by murderous tribal wars in which imported muskets more than decimated the Maori. Still, cruel experience and the persevering preaching of the missionaries gradually checked the fighting, and by the year 1839 it could be claimed that peace and Christianity were in the ascendant. So far the British government had resisted the considerable pressure brought to bear in Downing Street in favour of annexation. In vain Edward Gibbon Wakefield, organizer of colonizing associations, prayed and intrigued for permission to repeat in New Zealand the experiment tried by him in South, Australia. Lord Glenelg, the colonial minister, had the support of the missionaries in withstanding Wakefield's New Zealand Company, which at length resolved in desperation to send an agent to buy land wholesale in New Zealand and despatch a shipload of settlers thither without official permission. Before, however, the "Tory" had thus sailed for Cook Strait, it had become known to the English government that a French colonizing company — *La Compagnie Nanto-Bordelaise* — was forming, under the auspices of Louis Philippe, to anticipate or oust Wakefield. Further obstruction was manifestly futile, and the British authorities reluctantly instructed Captain Hobson, R.N., to make his way to northern New Zealand with a dormant commission of lieutenant-governor in his pocket and authority to annex the country to Australia by peaceful arrangement with the natives. Hobson landed in the Bay of Islands on the 22nd of January 1840, hoisted the Union Jack, and had little difficulty in inducing most of the native chiefs to accept the queen's sovereignty at the price of guaranteeing to the tribes by the treaty of Waitangi possession of their lands, forests and fisheries. Some French settlers, convoyed by a man-of-war, reached Akaroa in South Island in the May following. But Hobson had forestalled them, and those who remained in the country became British subjects. Meanwhile, a week after Hobson's arrival, Wakefield's colonists had sailed into Port Nicholson, and proposed to take possession of immense tracts which the New Zealand Company claimed to have bought from the natives, and for which colonists had in good faith paid the company. Other bands of company's settlers in like manner landed at Nelson, Wanganui and New Plymouth, to be met with the news that the British government would not recognize the company's purchases. Then followed weary years of ruinous delay and official inquiry, during which Hobson died after founding Auckland. His successor, Fitzroy, drifted into an unsuccessful native war. A strong man, Captain Grey, was at last sent over from Australia to restore peace and rescue the unhappy colony from bankruptcy and despair. Grey, much the best of the absolute governors, held the balance fairly between the white and brown races, and bought large tracts of land for colonization, including the whole South Island, where the Presbyterian settlement of

Otago and the Anglican settlement of Canterbury were established by the persevering Wakefield.

In 1852 the mother-country granted self-government, and, after much wrangling and hesitation, a full parliamentary system and a responsible ministry were set going in 1856. For twenty years thereafter the political history of the colony consisted of two long, intermittent struggles — one constitutional between the central government (first seated in Auckland, but after 1864 in Wellington) and the powerful provincial councils, of which there were nine charged with important functions and endowed with the land revenues and certain rating powers. The other prolonged contest was racial — the conflict between settler and Maori. The native tribes, brave, intelligent and fairly well armed, tried, by means of a league against land-selling and the election of a king, to retain their hold over at least the central North Island. But their kings were incompetent, their chiefs jealous and their tribes divided. Their style of warfare, too, caused them to throw away the immense advantages which the broken bush-clad island offered to clever guerrilla partisans. They were poor marksmen, and had but little skill in laying ambuscades. During ten years of intermittent marching and fighting between 1861 and 1871 the Maori did no more than prove that they had in them the stuff to stand up against fearful odds and not always to be worsted. Round Mount Egmont, at Orakau, at Tauranga and in the Wanganui jungles, they more than once held their own against British regiments and colonial riflemen. The storming of their favourite positions—stockades strengthened with rifle-pits—was often costly; and a strange anti-Christian fanaticism, the Hau-Hau cult, encouraged them to face the white men's bullets and bayonets. But even their fiercest fighting leaders, Rewi and Te Kooti, scarcely deserved the name of generals. Some of the best Maori fighters, such as the chiefs Ropata and Kemp, were enlisted on the white side, and with their tribesmen did much to make unequal odds still more unequal. Had General Pratt or General Cameron, who commanded the imperial forces from 1860 to 1865, had the rough vigour of their successor, General Chute, or the cleverness of Sir George Grey, the war might have ended in 1864. Even as it was the resistance of the Maori was utterly worn, out at last. After 1871 they fought no more. The colonists too, taught by the sickening delay and the ruinous cost of the war to revert to conciliatory methods, had by this time granted the natives special representation in parliament. A tactful native minister, Sir Donald McLean, did the rest. Disarmament, roads and land-purchasing enabled settlement to make headway again in the North Island after twelve years of stagnation. Grey quarrelled with his masters in Downing Street, and his career in the imperial service came to an end in 1868. His successors, Sir George Bowen, Sir James Ferguson, the marquess of Normanby and Sir Hercules Robinson, were content to be constitutional governors and to respect strictly the behests of the colonial office. Meanwhile the industrial story of New Zealand may be summed up in the words wool and gold. Extremely well suited for sheep-farming, the natural pastures of the country were quickly parcelled out into huge pastoral crown leases, held by prosperous licensees, the squatters, who in many cases aspired to become a country gentry by turning their leases into freeholds. So profitable was sheep-farming seen to be that energetic settlers began to burn off the bracken and cut and burn the forest in the North Island and sow English grasses on the cleared land. In the South artificial grassing went on for a time hand in hand with cereal-growing, which by 1876 seemed likely to develop on a considerable scale, thanks to the importation of American agricultural machinery, which the settlers were quick to utilize. Even more promising appeared the gold-fields. Gold had been discovered in 1853. Not, however, until 1861 was a permanent field found—that lighted upon by Gabriel Read at Tuapeka in Otago. Thereafter large deposits were prontably exploited in the south and West of South Island and in the Thames and Coromandel districts of the Auckland province. Gold-mining went through the usual stages of alluvial washing, deep sinking and quartz-reef working. Perhaps its chief value was that it brought many thousand diggers to the colony, most of whom stayed there. Pastoral and mining enterprise, however, could not save the settlers from severe depression in the years 1867 to 1871. War had brought progress in the north to a standstill; in the south wool-growing and gold-mining showed their customary fluctuations. For a moment it seemed as though the manufacture of hemp from the native *Phormium tenax* would become a great industry. But that suddenly collapsed, to the ruin of many, and did not revive for a number of years.

In 1870 peace had not yet been quite won; industry was depressed; and the scattered and scanty colonists already owed seven millions sterling. Yet it was at this moment that a political financier, Sir Julius Vogel, at that moment colonial treasurer in the ministry of Sir William Fox, audaciously proposed that the central government should borrow ten millions, make roads and railways, buy land from the natives and import British immigrants. The House of Representatives, at first aghast, presently voted four millions as a beginning. Coinciding as the carrying out of Vogel's policy did with a rising wool market, it for a time helped to bring great prosperity, an influx of people and much genuine settlement. Fourteen millions of borrowed money, spent in ten years, were on the whole well laid out. But prosperity brought on a feverish land speculation; prices of wool and wheat fell in 1879 and went on falling. Faulty banking ended in a crisis, and 1879 proved to be the first of sixteen years of almost unbroken depression. Still, eight prosperous years had radically changed the colony. Peace, railways, telegraphs (including cable connexion with Europe), agricultural machinery and a larger population had carried New Zealand beyond the primitive stage. The provincial councils had been swept away in 1876, and their functions divided between the central authority and small powerless local bodies. Politics, cleared of the cross-issues of provincialism and Maori warfare, took the usual shape of a struggle between wealth and radicalism. Sir George Grey, entering colonial politics as a Radical leader, had appealed eloquently to the work-people as well as to the Radical "intellectuals," and though unable to retain office for very long he had compelled his opponents to pass manhood suffrage and a triennial parliaments act. A national education system, free, non-religious and compulsory, was established in 1877. The socialistic bent of New Zealand was already discernible in a public trustee law and a state life insurance office. But the socialistic labour wave of later years had not yet gathered strength. Grey proved himself a poor financier and a tactless party leader. A land-tax imposed by his government helped to alarm the farmers. The financial collapse of 1879 left the treasury empty. Grey was manœuvred out of office, and Sir John Hall and Sir Harry Atkinson, able opponents, took the reins with a mission to reinstate the finances and restore confidence.

Roughly speaking, both the political and the industrial history of the colony from 1879 to 1908 may be divided into two periods. The dividing line, however, has to be drawn in different years. Sixteen years of depression were followed, from 1895 to 1908, by thirteen years of great prosperity. In politics nearly twelve years of Conservative government, or at least capitalistic predominance in public affairs, were succeeded by more than seventeen years of Radicalism. Up to January 1891 the Conservative forces which overthrew Sir George Grey in 1879 controlled the country in effect though not always in name, and for ten years progressive legislation was confined to a mild experiment in offering crown lands on perpetual lease, with a right of purchase (1882), a still milder instalment of local option (1881) and an inoffensive Factories Act (1886). In September 1889, however, Sir George Grey succeeded in getting parliament to abolish the last remnant of plural voting. Finance otherwise absorbed attention; by 1880 the public debt had reached £25,000,000, against which the chief new asset was 1300 m. of railway, and though the population had increased to nearly half a million, the revenue was stagnant. A severe property-tax and an increase of customs duties in 1879 only for a moment achieved financial equilibrium. Although taxation was seconded by a drastic, indeed harsh, reduction of public salaries and wages (which were cut down by one-tenth all round) yet the years 1884, 1887 and 1888 were notable for heavy deficits in the treasury. Taxation, direct and indirect, had to be further increased, and as a means of gaining support for this in 1888 Sir Harry Atkinson, who was responsible for the budget, gave the customs tariff a distinctly protectionist complexion.

During the years 1879-1890 the leading political personage was Sir Harry Atkinson. He, however, withdrew from party politics when, in December 1890, he was overthrown by the Progressives under John Ballance. Atkinson's party never rallied from this defeat, and a striking change came over public life, though Ballance, until his death in April 1893, continued the prudent financial policy of his predecessor. The change was emphasized by the active intervention in politics of the trade unions. These bodies decided in 1889 and 1890 to exert their influence in returning workmen to parliament, and where this was impossible, to secure pledges from middle-class candidates. This plan was first put into execution at the general election of 1890, which was held during the industrial excitement aroused by the Australasian maritime strike of that year. It had, however, been fully arranged before the conflict broke out. The number of labour members thus elected to the general assembly was small, never more than six, and no independent labour party of any size was formed. But the influence of labour in the Progressive or, as it preferred to be called, Liberal party, was considerable, and the legislative results noteworthy. Ballance at once raised the pay of members from £150 to £240 a year, but otherwise directed his energies to constitutional reforms and social experiments. These did not interfere with the general lines of Atkinson's strong and cautious finance, though the first of them was the abolition of his direct tax upon all property, personal as well as real, and the substitution therefor of a landtax of 1d. in the £ on capital value, and also of a graduated tax upon unimproved land values, and an income-tax also graduated, though less elaborately. The graduated land-tax, which has since been stiffened, rises from nothing at all upon the smaller holdings to 3d. in the £ upon the capital value of the largest estates — those worth £210,000 and upwards. Buildings, improvements, and live stock are exempted. In the case of mortgaged estates the mortgagor is exempted from ordinary land-tax in proportion to the amount of his mortgage. On that the mortgagee pays at the rate of ¾d. in the £. In 1896 municipal and rural local bodies were allowed to levy rates upon unimproved land values if authorized to do so by a vote of their electors, and by the end of 1901 some sixty bodies, amongst them the city of Wellington, had made use of this permission. The income-tax is not levied on incomes drawn from land. In 1891 the tenure of members of the legislative council or nominated Upper House, which had hitherto been for life, was altered to seven years. In 1892 a new form of land tenure was introduced, under which large areas of crown lands were leased for 999 years, at an unchanging rent of 4% on the prairie value. Crown tenants under this system had no right of purchase. In the same year a law was also passed authorizing government to repurchase private land for closer settlement.

On Ballance's sudden death in April 1893 his place was taken by Richard Seddon, minister of mines in the Ballance cabinet, whose first task was to pass the electoral bill of his predecessor, which granted the franchise to all adult women. This was adopted in September 1893, though the majority for it in the Upper House was but two votes. In 1893 was enacted the Alcoholic Liquor Control Act, greatly extending local option. In 1894 was passed the Advances to Settlers Act, under which state money-lending to farmers on mortgage of freehold or leasehold land was at once begun. The money is lent by an official board, which deals with applications and manages the finance of the system. In thirteen years the board lent out over five millions and a half, and received repayment of nearly two millions of principal as well as over one million in interest at 5%. Borrowers must repay ½% of their principal half-yearly, and may repay as much more as they choose. Profits are paid over to an assurance fund. No losses were incurred during the thirteen years above mentioned. The net profit made by the board in 1906 was £45,000. The same year also saw the climax of a series of laws passed by the Progressives affecting the relations of employers and workmen. These laws deal with truck, employers' liability, contractors' workmen, the recovery of workmen's wages, the hours of closing in shops and merchants' offices, conspiracy amongst trade unionists, and with factories, mines, shipping and seamen. In 1895 a law controlling servants' registry offices was added. In 1897 all shipowners engaging in the coasting trade of the colony were compelled to pay the colonial rate of wages.

Meanwhile the keystone of the regulative system had been laid by the passing of the Industrial Conciliation and Arbitration Act, under which disputes between employers and unions of workers are compulsorily settled by state tribunals; strikes and lock-outs are virtually prohibited in the case of organized work-people, and the conditions of employment in industries may be, and in many cases are, regulated by public boards and courts. The years 1896, 1897 and 1898 were marked by struggles over the Old Age Pensions Bill, which became law in November 1898. In 1898 the divorce law was amended on the lines of the Stephen Act of New South Wales, a change which helped to treble the number of petitions for divorce in the next seven years. In 1898 also the municipal franchise, hitherto confined to ratepayers, was greatly widened; in 1900 the English system of compensation to workmen for accidents suffered in their trade was adopted with some changes, one of the chief being that contested claims are adjudicated upon cheaply and expeditiously by the same arbitration court that decides industrial disputes. In 1895 borrowing on a larger scale was begun, and in twelve years twice as many millions were added to the public debt.

Before this the Ballance ministry had organized two new departments, those of labour and agriculture. The former supervises the labour laws and endeavours to deal with unemployment; the latter has done much practical teaching, inspection, &c. Butter, cheese and New Zealand hemp are by law graded and branded by departmental inspectors before export. For some years the government has worked two coal-mines profitably, chiefly to supply its railways. In 1907 the net profit on these was over £8000 The continued success of the government life insurance othce led in 1899 to the setting up of an accidents insurance office, and, in 1903, of a state fire insurance office.

The outbreak of the Boer War in October 1899 was followed in New Zealand by a prompt display of general and persistent warlike enthusiasm: politics ceased to be the chief topic of interest; the general election of 1899 was the most languid held for fifteen years. The desire of New Zealanders to strike a blow for the mother-country took the practical shape of dispatching to South Africa ten successive contingents.

After gaining office at the beginning of 1891 the Ballance-Seddon party had to struggle with the last four years of the period of depression. In 1895 began a marked commercial revival, mainly due to the steady conversion of the colony's waste lands into pasture; the development of frozen meat and dairy exports; the continuous increase of the output of coal; the invention of gold-dredging; the revival and improvement of hemp manufacture; the exploiting of the deposits of kauri gum; the reduction in the rates of interest on mortgage money; a general rise in wages, obtained without strikes, and partially secured by law, which has increased the spending power of the working classes. Undoubtedly also commercial confidence was restored by the reconstruction in 1895 of the Bank of New Zealand, and activity has been stimulated by large public loans, while more cautious banking and the systems of taxation and rating on land values, adopted in

1891 and 1896, have done something to check land speculation.

Between 1879 and 1908 seven governors represented the crown in New Zealand. Of these Sir Hercules Robinson and Sir Arthur Gordon had but brief reigns; Sir Arthur Gordon quitted the colony in June 1882. His successor, Sir William Drummond Jervois, arrived in January 1883, and held office until March 1889. The earl of Onslow, who followed, landed in June 1889, and resigned in February 1892. The next governor, the earl of Glasgow, remained in the colony from June 1892 to February 1897, and was succeeded in August of the last-mentioned year by the earl of Ranfurly, who did not retire until 1904. His place was then taken by Lord Plunket. The cabinets which administered the affairs of the colony during these years were those of Sir Frederick Whitaker, Sir Harry Atkinson (3), Sir Robert Stout (2), Mr Ballance, Mr Seddon, Mr Hall-Jones and Sir Joseph Ward. Mr Hall-Jones's short premiership was an interregnum made necessary by the absence of Sir Joseph Ward in England at the moment of Mr Seddon's death. Except in one disturbed month, August 1884, when there were three changes of ministry in eighteen days, executives were more stable than in the colony's earlier years. The party headed by Ballance, Seddon and Ward held office without a break for more than seventeen years, a result mainly due to the general support given to its agrarian and labour policy by the smaller farmers and the working classes. Sir Arthur Gordon differed from his ministers — Hall and Atkinson — on their native policy. Lords Onslow and Glasgow came into collision with Ballance over a proposal to nominate a large batch of Liberals to the then Conservative legislative council. The dispute was by consent referred to the secretary for the colonies. and the decision from Downing Street was in Ballance's favour. The governor's salary, reduced in 1887, was restored to £7500 a year in 1900. An Immigrants Exclusion Act voted by the general assembly in 1896 did not receive the royal assent; but, by arrangement with the colonial office, another measure, giving power to impose a reading test on aliens landing in the colony, became law in 1899.

The presence of New Zealand premiers at the imperial conferences in London in 1897, 1903 and 1907 helped to bring the colony into conscious touch with imperial public questions. Among the results were the increase of the naval contribution (first to £40,000 and then, in 1908, to £100,000), and the imposition in 1903 and again in 1907 of severe discriminating duties against imports from foreign countries.

Part II

Picturesque New Zealand

Chapter I

Far down beneath the Southern Cross, in the region of fabled Lemuria, is a long, bright land; a land of wondrous beauty and pleasing variety. There argent slopes of lofty ranges sweep down to forests of ineffable loveliness that shelter palm and fern and flowering tree. There great glaciers, littered with their rocky thefts from adjacent mountains, perpetually grind and groove, and eventually feed roaring, tawny rivers. There inroading sea and straggling lake, that fill ice-carved basins terminating far below the tides, form pictures of wild and captivating beauty.

In this land are astonishing contrasts. There the weird and the beautiful are seen side by side; fire and steam near snow and ice; spouting geyser beside cold stream; boiling, sputtering mud adjoining still, translucent depths.

Such, and much more, I found in months of travel in the Dominion of New Zealand, "The Long White Cloud," "The Far-stretching Land"; a land of the moa and the Maori. New Zealand is, indeed, a continent in miniature. No other country of the world has so great a variety of scenic charms within so small a compass. This insular unit of the British Empire is little larger than Colorado. Yet it has mountains that rival the Alps of Switzerland, and sounds that recall the fiords of Norway. It has weird fire-born wonders exceeding in extent those of the Yellowstone National Park; it has canyons with depths matching those of the Yosemite and the Grand Canyon of Arizona. In the wealth of its flora, in the poverty of its mammalia, and in its peculiar flightless avifauna, it is one of the most remarkable countries of the earth.

In the awe-inspiring, the majestic, the enchanting, the unique, Aotearoa abounds; in diversity it is equally rich.

Not all that I had read of New Zealand did I find there. Some of the glories detailed had departed with the advance of settlement. Further, some extollers of New Zealand scenery had exaggerated; others had misplaced words of praise, applying them to hills and deforested mountains in a delirium that would have been more excusable in descriptions of the shadowy lakes and sounds and the glittering, ice-worn Alps.

But in accounts of New Zealand's physical magnificence delirious touches may be expected, especially from the New Zealander; The New Zealander who knows Niu Tirani's "Cloud Piercer" and its myriad satellites, its fiords of lake and sea, and the moss and fern-grown cliffs of its rushing canyon rivers, is proud of nature's gifts to the land of Kia ora, and in his recitals thereof there is enthusiasm. The New Zealander's pride is justifiable, it is contagious. And they from overseas who have seen these wonderful creations are prone to join him in his panegyrics. To these fortunate ones, this "Italy of the South," this "Japan of the South Pacific," is one of the most fascinating quarters of the globe.

MOUNT COOK FROM THE HOOKER RIVER

Though this favored land is small, its total area being about 104,000 square miles, the boundaries within which its executive authority is administered are far apart. Including its island possessions, New Zealand has governmental jurisdiction within forty-two degrees of longitude and within forty-five degrees of latitude. Its northernmost possession, near the pearl-shell lagoon of Penrhyn, is only eight degrees below the Equator, while its southernmost limits, the mountainous Campbell Islands, are more than three thousand miles from Penrhyn's shoals. New Zealand itself throws its boot-like form a thousand miles along the Tasman Sea, which separates it from Australia, to the west, but its extreme breadth is only a fifth as great.

The largest land divisions of New Zealand are the North Island, about the size of Pennsylvania; the South Island, approximating the area of Florida; and Stewart Island, slightly more than half as large as Rhode Island.

New Zealand is largely mountainous. For this reason less than half its surface is suitable for agriculture. In the South Island, the more mountainous of the two main islands, nearly a fourth of the total area is valueless either for cultivation or grazing. In this island elevations of from eight to ten thousand feet are common, the highest peaks being in the Southern Alps, the island's backbone. In the North Island few of the mountains are more than four thousand feet high, and only on the loftiest of them, steaming Ruapehu, are glaciers found.

In its climatic conditions New Zealand has been likened to Italy, with which it closely corresponds in latitude. To a large extent New Zealand is a rainy land, but as the majority of its precipitations are at night and in the early morning, parts of it have sunshine records equal to some of the best obtained in Italy. In the North Island the annual rainfall is fifty-one inches, and in the South Island forty-six inches. One of the rainiest places is on the west coast of the South Island. At Hokitika, a worthy rival of Washington's Neah Bay, the annual rainfall has averaged one hundred and fifteen inches for more than a quarter of a century. Yet Hokitika is not New Zealand's rainiest place. In Dusky Sound an annual precipitation of more than two hundred inches has been recorded. Despite the assertion that New Zealand has a plentiful and regular rainfall, many parts less favored with moisture than Hokitika would like some of its rainy days, and none more so than Otago, where irrigation has been promoted to relieve the dryness of tussock plains.

Another distinguishing feature of New Zealand's climate is its windiness. Its mountains are the playground of terrific winds, and its four thousand miles of coast-line is pounded by some of the heaviest seas known to the world.

The climate of New Zealand is both varied and healthful, due to the Dominion's isolation, wide range of latitude, and the proximity of all its parts to the ocean. As for its healthful qualities, for the last twenty years the country's average annual death rate has been less than ten per one thousand inhabitants, one of the lowest death rates ever recorded anywhere.

Not for its physical charms nor its climatic characteristics, however, is New Zealand best known to the world. Its recent world fame rests mainly on its humanities to man. New Zealand has long been singled out as a striking example of the Utopian tendencies of this age. Its initiativeness, its independence and progressiveness have marked it conspicuously, and the world echoes and reechoes with its well-earned encomiums. Although New Zealand has abundant opportunity to become more democratic still, it has set an example for legislation in favor of the people that might well be imitated by earth's greatest nations.

In this stronghold of liberalism there is, in a happy degree, government of, by, and for the people. There the "interests" do not exercise a dominating influence; for "special privilege" it is practically a barren field. There the evils of private commercial monopoly are not tolerated. "Trusts" have been sighted from afar and warned off, and the growing menace of those uncovered within New Zealand has been curbed by legislation.

In New Zealand, Labor and Capital meet as "man to man." Wisely conceived labor laws provide protection for both, and, combined with rational land-tax and land-settlement legislation, have for more than twenty years assured general industrial peace and widespread prosperity. For poor and suffering humanity of all ages substantial State provision has been made. There the people are the predominating owners of public utilities; with them State ownership has become so varied and general that it has been called State socialism.

This land of model activities, now the home of multitudes from overseas, once was shunned and dreaded. In 1642, Abel Tasman, first of white men to navigate New Zealand waters, had little more than sighted it before he was attacked by Maoris, who slew three of the Zeehaan's crew, causing him to hasten back toward his Batavian base without setting a foot on shore. One hundred and twenty-seven years later, in the year of his discovery of New Zealand, Captain Cook, first of Europeans to land in New Zealand, was inhospitably received in Poverty Bay—so named by him because he could obtain no food supplies there. In an encounter between Maoris and members of his crew, one native was shot, and although the manner of his death astounded his comrades, they continued to defy the strangers.

For many years thereafter European navigators, terrified by these and other tales of deadly strife and, often, bloody feasts, feared to land on New Zealand's inhospitable coasts. It was then, in truth, a clime where men ate each other, and it was one of the most contentious places on the globe. From ghostly Te Reinga to the "Sea of the Greenstone," from treacherous Poverty Bay to the iron-sanded coasts of Taranaki, there was almost constant warfare among the natives. In later times they battled against their white invaders, and little more than forty years have passed since Maori and pakeha last clashed together in war.

New Zealand is no longer shunned. The influences of Christianity and civilization, first exerted on the Maoris by Marsden in 1814, and later by a host of other missionaries, have tamed the savage breast and forever stayed the hostile arm. The colony that the British Parliament once adjudged as too dangerous to be even the site of a convict settlement, and over which England delayed proclaiming her sovereignty until after seventy years of virtual possession, is now pointed to as a model in social achievement. To-day New Zealand is the home of more than a million white people, and every year it is the goal of thousands of immigrants.

On their arrival these immigrants find conditions remarkably different from those encountered by their predecessors of twenty-five years ago. No longer does the existence of great estates, of dog-in-the-manger land-lordism, compel them to become laborers, as that celebrated colonizer of New Zealand, Edward Gibbon Wakefield, would have had the plebeian poor among them become. They have the opportunity to become landowners, if not landlords as well, themselves. The great estates that obstructed closer settlement in early days have been acquired and subdivided by the State; those that still remain will meet a similar fate. The New Zealand immigrant of to-day can obtain land at a fair price and on easy terms, and if he wishes to borrow money to develop his acres the State will loan it to him on a long-time stipulation at a low rate of interest. If a worker, he can borrow money from the State to build himself a house, or the Government will build it for him.

New Zealand is still a young country; therefore its progress is the more remarkable. White settlement there did not really begin until about seventy years ago. Long prior thereto whalers had established stations in the colony, but they were indifferent settlers, and the districts they occupied are still among the least inhabited parts of the Dominion.

The remoteness of New Zealand was in itself no small obstacle to immigration in those days. For the twelve-thousand-mile voyage from England from three to six months were required, and the accommodations aboard ship were far inferior to those of to-day. Further, after reaching the colony there were exasperating differences and delays with the Maoris over land titles, followed by the growth of large estates near the ports of debarkation.

A TATTOOED MAORI

For years settlement proceeded slowly, though backed by lords and bishops, churches and colonizing laymen. Then the Provincial Governments began building railways, roads increased in length, bridges became more numerous, all carrying settlement with them. Next the Central Government inaugurated a vigorous public-works policy with millions of borrowed sovereigns, and thereby brought to the colony such prosperity—and wild scrambling for public money—as it had never before known. Immediately speculation became riotous, opportunities for development in all lines increased, prices advanced, and trade improved. Increase in immigration naturally followed, the name of New Zealand became more brightly emblazoned upon the pages of history, and its fame began to spread throughout the earth. Thenceforward, until the ascendancy of the Liberal administration in 1891, prosperity and adversity, advancement and retrogression, alternated, and government succeeded government in bewildering confusion. Then came the stable administration of John Ballance and his successors, bringing with it reformatory laws and prolonged prosperity.

New Zealand's prominence has not insured it against the exaggerations of many misconceptions and careless statements. Between what the world says of New Zealand and what it actually is, there is, in many particulars, a wide difference. This variance in opinions includes the Dominion's geographical location. Many Americans do not even know where Maoriland is. Although it lies eleven hundred miles east of Australia, some persons fancy it to be within sight of the land of ungainly kangaroos; others imagine it to be near South America, from which it is separated by four thousand miles of sea; or, worse still, off the coast of Greenland. At the Carnegie Museum in Pittsburg—but let a New Zealander tell the story:—

"I had been but a short time in the United States," said this man, a resident of Wellington, "when one day I paid a visit to the Carnegie Museum. I am proud of my country, and I then believed it was about the only place on the map. Innocently thinking that the words would serve as a sort of open sesame to a hearty welcome, I said to the doorkeeper: 'I am from New Zealand.'

"'Oh,' responded he, nonchalantly, 'we get them from all parts here. Last week we had visitors from New York, Philadelphia, Boston, and other cities. But New Zealand! Let me see. What state is it in?'"

As some persons have obtained their meagre information of New Zealand from hearsay, or from newspaper interviews or articles containing half-truths or totally erroneous statements, it is but natural that they should have mistaken ideas concerning the land that Tasman viewed from ship's deck, and that Captain Cook, at a more propitious hour, seized in England's name and stocked with pigs. Such have, among other things, heard or read that New Zealand is a Socialist country; that its government is in the hands of labor; that it has no millionaires, no slums nor paupers, no industrial strikes nor lockouts, no child laborers, no trusts, no selfish, stifling land monopoly, no private employment offices. Some of these have been informed, too, that the State owns all the land, the coal mines and the forests, and all public utilities, and, finally, that the entrance standards of this blissful land "are so high," to quote one admirer of New Zealand, "that only an English-speaking person with proofs of morality and good health and a certain sum of money can enter."

In this and consecutive paragraphs I shall deal briefly with these misconceptions and contortions of facts. In some particulars these people have heard aright, in others only partially so. First, and emphatically, New Zealand is not a Socialist country. Any well-informed Socialist will tell you that, and, if he be a New Zealand Socialist, perhaps with vigor. So far is New Zealand from being a Socialist stronghold, that in the national elections of New Zealand in 1911 the Socialist candidates polled less than 5000 votes out of a total of about 470,000 votes cast at the first ballot, according to the daily press, and not more than 9000 votes according to a statement made to me by the New Zealand Socialist Party's honorary secretary. Yet New Zealand is, in a measure, a socialistic land, where, curiously, Socialists form a small minority of the people. New Zealand has socialistic legislation,—or much that has been generally so labeled,— but it has never had a Socialist administration, nor is there any imminent likelihood that it will. As yet the New Zealand Socialists have not even one member of their own number in Cabinet or Parliament.

"Why has not Socialism grown faster in New Zealand?" I asked Fred R. Cooke, the New Zealand Socialist Party's honorary secretary, in 1912.

"Because the bulk of the people," he answered, "have been persuaded that they are living under a mild form of

Socialism. And then, the country has not reached the stage of capitalist evolution which forces the next stage, Socialism."

"What," I asked him, "is the New Zealand Socialist's opinion of the so-called socialistic legislation of New Zealand?"

"The New Zealand Socialist's opinion of the socialistic legislation," he replied, "is that it proves the futility of palliative legislation. The Conciliation and Arbitration Act has for many years been lauded as a piece of socialistic legislation all over the world, and the employing class, ever since it passed into law, have been pretending to fight it. Now, when the workers recognize its evils and are declaring against it, the employing class are trying to enforce conciliation and arbitration. There are many other acts which are supposed to be socialistic but they are not so."

"Is any of New Zealand's legislation truly socialistic?" I inquired of him.

"The only act passed in New Zealand which is *toward* Socialism is adult suffrage," he replied.

In New Zealand labor is a strong political power; yet, contrary to widespread suppositions, the Dominion has not, and never has had, a labor government. Still, labor has had much to say in, and to do with, the conduct of State affairs. Not as a separate political entity, it is true, but as the tandem mate of the Liberal party, which has been so strongly pro-labor that some have called it the Labor party. Labor will always be strong enough in New Zealand to have a voice in governmental affairs, and it is because it has had this voice for more than twenty years that it did not long ago form an enduring political party of its own and fight for supreme power, as labor did in Australia years before the formation of the New Zealand Labor parties of 1910 and 1912.

Labor has dealt capital staggering blows in New Zealand, both through land and labor laws. Yet these very laws have redounded to capital's benefit. True, they deprived it of many broad acres, through taxation and compulsory sale to the State, but this has resulted in widespread development and prosperity. They also forced capital to relinquish its dominance over labor; compelled it to abolish sweating and pay a living wage; to grant short hours and liberal overtime allowances; to provide mechanical and sanitary safeguards and conveniences for its employees; to establish a scale of compensation for accidents, with a maximum liability of $2500. At the same time, however, the exactions of labor obtained for the capitalist protection and stability; nevertheless, to many interested and disinterested observers it does seem that capitalism has been embarrassed and harassed by the multiplicity of labor acts and their amendments.

Industrially New Zealand is a comparatively peaceful land, but it is not true that it has no strikes or lockouts. However, such as it has had, since the passage of the Industrial Conciliation and Arbitration Act and its numerous amendments, have been few, and usually of trivial consequence. Possibly the strike in New Zealand would have been more frequent if it were not, as it has been for several years, a legal offense. So, also, are lockouts. Against both employees and employers penalties for violations of the strike and lockout clauses of the Conciliation and Arbitration Act are heavy.

For nearly twenty years after the passage of this act, strikes were practically unknown in New Zealand; but recently the growing dissatisfaction of workers, particularly those allied with the New Zealand Federation of Labor,—a strong organization with principles akin to those of the Industrial Workers of the World,—has caused the strike shadow to lengthen alarmingly. The most serious strike New Zealand has had since 1890 occurred in 1912, among the gold miners of Waihi, and it lasted five months.

Perhaps nothing in this interesting land impresses the investigating visitor more than the continual disputes and adjustments between capital and labor and the numerous and frequent changes in the labor laws. What one truthfully writes of New Zealand's labor statutes this year may not be true of them next year. In this political experimental station, this social laboratory, legislative labor acts are constantly, some of them almost regularly, appearing in wholly or partially new vesture. Repeals are infrequent, amendments are many.

This legislative tinkering, as irate New Zealanders commonly call it, has been responsible for a great deal of exasperation and uncertainty in the Dominion. At every session of Parliament, for years, labor bills have been a feature of the House of Representatives' proceedings. By no means can the majority of these be truthfully construed as detrimental to commerce or industry, but harassed employers continually fear them. In innumerable instances employers have fought against specific legislation, but what they object to more than anything else, apparently, are perennial amendments, on the ground that they unsettle and otherwise injure business.

For the prevention of child labor New Zealand has passed stringent laws, and with excellent results. Nevertheless, juvenile labor of a regrettable kind still exists there. In the factory, the shop, and the mine there are no youthful workers under a reasonable age; there age limits protect them. But on dairy farms, where so often parents are poor and cows many, less satisfactory conditions prevail.

The New Zealand Government has deeply interested itself in labor, but not to such a degree as to prohibit or monopolize employment agencies. The State does conduct scores of free employment agencies, but, under the name of servants' registry offices, many employment bureaus are run by private concerns.

In New Zealand there possibly are no millionaires,—in pounds sterling,—but there are New Zealanders worth a million dollars each, and more.

Nor are there slums in New Zealand, as slums are known in great cities of the Northern Hemisphere; but in at least two of the Dominion's chief cities slums of a character that had aroused public protest existed on my last visit. Generally speaking, there is no pauperism in New Zealand, but many families have experienced pauperism for short periods, and others have been on the verge of it. In dull winters thousands of free meals have been distributed by charity organizations, and deputations of men have besought State and municipality to save them from hunger by giving them employment.

On the whole. New Zealand is a prosperous land, far more so, proportionately, than most older countries. In the same degree it is one of the richest countries of the world, both with regard to the people's material welfare and in natural resources. Likewise it is one of the most heavily indebted nations of the earth.

The per capita private wealth of the country, according to a New Zealand Government publication, is about $1800. About one tenth of the private wealth is deposited in the banks of the Dominion, and of this between thirty-five and forty per cent is held by the post-office savings banks. In them the average deposit in 1912 was about $190. If a recent estimate made by Sir Joseph Ward is approximately correct, the combined private and public wealth of New Zealand exceeds $3,250,000,000, exclusive of the incomes of wage-earners, amounting, Sir Joseph estimated, to $230,000,000 annually, and excluding the incomes from salaries and professions, totaling about $20,000,000 yearly. On a population basis of 1,060,000, this, exclusive of the incomes named, gives a combined private and public wealth of $3065 per capita.

To what does New Zealand owe its prosperity? Why is its estimated per capita wealth greater than that of the United States, considering that, little more than twenty years ago, within its borders tramping "sundowners" were met on every road, and industrial conditions were so bad that empty, neglected houses with broken windows and unkempt lawns were common?

The answer is, that New Zealand has burdened itself with an enormous national debt. Borrowed money is the prime cause of its prosperity. And as one result of its borrowings there has developed a condition in which, it has been estimated, about every eighth person is dependent on the

Government for a living, either as a State employee or as a dependent of such.

In 1912, the net general indebtedness of New Zealand approximated $395 per European head. In the twenty-two-year period of 1891-1913, its net national indebtedness increased one hundred and twenty per cent, or fifty-six per cent more than its increase of European population in the same time. On the whole obligation the per capita interest charges yearly total more than the per capita principal of the United States interest-bearing debt! Much of the interest outlay, however, is regained by the State in loans to settlers, workers, and local bodies. In his 1911 financial budget, Sir Joseph Ward classified about sixty per cent of the national debt as "paying interest and making profit," while about ten per cent more was declared to be "indirectly interest-bearing."

Will New Zealand be able to meet its obligations? Will it be able to repay at the specified time the 26,000,000 dollars which the 1912 official Year-Book declares is due in 1914-15; the 150,000,000 due in 1929-30; the 81,000,000 due in 1939-40? Not without renewals and fresh loans. In the Public Debt Extinction Act, however, a plan is provided whereby, with renewals to repay short-dated debentures, the existing debt can be repaid within seventy-five years. This act—passed in 1910—also provides for the repayment of all future loans within seventy-five years of their contraction. Extinction is to be accomplished by annually setting aside a certain sum for investment. Possibly this scheme will succeed, but that has been questioned, among others, by Prime Minister Massey when leader of the Opposition.

Fortunately for New Zealand, it has good assets. In 1911, Sir Joseph Ward valued its public assets at twenty per cent more than its national liabilities. Crown lands alone are worth considerably more than one hundred million dollars, and railways fully one hundred and sixty million dollars. As for the public works assets, however, it is difficult to reach an actual valuation, because these grow in value with increase in population and general development. Upon the latent water power which the State is to exploit, only a vague value can be put at this time. Ultimately water power, so abundant in New Zealand, should become a very valuable asset to the State.

THE RIGHT HON. SIR JOSEPH GEORGE WARD, BAR., P.C., K.C.M.G.

Respecting State ownership, it is not so extensive as some persons imagine. The New Zealand Government is a great landlord, by far the greatest in the country, but not by many millions of acres does it own all the land. Its ownership is of such a magnitude, however, that, combined with constructive land laws, it has made private land monopoly impossible.

Neither does the State own all the coal mines, the forests, and public utilities. It has only three collieries, which produce less than twenty per cent of the Dominion's total coal output. The State holds immense areas of forest, but other vast sylvan domains are private freehold. It owns the railways,—excepting a few short private lines,—the telegraph lines, and, barring a few rural lines, the telephone systems; but water, gas, electric lighting and power, and street railway services are the properties of local bodies or private concerns.

Discounting exaggerated conceptions, no person, no institution in New Zealand is so busy, so versatile as that vague yet substantial entity, "The Government." Its hands are in many enterprises and benevolences, and for years it has been constantly on the lookout for new ways to occupy itself.

Today it does business with one hand and distributes philanthropy with the other. As a direct commercial institution it operates railways, telegraph and telephone systems, coal mines, tourist steamers and motor coaches, and soon it will be selling electricity. It conducts hotels, sanatoriums, life, fire, and accident insurance offices. It is a banker, money-lender, landlord, and public trustee. As an indirect commercialist it aids dairymen by inspecting and grading their produce; it aids stockmen by keeping blooded stock for breeding; and it assists beekeepers and poultrymen by giving them free instruction.

As an altruistic institution it has established old-age and widows' pensions, superannuation funds for its employees, national endowments for pensions and education, national scholarships, and a national. State-subsidized provident fund. It has provided general protection and assistance for the laborer and assisted passages for immigrants. Industrial peace it has secured by arbitration and conciliation.

In the exercise of its purely philanthropical functions, the New Zealand Government's most noteworthy act is its gift of old-age pensions. These, which now number more than sixteen thousand, are paid to all persons who are more than sixty-five years of age and who have resided in New Zealand continuously for twenty-five years, barring allowances for absences from the country. At first the maximum annual pension was ninety dollars; now, excluding a special increase granted in 1911 to pensioners having dependent children, it is one hundred and thirty dollars, and the average pension paid is very nearly as much. To men of sixty years of age and women fifty-five years of age who have dependent on them two or more children under fourteen years of age, an annual pension of one hundred and ninety-five dollars may be paid.

In 1911, the State added to its paternal benefits pensions for widows. For widows with children and small incomes the annual pension ranges from sixty to one hundred and fifty dollars.

Another pension scheme of the State, one that is maintained partly by contributions from the beneficiaries, is the Public Service Superannuation. This provides pensions for the superannuated officials of all branches of the public service, excepting the Railway Department officials and teachers of the public schools, who have separate pension funds. The solvency of the superannuation fund is guaranteed by the State, which contributes to it a fixed sum annually.

Still another coöperative, State-guaranteed pension scheme is authorized by the National Provident Fund Act. To this fund any New Zealand resident between the ages of sixteen and forty-five, whose annual income does not exceed one thousand dollars, is entitled to contribute. One fourth of the fund is contributed by the State, Ultimately, if those whom it is intended to benefit take a proper interest in it, this fund should largely supersede old-age pensions.

After reaching the age of sixty, contributors to the fund are entitled to a weekly allowance for the rest of their lives. Other features of the scheme are the incapacity allowance, which may be drawn for a maximum period of fourteen years, and an allowance of thirty dollars for medical attendance on the birth of a contributor's child.

As for New Zealand's entrance requirements, sane mentality and morality are demanded of all its immigrants, but no white immigrant is obliged to possess any specified sum of money on landing, unless he is deemed likely to become a public charge, or is a State-assisted farmer or farm laborer. No Chinese, however, can enter New Zealand lawfully without the payment of a five-hundred-dollar head tax.

As I have said, New Zealand is a land of amazing variety, but its diversity is not confined to its physical gifts. It applies as well to its industrial and political activities. Industrially New Zealand is a beehive in which drones are relatively scarce. For those of its inhabitants who choose to work there is little excuse for idleness. Forest, farm, and factory; mine, swamp, and sea; gold and coal, flax and fish, the kauri and its gum, wool and frozen mutton, butter and cheese, a hundred manufactured articles—all these keep this land of labor busy, well fed, and well clothed.

THE HOT WATER BASINS, WHITE TERRACE

Its export trade approximates from one hundred to one hundred and ten million dollars annually, and its imports, of which about eight per cent are received from the United States, have a total value of from eighty-five to one hundred million dollars yearly. Its wool exports yield it forty million dollars; its frozen meats, twenty millions; butter, ten millions; cheese, six millions; gold, ten millions; flax, from two to four millions; grains, provisions, and timber, twenty millions.

The greatest of all the sources of New Zealand's industrial life is the sheep. Without sheep New Zealand could not so soon have reached the commercial position it holds to-day. Its most important export is wool, which yields about one third of the total value of all exports.

In nearly all parts of the country are pastoral runs, and there are few places where I have not heard the bleating of sheep and the barking of shepherd dogs. I have startled ewe and lamb on lonely tussock plains, and have seen them feeding high on the slopes of grassy ranges. On rural roads sheep raised clouds of dust, and at many railway stations they struggled for standing room in crowded cars. In New Zealand's pastures to-day there are twenty-five million sheep,—nearly half as many as there are in the United States,—and every year between six and seven million bleat for the last time in its slaughter yards.

To shear the twenty-two thousand sheep flocks of New Zealand and handle the clip, thousands of men are employed for about six months each year. In the North Island many of the shearers are Maoris, and in the clipping sheds Maori girls are commonly employed to clean and roll the fleece. In Maoriland no industrial workers earn money faster than expert shearers. On every large station are men who shear from two hundred to two hundred and fifty sheep every day, which means a daily wage of from ten to twelve dollars.

Sheep have made many New Zealanders rich. Of the wealth of more than one dominant character in the Dominion it can be truly said, as to me it was said of Sir George Clifford, "He made it all out of wool and mutton." One sheep farmer stated in a Wellington court that he had loaned one hundred and seventy-five thousand dollars to South Americans, and that he had invested large sums in Australia and in his own country.

Politically New Zealand is a democratic Dominion, with a leaning toward imperialism. Its democracy is shown in its legislation for the masses. Its imperialistic sympathy—due to its relationship to a monarchy—is manifested by a zealous regard for, and keen efforts in the behalf of, the solidarity of the British Empire, and by heavy contributions to England's imperial navy and army,—to the first in money, to the second, as in the Boer War, in men.

Democratic as New Zealand is, it is not so democratic, in some ways, as Switzerland or certain American states. Not yet, for example, has it the initiative, the referendum, or the recall. It is officially connected with a monarchy, it likes kingly honors, and it has its knighted citizens. But it cares not for all the glittering bestowals of a king. With all its love for "Home,"—in some measure due to the extensive trade relations between itself and the mother country, which buys about eighty per cent of the Dominion's exports,—New Zealand desires no hereditary titles on which to found a permanent aristocracy. It prefers a "Digger Dick" or a "Plain Bill" to a baronet.

Despite their official obligations to a kingdom, the New Zealanders govern themselves. On questions affecting Great Britain's international and intercolonial interests, imperial authorities are consulted, but otherwise New Zealand is free to legislate and govern as it chooses. In national issues both men and women have a voice. Even the Maoris enjoy universal suffrage and elect members of their own race to Parliament, and they also have their own representatives in the Legislative and Executive Councils.

At first—excepting during the year the colony was a dependency of New South Wales—the government of New Zealand was vested entirely in a Governor, who was answerable only to the Crown. In 1852, the British Parliament granted the colony a General Assembly, comprising a Legislative Council, nominated by the Governor, and an elective House of Representatives. By an act of the same year the colony was divided into six provinces, each empowered to have a presiding Superintendent and an elective Council, which was authorized to legislate on all but a few specified questions. Eventually the provinces were increased to nine, but in 1876, after bitter protests and years of widespread controversy concerning them, they were all abolished by the General Assembly.

In 1855, fifteen years after British sovereignty was proclaimed over it by Captain Hobson, its first Governor,—whose tomb is in Auckland,—New Zealand was granted a responsible system of government, under which the Executive Council became responsible to Parliament.

As New Zealand grew in wealth, fame, and prestige, it became dissatisfied with the term colony, and in 1907, at its request. King Edward VII was "graciously pleased" to advance it to the status of a Dominion. As now constituted, the government of New Zealand consists of a Governor, an Executive Council, a Legislative Council, a House of Representatives, and more than forty departments and offices.

As its official head the Dominion has a titled Governor, appointed by the King. He has many State duties but nevertheless he is little more than a graceful ornament, and as an executive official he could readily be dispensed with. The real government head is the Prime Minister.

The Governor presides over the Executive Council, an advisory aid to him, whose members he appoints, and under writs of summons from him the members of the upper house obtain and hold their seats. The Governor also has power to dissolve Parliament and to authorize the formation of another ministry. Although he possesses considerable power and authority, he seldom, it is said, exercises his initiative rights, but usually acts as advised by the Executive Council. The Governor receives annually a salary of $25,000, a household allowance of $7500, and $2500 for traveling expenses.

The Executive Council—which many New Zealanders wish to see made elective—is more forward and independent in its actions than its presiding officer. In the name of the "Government," it habitually leads the way in legislation, proposing and introducing many measures. "I propose," or "It is proposed," says the Prime Minister, in Parliament or in public interview; and Parliament, if favorably disposed, incorporates the proposals into acts which become law when approved by the Governor or assented to by the King.

The busiest officials of the New Zealand Government, apparently, are the members of this Council. They are only eight, aside from the Maori representative, yet they hold about forty portfolios. The most overworked of them, probably, is the Prime Minister. For $8000— irrespective of allowances, which are granted all ministers— he sometimes discharges the duties of as many as seven portfolios, and he never has less than five or six. The other ministers usually have from three to four portfolios each. Of these the Minister of Railways receives a salary of $6500; the other ministers get a salary of $5000 each.

The Legislative Council, the membership of which is not limited, has thirty-nine members. Prior to 1891 the members were life appointees, but since then appointments have been tenable for only seven years, though reappointments are allowed.

With its upper house New Zealand is not wholly satisfied. It admits its usefulness,—as, for instance, in protecting the people from hasty legislation. But a very large percentage of the electors are opposed to it, notwithstanding. Like Sir George Grey, sixty years ago, they want an elective Legislative Council. They maintain that the members cannot truly be representative while their nomination and tenure of office, with respect to holding over through renomination, are, they believe, dependent on the wishes of the government in power. Twenty years of continuous government, by the party responsible for the abolition of life appointments, so fully persuaded them of this that the reform of the Council was adopted by the Conservatives as a party principle in 1911, and they entered the electoral field pledged to make the upper house elective. In this effort, however, they have as yet been unsuccessful.

The House of Representatives is quite a democratic assemblage. Of its eighty members about half are industrial workers, and in 1911 seventy-five per cent of these were farmers. In that year the twenty-five agricultural and stock farmers in the House outnumbered barristers and solicitors three to one. Altogether more than thirty occupations were represented on the membership roll, ranging from blacksmith to "gentleman." Four members of Parliament are Maoris.

HEAD OF LAKE WAKATIPU FROM PIGEON ISLAND

Members of the House are elected for three-year terms, and, unfair though it may seem to suffragettes, all of them are men, despite the fact that New Zealand women have had the right to vote for more than twenty years. Women voters are allowed to hold minor public offices, but for election to Parliament they cannot qualify. In one way members of the House are more fortunate than the Councillors—their individual salaries of one thousand five hundred dollars is five hundred dollars greater than the salary drawn by an "Honorable." But the average member of the House probably earns the difference, and if he does not, he ought to have it, and needs it, to pay his campaign expenses, items which do not trouble the "M.L.C.'s." Were it not for a legal prohibition limiting campaign expenses, some of these parliamentary seekers would have very little salary left after deducting election obligations. Fortunately for the campaigner, the law specifies that no parliamentary candidate's election liabilities shall exceed one thousand dollars.

The electoral system of New Zealand has some commendable features, but it needs still further reformation. In 1890, the Dominion established the one-man-one-vote principle; in 1893, it granted woman's suffrage; and three years later it abolished the property qualification. Now any man or woman who has been a resident of the country for one year, and of his or her district for three months immediately preceding registration, is entitled to vote. Maoris do not have to register.

No reference to the electoral system of New Zealand and the progressive laws which it has made possible would be complete without an acknowledgment of the part taken by women voters. A good percentage of the best legislation in New Zealand is in large degree attributable to the interest and energy displayed by women. The great Seddon, who obtained the franchise for women in his first year as Premier, realized this soon after the measure became law. Mr. Seddon, who pressed for the bill's passage more on account of his late superior's advocacy of its principles than because of his personal approval, also found that the women greatly strengthened his party's position at the first election in which they participated. Yet he had pictured Parliament as "plunging into an abyss of unknown depth by granting the franchise to women."

Evidently woman's suffrage has had no baneful effect on New Zealand. It was obtained without prolonged and bitter dissensions, and without the riotous, disgraceful scenes attending campaigns in its behalf in England. New Zealand's women obtained their victory quietly, and unobtrusively they have enjoyed its fruits; but though they take practically as much interest in politics as the male electors, as indicated by the number of their votes, with their present limited electoral rights they appear to be satisfied.

As a body they do not aspire to the higher political honors, and among them there is no concerted action in that direction. By male office-seekers and by Government alike, they are sought and welcomed as valued supporters of men and men's measures, but this is virtually as far as an invitation to their participation in political rewards goes. The women of New Zealand are not encouraged to seek political preferment; rather they are discouraged, directly and by palpable insinuation. Their political remunerations are exceedingly disproportionate to the value of services rendered. Even England, where the enfranchisement of women is still a burning question, gives its women a greater share in public affairs than the women of New Zealand possess.

New Zealand is a developing, a changing land. It is still, as it has been for the last quarter of a century, mainly a pastoral domain. But it is developing from an agricultural land into an industrial one, with cities and towns as its pulsating centres. Necessarily and naturally, in the wake of these transformations there must come, as there already have come, important political changes. Once the owners of great estates wielded the most powerful influence in affairs both national and local. Then, with the fairer taxation and the division of these little kingdoms, came the small freeholder, the leaseholder, and the workingman, and usurped this predominance. But, fortunate as they have been, these classes are not fully satisfied with the results obtained since the eventful days of '91. Freehold exponents, allied politically and otherwise, have been demanding a wider application of the freehold,—which the Conservatives have promised to give them,—and the working classes continue to complain of laws existing and to clamor for others yet undrawn. They have even secured union preference in a multitude of industrial agreements and Arbitration Court awards, and now they cry for the establishment of union preference by statute. In New Zealand union labor has become so strong that men have actually been fined in courts of justice for failure to join labor unions when ordered by the courts to do so, in accordance with industrial agreements or awards.

But despite it all—despite the insistent, annual demands of the laborer, "Give us more," "Give us statutory union preference," "Give us this, give us that"—despite the solemn, indignant assurances of employers that business will be ruined, and that the labor laws are killing the country—despite all this, New Zealand continues to grow, in population and trade, in public and private wealth. And it will continue to prosper, as it has for the last twenty-two years, so long as the world prospers, and so long as it is as well governed as it has been since the reforming hand of John Ballance grasped the helm of the ship of state. New Zealand has a brilliant past, but it has a still more luminous future.

Chapter II

And now what can be said of them who have created this meritorious State? Are they, because they have accomplished so much in so brief a time, an extraordinary people; are they mentally, morally, socially superior, as individuals? In one respect, perhaps, the New Zealanders differ from the majority of mankind. As a democracy they have made more of their opportunities. They have run where others walked or wallowed. They have exhibited humanitarianism where others displayed brutality, uncharitableness, or indifference.

New Zealanders are so far from being extraordinary that they have been called parochial and conceited. On criticism laudatory of their country they smile, and, some charge, on censure frown. Many parochial and conceited New Zealanders there are, but I cannot candidly say that the average New Zealander is more parochial or conceited than are millions of people in the United States or in Europe. On subjects affecting his native heath the New Zealander undoubtedly is sensitive, but what nationalities are not so?

On the other hand, prolonged prosperity apparently has created in the New Zealander some indifference to criticism which, if heeded, might have beneficial results. It is possible that, for the development of character, New Zealand has had too much prosperity.

World-wide praise also has contributed to the New Zealander's self-complacency. With the world's eyes upon him, he sometimes proudly asks the visitor, "What do you think of our little country?" But his national pride is excusable. His land has accomplished something worthy. It has labored to alleviate the burdens of the commonalty; it has set the world a bright example.

New Zealanders are a busy, independent, and pleasure-loving people. Their popular sports are horse-racing, football, cricket, tennis, golf, swimming, and yachting. In every part of the country there is a weekly half-holiday for factories, shops, offices, the building trades, etc., and in addition there are from six to seven full holidays each year. Proof that New Zealanders enjoy themselves may be seen on any clement Saturday night, when, in the cities, thousands leisurely stroll the streets, crowding the footpaths and filling the roadways from curb to curb. Noteworthy, too, is the observance of the Sabbath. On that day scarcely a train moves; in some cities street cars do not run during church services; and all shops and hotel bars are closed. To those persons who find the customary fishing expedition or steamer excursion a tame diversion, Sunday in Aotearoa often is most pronouncedly dull.

Another noticeable characteristic of the New Zealander is his friendly feeling toward the United States. One of the stanchest supporters of friendly relations with the United States is New Zealand's Chief Justice, Sir Robert Stout. "I have always been of opinion," he told me, "that we ought to have close relations with our kin beyond the sea on the Pacific. This is why I have ever advocated social and trade relations between New Zealand and the United States. And personally I have always liked the Americans I have met."

MAORI MEETING HOUSE

Apparently one cause of New Zealand's friendliness toward the United States is the fear of an Asiatic armed invasion. At present New Zealand appears to have little reason for such apprehension, yet, as mirrored in the press, it is held to be a possibility of the future. There are now only about three thousand Chinese in the country—much less than formerly—and in the last decade less than one hundred Japanese have entered New Zealand. It is apparent also that an imperial war with Germany has not been overlooked.

A determination to be prepared for war has caused New Zealand, partly at the suggestion of Lord Kitchener, to adopt compulsory military training. This action, though perhaps popular with the majority of New Zealand men, has been received with bitter hostility by thousands of them, and many have preferred prison sentences to enforced service. From all able-bodied males over twelve years of age military training is required until the age of twenty-five, followed by enrollment in the Reserve Force until the age of thirty.

New Zealanders are intelligent; and, answering the American woman who asked, "What language do New Zealanders speak?" they speak English. The country has one of the best public school systems in the world, and eighty-five per cent of its people can both read and write. It has primary, secondary, and high schools, technical and industrial schools, training colleges for teachers, and schools for the Maoris. It has a limited free-book system, various free scholarships, and evening continuation classes. With the exception of fees charged for instruction in the higher branches at district high schools, education in the public schools is free, and, between the ages of seven and fourteen, compulsory.

My prefatory reference to the New Zealanders would be incomplete without an accompanying introduction of the Dominion's romantic brown people. Beneath the ensign of the Southern Cross and the Union Jack dwells a race of imposing stature, almost the tallest among men. Its members, dark-haired, smiling, and robust, are intelligent, in land collectively wealthy, independent, proud, and jealous of their rights.

Such are the New Zealand Maoris, the venturesome sailors of Hawaiki, the greatest fighting people of the South Pacific. A man-eating, blood-drinking race, they yet had their poets, their orators, their astronomers and wise men. Long before Columbus braved the dangers of unknown seas the Maoris roved the wide Pacific. For thousands of miles they pushed outward from the east, west, and north in naught but canoes, discovering and populating many islands, and in New Zealand reaching their *ultima Thule*. The Maoris have a remarkable history, one rich in stories of the human passions, of love and hate, of merciless warfare, of cannibalism, of multitudinous superstitions and amazing, deadly suspicions. To those who love to delve into the mystic past of primitive people the history of the Maoris is a romance of romances. It carries the investigator from Arabia to America, from Northern India and Hawaii to the pathetic remnants of the Morioris in the Chatham Islands. It involves the rise and fall of nations. It tells of many migrations, of almost constant intertribal warfare. It is replete with tales of gods and demigods, of monsters of land and sea. It is bright with charming recitals of love escapades of man and maiden.

Stirring, indeed, were the days of old. For hundreds of years the militant cry of the toa rang through the land, from Hawke Bay to Taranaki, from Auckland to the greenstone isle. War was waged on a thousand pretexts: over land, women, curses, insults. Until 1869 cannibalism existed, although it had long been uncommon; and as late as 1871 Maoris warred against the colonials.

Whence came the Maoris? From Hawaiki, they say. But where is Hawaiki? There are many Hawaikis. All the myriad islands of Polynesia, from Easter Island to Ponape, from Hawaii to New Zealand, say that Hawaiki, or its equivalent in the various Polynesian dialects, was their original home; but their ideas respecting the exact location of this ancestral abode are somewhat vague. According to S. Percy Smith, at least seven Hawaikis are known, among them Hawaii, Samoa, Tahiti, and neighboring islands, and Rarotonga. Mr. Smith believes the Hawaiki of the Maoris to be Tahiti and adjoining islands. Maoris themselves say that they came from Tawhiti-nui, but it is doubtful if the first Hawaiki was situated in that part of the world.

Tentatively Mr. Smith has traced the Maoris back to India. Judge Pomander, of Hawaii, held that these Polynesians, and Polynesians in general, were a branch of the Indo-Europeans. Other investigators have traced them to Arabia, thus giving them a Caucasian origin. Professor J. Macmillan Brown has traced them to the Mediterranean's shores. By Judge Francis Dart Fenton the Maoris were accorded kinship with the Sabaians, the most celebrated of all the people of ancient Arabia. The Sabaians were "men of stature," says Jeremiah, and one of their rulers was the Queen of Sheba.

The date of the first arrival of the Maoris in New Zealand is not positively known. Judge Fenton says that apparently there were thirteen expeditions to New Zealand of which traditional accounts have been preserved, and others of which only uncertain stories exist. According to Mr. Smith, the original discovery of New Zealand by a Maori was made in the tenth century by Kupe, a high chief of Tahiti. About 1350 A.D. there reached New Zealand a fleet of six double-decked canoes. This is the greatest Maori migration known to-day.

If the Hawaiki of the Maoris was Tahiti, it was a long, dreary, and dangerous voyage they were forced to make to reach New Zealand. After leaving Rarotonga, there were about two thousand statute miles of sea to navigate before reaching the northern part of Aotearoa, where nearly all the canoes landed, and there were but a few wide-scattered islands en route, at which the voyagers may or may not have halted.

When the Maoris settled in New Zealand they found it inhabited by a race generally believed, though not absolutely known, to be the Morioris, a branch of the Polynesians.

Whatever race it was, it is certain that its members were soon conquered and enslaved, and many of them eaten, by the Maoris. If they were not Morioris, they have been long extinct; if they were, they have been so nearly exterminated that to-day not more than a half-dozen pure-blooded members of the race exist, and all of these live on the Chatham Islands, about five hundred miles east of Lyttleton.

MAORI WARRIOR

Possibly the people inhabiting New Zealand prior to the Maoris were Melanesians; but the Melanesian taint seen in a few Maoris to-day is not generally regarded as evidence that a black race once lived in the Dominion. Yet one tradition says that Melanesians reached New Zealand in a canoe about 1250 A.D. Probably this relationship to the black is due to intermarriage in Fiji and westward centuries ago.

After establishing themselves in New Zealand the Maoris did not organize any intertribal governments or make any efforts to form a nation. From the first every tribe, with occasional exceptions inspired by policy, lived and fought for itself. Changes of scene, of climate, and the possession of greater chances for development, did not modify the militant propensity of these barefooted colonists. They warred as they did in Hawaiki. Over all the land blood was spilled; whole tribes were destroyed, and cannibal feasts were common. Every able man was a warrior, ready at an instant's notice to exchange the peace of home for the strife of battle-field. On fortified hills the Maori ensconced himself, and there, day and night, watched and waited for his enemies; or, with spear, sword, club, and tomahawk, sallied forth for conquest.

Apparently the Maoris were constantly at war because they loved it, but John White says they did not, "though when once in it they are so proud that they cannot think of wishing or offering terms of peace." Undoubtedly the majority of Maori wars were due to violations of the Maori's code. Possibly no people had a nicer sense of honor, "in the old acceptation of the term," says Gudgeon, than the Maori. To him the slightest insult or injury "was unbearable, and therefore quickly avenged, even when the injured tribe was weak compared with the enemy." A single tribesman could start a war merely by a verbal insult. Even a fancied insult from a child has caused war.

A feature of Maori warfare was cannibalism, the worst stage of which was reached in Hongi's wars. Long prior to this, cannibalism had gratified appetite both in war and peace. This was so generally known to early navigators to New Zealand that for years, the terror of cannibalism prevented intercourse with the natives. In 1780, when in the House of Commons New Zealand was proposed as a suitable place for a convict colony, "the cannibalistic propensities of the natives was urged in opposition and silenced every other argument."

By many Maoris human flesh was classed as the best of all flesh. Some Maoris were so eager for food of this sort that they lay in wait for victims "like the tigers of India." Many of the victims of cannibalism were slaves, some of whom were eaten in peaceful times. One writer says that occasionally even children were eaten. Yet the Maoris liked children so well that they spoiled them. When children were the offspring of an enemy, however, it was considered proper to eat them.

As the Maoris increased in numbers in New Zealand, they spread over the land until, from the North Cape to the Bluff, not an inch of soil remained unclaimed. And all land claims were guarded with the most jealous care. The Maori was always sure of his boundaries. His landmarks were trees, streams, stones, holes, posts, rattraps, and eel-dams. These boundaries were thoroughly memorized. Patiently and minutely their names, location, and characteristics were implanted in the minds of Maori youth by father and grandfather. Instruction also was given in all important history connected with the acquirement and possession of the land. And all these lessons were treasured by the pupil with a memory that, says Judge Fenton, was reliable up to twenty Maori generations, or five hundred years.

A dispute over landmarks among such positive, combative memorizers was sure to lead to serious trouble. That which the Maori regarded as his "mother's milk," and his "life from childhood," he at all times was ready to risk his life to retain. Considering the complex nature of Maori land titles, it is not surprising that there was a multitude of land disputes, or that many land title tangles try the patience of the Native Land Court to-day.

Some of the claims made by native landowners are amazing. One Maori believed he was entitled to a tract of land because he had been cursed on it. Another claimed ownership because he had been injured on the property involved. By the Colonial Government one claim actually was allowed because one of the claimants swore that he had seen a ghost on the disputed land.

The Maoris have always held land in common, and to a very large extent they so hold their five million acres to-day.

To them communal ownership seems to be satisfactory, but when a white man leases a piece of their land he may not find the system so agreeable. When the first rent-day arrives he, like the Bay of Plenty physician I heard about, may be harassed by several landlords and landladies.

A MAORI VILLAGE

In answer to a knock one day, this doctor opened his front door to find his veranda occupied by three or four generations of Maoris. What did they want? "Money for the rent." The lessee did not want to deal with what looked to him like a tribe, and, summoning a frown, he shouted: "Get out of here!" The rent collectors got, but outside the gate they halted, and after a parley they sent back, with better results, one of their number to collect for all.

Among Maoris land was a frequent cause of war, and it was often a bloody bone of contention between them and the white settlers. An early result of the "king movement," culminating in 1858 in the proclamation of Potatau Te Wherowhero as the first Maori king, an act that was prompted partly by a desire to retain native lands in Maori hands, was war. In this thousands of troops, including ten thousand imperial soldiers, were engaged for months. The Maoris displayed great bravery, first-class fighting ability, and remarkable cunning. The end of the war was dramatic, and typical of the Maori spirit.

In a hurriedly built fort about three hundred natives, among them women and children, for three days withstood the artillery and rifle fire and bayonet charges of fifteen hundred soldiers. When called upon to surrender, Rewi, the chief in charge, wrote to General Cameron:—

"Friend, this is the word of the Maori: They will fight on forever, forever, forever."

The women, declining an opportunity to leave the fort in safety, said:—

"If our husbands are to die, we and the children will die with them."

Finally, however, the pa's defenders dashed out in compact formation and scattered for freedom, leaving about half the garrison dead and wounded.

Of men the Maoris never were afraid, but the boldest among them quailed at thoughts of incurring the displeasure of gods and spirits. They still are superstitious, but not to the degree they once were. At all times their lives were regulated by a strict regard for the supernatural. In their memory the respected, dreaded tapu was deeply engraved in large letters. To break it often meant death. From the legendary day that the god Tanemahuta separated earth and heaven by standing on his head and kicking upward, "the whole Maori race, from the child of seven years to the hoary head, were guided in all their actions by omens."

In those days witchcraft was rampant, and persons accused of it were put to death. Curses, which were believed to be the main causes of bewitchery, were so dreaded that whole families were sometimes driven to death merely by the knowledge that they had been cursed. When a Maori believed himself to be bewitched he consulted a priest, or tohunga, who, with much ceremony, including many incantations, tried to destroy the effects of the curse.

The number of objects to which tapu applied among the Maoris was astonishing. This touch not, taste not, handle not perturber was always exercising its baneful influences. Even to those it protected it was dangerous. Also it was inconvenient. The possessors of tapu, according to an authority, did not even dare to carry food on their backs, and everything belonging to them was tapu, or prohibited to the touch or use of others. The suggestions of punishment conveyed by violations of tapu were so strong that sometimes they frightened the culprits to death.

Some forms of tapu were removable by tohungas, as those existing at the baptism of children and at tattooings. It would seem that tohungas—who, often priests, also were wizards, seers, physicians, tattooers and barbers, and not uncommonly builders of houses and canoes—had enough to do merely in lessening and preventing the results of tapu violations; but it was not so. Much of their time was spent as physicians. As such their services were required for ills both real and imaginary. Their cures were effected mainly by suggestion, and to create and convey curative fancies they employed a great variety of invocations. Also they called to their aid the properties of barks, roots, and leaves, supplemented by the planting and waving of twigs, clawing of the air, and bodily contortions. They were surprisingly successful, despite the fact that many of their cures were secured under such rigorous treatment as bathing in cold water to eradicate fever and consumption.

Tohungas did not claim ability to raise the dead, but they did undertake to revive all who were on the verge of the grave, on certain conditions. Then even the stars were required as assisting agencies. The Pleiades had to be at or near their zenith and the morning star must be seen when Toutouwai the robin caroled his first song of the day.

When the patient recovered, the tohunga was a great man. But when the patient died, there was weeping and wailing.

Then it was the mournful tangi was held; then men and women came from far and near to condole with the sorrowing, to cry loudly, to feast even while their hearts were heavy and their eyes red with the deluge of many tears. Then were heard wild songs, then were seen frenzied dances, then flowed the blood of lamenting ones, usually women, who in their mad grief slashed their bodies and sometimes their faces. Sacrifices of slaves were occasionally made, that the bewailed might have attendant spirits. Sometimes even suicide was committed, as when the wives of a chief strangled themselves; and sometimes, too, wailing ones fell dead from exhaustion, and in Te Reinga joined those for whom they had so passionately mourned.

The tangi is generally observed among the Maoris even to-day. Still are heard, for days at a time, the moan, the wail, the startling outburst of pent emotion. Still tears flow copiously, noses are rubbed against each other in grievous salutation, and there are collected the great commissariat stores so indispensable where the hangi (oven) is necessary to the prolonged continuance of the tangi.

A modern tangi is a very lamentable event. The largest tangis are attended by hundreds of natives, as well as by some white men. There is food for all. When there isn't,—then it is time to stop the tangi. A tangi without food! Taikiri! Impossible! At the greatest tangis tents and specially built houses are provided for the overflow attendance. At the tangi over King Tawhiao, which was attended by three thousand persons, hundreds of tents and extra whares were erected.

After death, what? This question, in so far as it relates to rewards and penalties for deeds done in the body, would have been answered hazily by the ancient Maori. Of this phase of the world beyond, the Maori knew little. Yet he had so far progressed in religious inquiry as to recognize ten heavens and as many hells. He also believed that some souls returned to the earth as insects; and like many Caucasians to-day, he held that when persons were asleep their souls could leave their bodies and commune with other souls. His belief also embraced recognition of the Greater Existence (*Io*), the dual principle of nature, and deification of the powers of nature. The spirits of dead ancestors he propitiated. A possible symbol of the Maori's belief in theism I saw in the heitiki, a grotesque, distorted representation of the human form, usually composed of greenstone and hanging pendant from the necks of Maori women.

In olden days the Maoris associated their chief rulers with the gods. In the men of highest rank, the arikis, gods were believed to dwell, and other gods were supposed to attend them. Arikis were the wise men of the tribes, and their powers and duties were manifold. They were the people's guides, they discharged many offices in times of peace, and exercised much authority in times of war. In all cases, however, their authority as priests was limited to things in which the interference of the gods could be discerned.

To-day the Maoris, as a people, know not the religion of their forefathers. In the main the pakeha's religion has become their religion. Thousands of them are church communicants, many of them can quote long passages of Scripture from memory, and the voices of others are heard in daily family worship. A Mormon missionary told me that some native families are such zealous Christians—outwardly, at least—that they have family prayers both morning and night. The majority of Maoris are communicants of the Church of England, but within recent years an astonishing number have embraced the Mormon faith.

Although, generally speaking, the Maori has accepted the fundamental principles of Christianity, his ethical viewpoint often is totally different from that of the European. This was well illustrated in a parliamentary inquiry into alleged "grafting" by a native member of Parliament. The charge, "accepting payment in connection with petitions," apparently astonished the Maoris. In this they could see no more wrong than in the Opposition leader's legitimate acceptance of a present of one thousand pounds from his constituents. In defending his colleague, Dr. Te Rangihiroa said that "the

Maori could not be expected to understand pakeha ways, as the pakeha could not himself. The Maori and European ethical systems are totally different."

Singular illustrations of Maori ethics are furnished by native marriage customs. In a trial where one Maori woman was charged with assaulting another wahine, counsel for the complainant said that Maoris believed that "when a husband has been away for seven years he is as good as dead, so that in this case the wife was considered divorced, and in consequence was treated somewhat lightly."

A further illustration is furnished by the murus, or punitive expeditions, that sometimes raid Maori households. With Maoris it has always been a recognized rule that when there has been misconduct on the part of either husband or wife a raid may rightfully be made on the offender's property. By the raided couple a muru may be regarded as the equivalent of a formal divorce. In one plundering excursion I learned that property to the value of five hundred dollars was seized.

The Maoris of old were industrious; idlers they did not have, as they have to-day. Every man able to do so was expected to work, and when the Maoris were not engaged in war they occupied themselves in many ways. On hills they built and fortified their important villages. Around them they dug ditches and sometimes built as many as four palisades, which they adorned with wood carvings that represented years of toil with stone implements.

They built canoes for war and peace; they chiseled and polished weapons of strife; they made ornaments of greenstone, whalebone, and wood, and from the fibres of the flax, the kiekie, and the cabbage tree they wove clothing, mats, and baskets. They were rude surgeons, clever tattooers, hunters, fishers, tillers of the soil. Time they divided into seasons (summer and winter) and moons, and they searched the heavens; for many stars were known to them by name, and comets they dreaded. When the Maoris saw a comet headed toward the earth they recited incantations to prevent a collision.

In the moon the Maoris made a discovery that, if it should ever be substantiated, will forever relegate to the shades of oblivion the blithesome affirmation, "My lover's the man in the moon." For in Marama the Maoris found not a man, but a woman. Her name was Rona. And was Rona a divine and angelic creature? Ah, no. She was only a cook. At Kaipara, says legend, Rona was cooking, and was on her way to get a calabash of water, when she stumbled and fell. In her rage Rona cursed the innocent moon. The moon, becoming nettled, descended, and seized the angry wahine. The woman stoutly held to a tree, but the moon prevailed, and carried Rona, tree, and calabash to the sky.

One of the commonest of old Maori occupations was tattooing. Among both men and women it was the fashion to be tattooed. The men tattooed because they believed it improved their faces and made them look more resolute; and, further, because Maori women did not regard the attentions of untattooed men with the highest favor. The women tattooed (usually only on lips and chin, as to-day) because the Maori tangata, unlike the Caucasian man, did not like red-lipped sweethearts or wives.

But that was in the long ago. Tattooing, excepting among women,—and many of them are no longer tattooed,—is out of fashion. Not for forty years have Maori men been tattooed.

The busy Maori of the past did not spend all his peaceful days working. He amused himself in a variety of ways. He danced, he sang, and on drums, whistles, and nose flutes he played. His ear for music was keen; in rhythm he was skilled; and his voice was deep and well matured. He engaged in many sports and games, and in the wharetapere, the house of amusement, he sometimes entertained himself all night. There was wrestling on land and in water; there were tobogganing, rope-skipping, stilt-walking, and kite-flying. Tops were spun, hoops were rolled, and for the children there were games of see-saw and hide-and-seek.

MAORI WAHINE WITH MAT OF KIWI FEATHERS AND
PENDENT HEITIKI

And the Maori also feasted. At the hakari, greatest of his ancient festivals, he piled food on high pyramidal stages. There sweet potatoes, taro, eels, fish, gourds, and many foods of tree, creeper, and fern were heaped in profusion. There, welcomed by songs and by speeches of pacing orators, visiting tribes assembled to partake of prodigal hospitality.

The Maori also spent many hours in making himself as attractive as possible. His vanity was appeased with ornaments, paint, and bright colors. To the hair much attention was paid by persons of rank, including chiefs, whose hair usually was long in peaceful days. For beards the majority of men did not care, because they hid the tattooing, and so facial hairs were extracted with mussel-shell pincers.

Those were the days of knobbed heads. Hair knobs were "the rage." On the back of some heads there were from three to six or more. They were fastened with combs, and their possessors were very careful to keep them in place. The coiffures were brightened with the feathers of birds, and one feathery decoration was a war plume of twelve huia feathers, single ones of which are worth now, I was told, as much as five dollars. But time has wrought her changes in this land as elsewhere. Befeathered Maoris are still common in New Zealand, but their feathers are worn in European hats. The war plume is no longer seen, the strife-provoking suspicions of early days exist no more. Rongo, god of sweet potatoes, has more followers than the warring Tu.

The modernized Maori is not much like his mat-clothed, tattooed ancestors. The flax mat and kilt have been superseded by European apparel, in many cases by carefully pressed suits and other demands of modern fashion. Even such conveniences as telephones and automobiles are possessed by Maoris.

The Maori is absorbing the education and customs of his vanquishers, but in turn he himself is being absorbed. Hear the lament of Chief Te Huki, uttered in 1911:—

"You Maoris are being superseded, absorbed by the pakehas. We have Maori features, true, but our skins are pakeha. The tide has turned, and is slowly but surely flowing out into oblivion. When the tide turns again, it will be salt, it will be pakeha. While the river Ruamahanga flowed and rippled across the land it was sweet, pure, and fresh; but when it reached the sea of Kiwa, it was lost, lost, lost!"

Chapter III

Travel in New Zealand is a pleasure; yet it has its inconveniences and discomforts. In almost every part of the country there is frequent steamer service, and about three thousand miles of railway are in operation; but many of the finest scenic districts can be reached only by stage-coach. There are still about as many miles of coaching routes as there are of railways, and for years horse and motor coaches will be important vehicles of transportation in New Zealand.

On the other hand, there are laudable conveniences. The tourist can avoid work and worry by having itineraries arranged by private booking agencies or by the Government Department of Tourist and Health Resorts, This department will book him to all parts of the country without charge; it will feed and lodge him in its hotels and accommodation houses; in its sanatoriums it will treat his diseases; it will furnish him with baths, pilot him on tours, provide him with recreation on bowling, tennis, and croquet grounds, and sell him books, photographs, and postcards.

Another convenient feature of travel in New Zealand is furnished by the express companies. These are as efficient as personal servants in calling for and delivering baggage to all parts of the Dominion. In this case, however, "express" does not imply quick dispatch, as it would in America. I had occasion to leave an order with New Zealand's largest express company for the dispatch of a valise from Auckland to Palmerston North, three hundred and forty miles distant. Several days after filing the order I called for the parcel. It had not arrived.

"Why," said I to the agent, "I thought the parcel would get here in one day."

"Oh, no," he replied; "it generally takes three days for that distance."

"What! Three days by express train?" I cried in amazement.

"It would come by goods train," the agent explained. "There are no express cars in New Zealand. Parcels must be forwarded in railway parcel vans or by boat. Usually parcels handled by the carrying companies are sent by steamer; it is cheaper."

Traveling in New Zealand is safe, especially on trains. Railroad wrecks are exceedingly rare. There are no mile-a-minute trains, no record-breaking specials, no strivings at all for what Americans call speed. With one exception, on its fastest runs the Government is satisfied with an average hourly speed of twenty-five miles, including all stops. The exception is on the Christchurch-Dunedin division, where the average speed for the two hundred and thirty miles is about thirty miles an hour. Nevertheless, there are New Zealanders who believe the railways of their country are nothing less than speedways.

"My! you go so fast on the Main Trunk Express that you can hardly see anything," said a New Zealand woman excitedly to a neighbor.

It was worse than this on the daylight-to-dark section of the Midland Branch. So rapidly did the train cover the ground in the tussocky hills that one frightened passenger publicly complained of the speed. The oscillation was so severe, said he, that women were thrown off their seats, and articles fell from the parcel racks. Probably this train was one of those composed of old and light carriages that, as I found, often rock like ships at sea.

West Coast trains are more conservative. One of these plodders participated in a handicap race on the Greymouth-Reefton line with two young men—and the men won! They missed the train at the depot, but they started in pursuit, and though it had twenty yards' start, they overtook it after running about two hundred yards. This was a splendid performance for an untrained scratch team, but a magistrate saw in it a violation of the trespass law, and fined the men.

Speed in construction is another popular joke subject with New Zealanders. A hundred miles of railway takes many years to build.

"When will the North Auckland line be completed?" I asked an Auckland manufacturer.

"God knows," he answered, with a sigh.

GOVERNMENT HOUSE, AUCKLAND

"When do you expect railway connection with Gisborne?" I inquired of an Opotiki hotel-keeper.

"Not in our day," he grimly replied.

Once a Government minister assured a deputation that the Opotiki-Gisborne line was "pushing ahead rapidly"; whereupon a member of the delegation inquired:—

"Do you think the railway will reach our district during the life of our leases?"

"What is the term of your lease?" asked the minister.

"Nine hundred and ninety-nine years," responded the delegate.

With the exception of a few short lines built chiefly for freight haulage, all the railways of New Zealand are owned and operated by the State, and have been since 1876. Within this period more than $160,000,000 has been spent on

Government railways, all of which are narrow-gauge. From its railways the State derives a gross annual revenue of about $20,000,000. The present net revenue approximates four per cent of the capital cost, or more than enough, according to an official statement, to pay the interest on the money borrowed for the system's construction.

Very likely the railways of New Zealand would be more profitable, or, at least, better managed, were they under the direction of a minister thoroughly experienced in railway affairs. Here is one just cause of complaint against Government ownership of public utilities. Too often their ministerial directors have had insufficient experience, or no experience at all, in the field over which they assume control. New Zealand's Railway Department has been fortunate for many years in the possession of an experienced general manager, but such an official, however efficient, can scarcely compensate for a less well-informed minister, particularly if that minister should not be inclined to heed the suggestions of tried assistants.

The equipment on New Zealand railways includes American-built locomotives and carriages based on the American saloon-car principle. This style of carriage is provided mainly for first-class passengers, though more are being built for second-class patrons. On nearly all trains I saw second-class passengers facing each other on uncomfortable leather-bottom seats running the full length of the car. In old coaches the distinction between first and second classes often is not pronounced. Sometimes the only advantages possessed by the first-class passengers are rough floor mats, leather backs to second-class seats, and a bit of gilt.

It is intended that every passenger shall have a seat, or, at any rate, that coaches shall not be overcrowded. New Zealand trains often are uncomfortably filled, but only with the consent of the passengers is this permissible. "No person," says a rule, "shall remain in a car with the full number of authorized passengers without the consent of the passengers." This rule is not always literally regarded, however.

Equally considerate is the no-tipping rule, which reads: "No railway servant shall receive any gratuity on pain of dismissal, and no person shall give or offer a gratuity to any such servant." New Zealand is no place for Pullman-car porters.

Of railway stations New Zealand has only one worthy of special mention, and that is in Dunedin. With this exception all the main depots are long, one-story brick buildings, with verandas running their full length and furnishing a roof for the platforms. The most conspicuous feature of the average station is its name. The majority have Maori names, and they are not noted for their brevity. On some lines seventy-five per cent of the stations have native appellations. The pronunciation of many of these is hard enough for the porter; to me they often were impossible. Soon after starting to pronounce them I found myself tacking like a ship in an adverse wind.

"The cost of travel is moderate," says a New Zealand authority, speaking of the Dominion's railways. It is reasonable, but equipment considered, it is, for "ordinary" tickets, quite enough. The rate is three cents per mile for first-class and two cents per mile for second-class. Holiday excursion tickets, mileage counted one way only, are respectively four cents and two cents per mile. For fifty dollars one can get a ticket valid for seven weeks on the lines of both islands, or for thirty dollars one can ride for four weeks on the lines of either island. Extensions of these tickets are granted up to four weeks for seven and one-half-dollars per week. Cheap tickets also are issued to workers, commutators, families, and to other classes of travelers. Schoolchildren not more than nineteen years of age and members of Parliament ride free. Children, however, are limited to a maximum distance of sixty miles.

The ticket system of the New Zealand railways has, with some warrant, been called cumbrous and antiquated; yet it is not so deficient as many complaining travelers allege. It is not true, as has been charged, that tickets can be purchased only on the day of departure. At all the chief cities and at about a dozen other places tickets can be purchased at railway stations the day before entraining. Nor is it wholly true that tickets cannot be purchased until within fifteen minutes of the departure of trains, but it is almost so, for only in a score of towns can they be bought at any time during the hours of business. At all other stations the fifteen-minute rule prevails, excepting on race-days and holidays. It is true, however, that the Railway Department has no uptown ticket agencies. This is an item of economy that means a large saving to the Government, but to the traveling public it is a cause of annoyance and inconvenience, second only to that occasioned by the apparently unnecessary time limit on ticket purchasing. Still it is compensated for in the principal cities by the passenger's ability to buy tickets at private booking agencies or at those of the Department of Tourist and Health Resorts.

Another very annoying circumstance is the lack of facilities for selling tickets on days of heavy travel. At the Auckland railway station, for example, only one ticket window has been open when two or three fast-filling trains were at the platform, with the result that passengers who were unable to get tickets before their train departed were subject to a surcharge of twelve cents on their fares.

Chapter IV

On a South Sea steamer redolent of the scented products of dreamy coral strands, I first saw the long white cliffs that, five hundred and sixty years before, had brightened the leaden eyes of the emaciated passengers of the Maori fleet from remote Hawaikian shores. From one land of stirring romance to another I had come; from Hawaiki, fatherland of the Maoris, to their last and most beautiful home; from a region of drowsy song and laughter to a country of brisk activity. It was early morn, a fresh breeze blew, and the sun, brilliant and unclouded, gave no evidence of the legendary beating it received at the hands of Maui and his brothers in New Zealand's cradle days.

New Zealand has many beautiful marine gateways, and toward the most beautiful of them all, Auckland, once the country's capital and now its largest city, our steamer plowed its way. One of the finest harbors of the world is possessed by this mistress of the Dominion's South Sea trade, a harbor with a setting as pretty as Sydney's Port Jackson.

Auckland not only has an exceptional harbor; it has two harbors, the arms of separate seas. On the east, where the city stands, is the Pacific Ocean; on the west, across a narrow isthmus, is the Tasman Sea. To the first comes traffic from overseas; to the second ply small coasting-vessels, which anchor in the port of Onehunga.

The eastern portal of "The Long Bright World" is reached through the tranquil, island-dotted Hauraki Gulf, one of the greatest yachting centres of the Southern Hemisphere. On the distant right as we entered the gulf on this smiling day were the forested heights of the Great Barrier, an island with charming bays and inlets possessing the unique feature of a "pigeongram" service to the mainland. On the left were the higher wooded ranges of Coromandel, the peninsula of gold. West of the Great Barrier towered the mountainous Little Barrier, a Government bird preserve.

AUCKLAND FROM MOUNT EDEN

"Most striking of all the islands in the gulf was Rangitoto, an extinct volcano, with long, dark slopes terminating in a ridge with twin shoulders. At its base, totally differing in form and substance, was sandy, pastoral Motutapu, one of the main picnic islands of Hauraki. As we turned into Rangitoto channel the view broadened. In the foreground rose the sandstone cliffs of peninsular Devonport, the green, terraced slopes of Fort Cautley, and Mount Victoria and its signal station, overlooking the wide shell beach of Cheltenham. Here were pretty pictures of lawn and meadow, of imported pine and cypress trees sheltering neat cottages with gray or red iron roofs.

Southerly, across the harbor, were the terraced bulks of volcanic Mount Eden, One Tree Hill, and Mount Hobson. Rounding Cautley's hidden guns, the steamer plowed the Waitemata, "the waters of affliction." On the mainland to the left were long, indented walls of sandstone, green, rolling meadows, groves and hedges of trees, scattered homes, and beach resorts; on shrub-mantled cliffs to the right, the pretty suburbs of Devonport, Stanley Bay, Birkenhead, Northcote, and Chelsea, where the Colonial Sugar Refining Company extracts sugar from Fijian cane.

Straight ahead, climbing hills and filling valleys, was Greater Auckland, one hundred thousand strong. Away beyond, overlooking the Tasman Sea, hung the blue haze of the Waitakere ranges, where the city gets its water supply. Well back from Auckland's shore, across Cemetery Gully, swung the great arch of one of the largest ferro-concrete bridges in the world. On an elevation overlooking the gully stood the huge pile of Auckland Hospital, maintained partly by a Government pound-for-pound subsidy. Nearer the shore the eye was quickly attracted by the shapely tower of St. Matthew's, the city's handsomest and costliest church, and the spire of St. Patrick's. Between these churches rises a building which Aucklanders call a sky-scraper. It has only seven stories, but its position is so elevated and the buildings around it are so low that it looks much higher than it is.

Only two other buildings in New Zealand have as many stories. When it was first proposed to erect a seven-story building in New Zealand, timorous residents of Christchurch, where it was finally built, protested against such emulation of America. "Earthquakes might shake it down," they said.

"Cab, sir!"

This was my first shore greeting as I passed down the steamer's gangway to encounter cabbies, express-men, customs officials, and policemen. I had hoped to hear the welcoming voice of a friend, but he had gone to Wellington, expecting me on a steamer which I had missed in Tahiti through an agent's inability to distinguish the difference between eastern and western time.

No, I did not want a cab; I wanted a ride in a "tram." The factory whistles were blowing five o'clock when, soon after landing, I saw a sign reading: "No standing in this car." Recollecting street cars of the United States with passengers crowding platforms, fenders, and roofs, I thought: "That's the car for me." Following the example of a score of workmen, I slid hastily into a seat. It was bare and hard, but that sign was so comforting that I read it again, and wished for a similar order on American car lines. Then I chanced to look at the aisle. It was little more than a foot wide! All the seats were narrow, too, and shoulders and legs necessarily encroached on the aisle, to the discomfort of the conductor.

Along this passage the conductor squirmed with a leather pouch or bag slung in front of him. In his hand he carried a box-like affair holding a row of tickets in blocks of various colors. To aid him in removing the tickets he carried on his breast a small sponge, with which he frequently moistened his thumb and forefinger. When I handed him a coin, his hand dropped into the bag. Immediately there was a great rattling. The conductor was drawing on his stock of coppers, each as big as a half-dollar, but worth only two cents. As most of his fares were pennies, quarts of coin seemed not unknown to him.

Just past a corner our car was stopped. Something had happened.

"What is the trouble?" I asked a man.

"They put a bloke off," said he. "There were too many in the car."

Too many in the car! Oh, America!

To me Auckland held a special interest. Here the globe-girdling fleet of the United States Navy had been generously entertained in 1908, and I knew that New Zealand's second capital had begun life on the banks of a creek seventy years before. At that time this stream flowed undisturbed into Waitemata Harbor; on this day its channel, filled, and paved with asphalt, was known as Queen Street, the business centre of the city.

New Zealand has no other street like Queen Street It is the city's connecting link with the world beyond the sea. At its foot anchor steamers that trade to all the continents and to the islands of the South Seas. There I have seen lumber from California and Oregon, kerosene from New York, mixed cargoes from Europe, and oranges, bananas, cocoanuts, and pineapples from the South Pacific. On it front handsome business blocks of from three to five stories; also a costly post-office, and a new town hall containing what is said to be the finest pipe-organ in Australasia.

On Queen Street there are bustle and entertaining details of life. There are lorries, black-roofed furniture vans, carts, two-wheeled drays, motor-cars, and, last and least, baggage-carts with old men lounging on them. Near these aged carters are other old men—bootblacks whose charge for a shine is "sixpence and as much more as you like to give," as one of them said to me. On this same corner from a half-dozen to a score of Maoris are always taking life leisurely—well-fed men who at all times are ready for a "long beer"; and women with pipes and papooses. And if it is Sunday night, at the junction of Queen and Grey streets there usually may be found Billy Richardson, stanchest of Prohibitionists, sternly reprimanding lovers of "shandy-gaffs" and things stronger, and perhaps once more telling his auditors that the Germans will be upon them and theirs if they don't soon reform. Then, too, there are always to be heard on this street Socialists and the Salvation Army, each claiming to possess the millennial formula.

QUEEN STREET, AUCKLAND

In my opinion, Auckland is seen at its best from the summit of Mount Eden, but there are others who prefer the vistas of One Tree Hill. Mount Eden, like so many volcanic hills of New Zealand, looks like a succession of terraces or steps. This was not its original shape; the terraces were made by warring Maoris. Eden is a great scoria heap that rises six hundred and forty feet above the sea. In it deep pits have been dug to get scoria for building material, streets, and railroad ballast, and at its base to-day stone quarries are worked.

Mount Eden is surely one of the most romantic and historical spots of New Zealand. Around it hover memories of war and intrigue, love and shadowy tradition. Where sheep now peacefully browse, human blood flowed and hideous clamor rose, for it was long the chief fort of the Tainui tribe, which started the first Maori war in New Zealand, and in the large earthworks food-pits of warriors are still seen to-day.

On Mount Eden I stood in the midst of a volcanic region, and on the verge of a crater one hundred and twenty feet deep. At its bottom were scoria stones that once were red-hot, and from its grassy slopes, everywhere marked by sheep tracks, red scoria obtruded. Over the tops of the mountain's pines I saw many isolated terraced hills, set in wildernesses of broken stones; all fiery furnaces once. Within a radius of five miles of Mount Eden there are said to be fifty extinct volcanoes. First nature threw missiles from them; centuries later came the Maoris, who converted them into forts, and from their heights hurled spears and swung stone axes, and heavy clubs of stone and wood.

The view from Eden's summit is one of the finest panoramas of the world. There are more majestic views, but scarcely any more varied. New Zealand, at least, has nothing to equal the picture I saw on my first tramp to Eden's grassy crest. Eastward stretched the distant mountain shores of Coromandel, the intruding Pacific and its island barriers, and the manifold reaches of Hauraki Gulf. Almost lost in the haze were the Barriers; in the foreground were rock-strewn Rangitoto and islands of flatter mould; nearer still was the slender green arm of the North Shore, once probably an island. Northward lay the white clay expanses of the kauri-gum land, sparsely inhabited hills covered with scrub and fern, and the Waitakeres and their native bush. To the south were low mountains.

In the west, between Waitakere's shores and Manukau Heads, was a glimpse of blue. It was the Tasman Sea, which under the name of Manukau Harbor pushes itself so far inland that it almost mingles with the Pacific. Where the waters of the two seas so nearly meet, two inconcurrent tides ebb and flow. When one tide is high the other has receded, yet at high tide they are only a thousand yards apart.

Auckland has been called a city of parks. It is more. As seen from Mount Eden it seemed a park itself,—a rolling park with meadows, fertile hills, trees and hedges, bowling-greens, football and cricket grounds, race-courses, and harmonious intervals of water.

Fronting Hobson Bay rambled Remuera, a dream of beauty; farther west were the sequestered homes of Parnell's wooded shores; back of them were the meadows and forested nooks of the Domain. In Auckland proper appeared the masts of shipping, smoking factory chimneys, church steeples, the dull-gray of cement-surfaced business blocks, the lighter gray of cottage roofs, and the rose tints of painted siding. This monotony of color was relieved only by isolated red roofs and verandas and red and yellow brick walls. In Ponsonby, Grey Lynn, and Newton were row after row of workmen's homes with scarcely a variation of color.

In the suburbs of Kingsland, Mount Eden, Epsom, and One Tree Hill, and in Parnell and Remuera, were flashes of color, and red roofs were in greater number.

In these suburbs many Auckland business men have their homes. The majority of these are cottages, inclosed by hedges or fences of pickets or galvanized iron. They are neat and cozy, standing in grounds beautified by flowers, shrubs, and trees, and frequently by lawns. Usually far more attention is given to the shrubbery than to the lawns. In all parts of New

Zealand parked walks border ragged, neglected grass. Many of these homes have names, and their owners show a love of privacy. Like the Englishman, the British colonial loves seclusion, and to obtain it he sometimes raises hedges from ten to fifteen feet high.

Of Auckland's parks, Albert Park, in the downtown district, is the prettiest, and Cornwall Park, sweeping down from and including One Tree Hill, is the most magnificent. Cornwall Park was presented to the city by the late Sir John Logan Campbell, "the Father of Auckland," and its three hundred acres have been estimated to be worth more than one million dollars. In Albert Park are cannon from Waterloo, Crimea, South Africa, and New Zealand battle-fields; and around the bandstand Admiral Sperry and other officers of the United States Navy planted sixteen oak trees in August, 1908.

ALBERT PARK, AUCKLAND

Another attractive reserve is the Domain, an area of two hundred acres embowered in wild and cultivated verdure. On its reclaimed swamp are cricket grounds where nearly a dozen cricket matches are played simultaneously every bright Saturday afternoon in the cricket season.

From Albert Park it is worthwhile to step into the public art gallery, adjoining. In this art exhibition, the best in the Dominion, are good examples of landscapes, marines, and portraits by New Zealanders.

In the Auckland Museum, also near Albert Park, is to be found New Zealand art of another sort. There, in the best display of its kind in the Dominion, are exceptional specimens of the intricate carvings of the Maoris. The section is populated by a multitude of carved wooden figures with miens ferocious, grotesque, solemn, and dull. There are tattooed faces, rows of big teeth that seem eager to crunch; tongues from one to two feet long that silently defy; three-fingered hands grasping war-clubs; other hands resting on abdomens, as though their owners had the stomach-ache. From pataka and whare, from isolated panels, statues, and ancient village gateway, large staring eyes of wood and shell glare at one inquisitively, contemptuously, or ignore the visitor altogether. All these effigies in wood are painted dull red with a preparation of powdered clay mixed with fat, and some of them are generations old.

On the right of the entrance to these labyrinths in wood where I entered, were the remains of a huge statue, perhaps originally twenty feet high. Its tongue was two feet long, its mouth was as large as a whale's, and in its right hand it held a weapon, as if on sentinel duty. In the rear of the hall stood an immense tiki, representing a mother with two children in her lap. The chest expansion of this figure, which once probably was at least fifteen feet high, was so great that not less than ten or twelve feet of tape would be required to take its girth.

Beneath this statuary was a great war-canoe. It was eighty-two feet long, had a maximum beam of seven feet, and could have seated at least one hundred men. It was one of the largest of Maori war-vessels, yet not nearly so large as some ancient canoes of New Zealand. One of these had a hull one hundred and eight feet long, but including its elaborated stern and bow, its total length was nearly two hundred feet. So wide were some canoes that four or five paddlers could sit abreast, the inside men being reliefs. Two hundred years ago double canoes were common in New Zealand, and there were outriggers also.

More interesting than the war-canoe were the museum's carved native houses. The largest and finest was about fifty feet long and half as wide, and several years were spent in its construction. The first of its features that impressed me were the wide gable boards, the large carved figures of men, and the ridge-post terminating in tikis. The tiki at the base of the post seemed to feel the weight above him severely. He was like Atlas with the world on his shoulders. His hands were braced against his sides, and in fancy I could almost hear him groan. The fellow at the top was almost, grinning; he had his feet on the man below and carried no burden.

The veranda was very different from European verandas. Instead of stepping on it, I stepped in, as in Maori houses generally, over a board running the full length of the porch. In this thatched, low-walled house the rafters were scrolls of red, white, and black; the sides were lined with heavy slabs of wood bearing carved illustrations of noted ancestors; and in the space between these panels were varied designs of split rods, painted red, white, and black, and flax strips.

The food-houses in the museum are, like all patakas, raised on posts. They were built thus to protect the food, seeds, and personal belongings of the leading tribesmen from rats, which once were so numerous as to provide the Maoris with one of their chief articles of diet. As a rule they were built with more care than other houses and were more finished and decorated. Frequently the carved panels were lashed to studs adorned with feathers, and nearly all the carvings were on the outside of the building. In this way the pataka differs from the wharepuni, or sleeping-house, which is carved mainly on the inside. The embellishments of a pataka would not be complete without an effigied warrior on the apex of the front gable boards with extended tongue betokening defiance, and hands on abdomen as an indicative, if not an actual, sign of plenty.

The larger of the museum patakas must have been a very important storehouse, for on its gable boards were carvings of the mythological manaia, a taniwha, or supernatural behemoth, and on its ridge-pole running lizards were portrayed. To the average Maori a lizard is a terrifying spectacle, but just why nobody knows. Perhaps the Maoris originally came from a land where their progenitors battled against crocodiles.

In a glass case below the patakas were burial chests probably two hundred years old. They were strange creatures of wood crudely representing the human form. One was short and very bow-legged, and he was all abdomen from thigh to neck. His eyes were closed and he was yawning heavily, as befitted one going to his last sleep.

In this same room were more impressive reminders of shroud and bier. In glass cases were preserved heads of ancient warriors, tattooed, and with hair attached. Among the Maoris the preservation of the heads of enemies as trophies of war was a common practice. This was done by removing the brain, eyes, and tongue, cleaning the interior and filling it with dressed flax; and by curing. The dressed head was first steamed in an oven, followed by several weeks of sun drying and smoking over wood fires at night. Once the Maoris sold many of these preserved heads to traders in the Bay of Islands, who sent them to Sydney, whence they were shipped to Europe. The traffic finally was stopped by the New South Wales Government.

A block from the museum, standing in beautiful grounds, is a wooden building of peculiar interest. It is Government House, in which New Zealand's Governor resides for a time each year. In Government House it is easy to imagine one's self under the roof of Napoleon's St. Helena residence, for it is a counterpart of the exile's home.

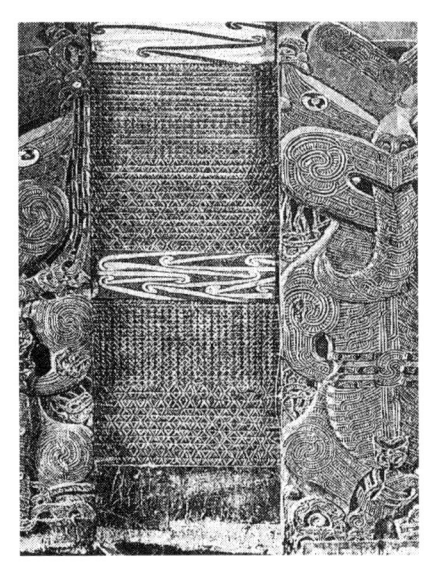

MAORI CARVINGS

In every New Zealand city there are reminders of America. They range from perambulators to harvesting-machines, from go-carts to railway locomotives, from whiskey to kerosene oil, from leather goods to sausage skins. All these and many other articles of commerce New Zealand imports from the United States. It has remained for Auckland, however, to introduce that cherished institution of America, the peanut roaster. On busy corners of Queen Street and Karangahape Road its cheery whistle is often to be heard. In New Zealand the peanut has been very much neglected. Perhaps its virtues are not appreciated, for it is still, in a measure, an alien struggling for deserved recognition. There were peanuts in Maoriland long before the arrival of the peanut roaster, but they usually were seen in disregarded heaps in small grocers' shops, and though they bore the legend, "Fresh roasted," they had the appearance of having been in one spot for months, like a homesteader.

The introduction of the peanut roaster into New Zealand was a praiseworthy bit of pioneering, but another popular accessory of American life is still lacking in that land. It is the buttered popcorn wagon. It will be an eventful day in the Dominion's history when the first popcorn wagon, with peanut roaster attached, sends forth appetizing odors in Aotearoa.

But think not that New Zealand has no savory street odors of its own. It has, and very pronounced they are, too. They were often wafted to me from fish shops, where "fish and chips " and soft drinks always were to be had. At night, when these shops cooked for the following day, the downtown streets of coastal cities were strong with the scent of fish and fried potatoes. This reference to shops is a reminder that when one goes shopping in New Zealand one does not go to "stores." There are stores in New Zealand, as wool stores, kauri-gum stores, and grain stores, but there are no dry goods stores, grocery or hardware stores. Instead there are drapers, general providers, greengrocers, and ironmongers. There are some attractive shops in New Zealand, but in looking at the average shop-windows I concluded that proprietors were crowded for space. Their windows were congested with goods, indicating a desire on their part to display to the passerby a sample of everything they had in stock.

It is a pleasure to go shopping in New Zealand, the attendants are so polite. They thank you for everything. With each purchased article I seldom got less than two "Thank yous," and sometimes three. The number depended upon the multiplicity of moves between buyer and seller. Usually there was one for each move. By an Auckland salesman I was thanked thrice when purchasing postcards, first when I handed him the cards I had selected, again when I paid, and lastly when he gave me my change.

Shopkeepers and their assistants are not the only polite people in New Zealand. Everybody who waits on the public has a supply of "Thank you" at tongue's end, ready for instant service. Some of these came at me on the jump; others were delivered with prim, pleasant formality; while others, and they were legion, "dragged their weary length along" as if the speakers were loath to part with them.

Chapter V

In the South Island the traveler is fascinated by ice and snow. In the North Island he is awed by fire and steam.

In the north, from Ruapehu's snows to Ohaeawai's tepid springs, full three hundred miles away, is a violent, vaporous land. It is ulcerous with turbulent, nauseous mudholes, and scabby with the white sterility of silica. Earthquake tremors frequently shake it, and it throbs with the pulsations of subterranean boilers. It has steaming lakes, pools, and streams, healing baths and springs, acidulous basins of emerald, opal, and orange, and tinted terraces of sinter. From smoking crater come deadly gases, and on mountain-top is heated turmoil amidst snow and ice.

Here are thermal islands in the sea, and buried villages ashore. Here, in this warming-pan, this outdoor kitchen, are roaring steam vents, simmering shallows and sweating sulphur. In populous centres, in untenanted swamp and manuka waste are plutonic vapors, infuriate mud, and spouting water. In this realm of hidden fires are clear, cold lakes in the shades of lovely forests.

All these and much more I found in the Hot Lakes Wonderland. The Hot Lakes District has been hastily, extravagantly named. It is rather a region of cold lakes, although there is plenty of hot water in all its parts, and some of it is present in lakes, but more generally so in pools and ponds.

The cause of all this thermal activity, I naturally supposed, was volcanic agencies and probably the chemical action of sulphuric acid on water. Not so, a Maori legend informed me. These volcanic fires were caused by two women, sisters of a high priest named Ngatoroirangi, who acted in his ecclesiastical capacity in the Arawa canoe on its voyage from Hawaiki to New Zealand. Ngatoroirangi and a man named Ngauruhoe ascended Tongariro Mountain, and there the priest's companion froze to death. Calling to his sisters in

Hawaiki, he asked them to bring him fire. On the back of a taniwha they came, and as they journeyed they produced geysers, the first one on White Island, an active volcano in the Bay of Plenty. The fire they brought saved their brother and converted New Zealand into a steam heater.

The centre of this wonderland is Rotorua, or "Rotterrua," as some careless people call it. It is one hundred and seventy-one miles by rail from Auckland, overlooking Lake Rotorua at an elevation of nine hundred and thirty-two feet above sea level, and is reached daily by express trains. Rotorua is more than the chief health and tourist resort of the Dominion. It is a Government town, controlled by the Department of Tourist and Health Resorts, and has been since 1907.

"Tenakoe" (Hello)!

It was a welcome to the sulphurous heart of the Arawa country that greeted me. The Maoris at the station seemed glad to see me, but they were not half so glad or effusive as the mob of hotel and boarding-house keepers and bus drivers beside the railway gate. There were nearly enough of them to populate a town.

As I went toward my hotel an odor of sulphur was wafted to me. It came from the sanatorium grounds by the lake shore, and the steam columns I saw in the same area rose from the artificial Malfroy geysers in a concrete basin.

Before sight-seeing in Rotorua I wanted a bath. Nothing was easier to get. I could have had scores of different kinds of baths before bedtime had I desired them. Rotorua is one of the cleanest towns in the world, for everybody there bathes frequently. In the midst of its bathtubs and pools the professional tramp would feel woefully out of place. Every morning before breakfast I saw men and women with towels on arms or shoulders on their way to bathhouses. Verily, if cleanliness be next to godliness, Rotorua must be especially near and dear to the gods.

As the baths of Rotorua are many and varied, so also are the places in which they are housed. They were offered to me in low, unpretentious buildings; in the Duchess, opened by King George V of England when he was Duke of Cornwall and York; and in the one hundred and fifty thousand dollar bathhouse of European design. I was invited to swim in the mild Blue Bath; to disport in the stronger Priest; to test my endurance qualities in the powerful Postmaster; to feel the drawing power of the Sulphur Vapor Bath; and to spatter myself with mud. Altogether there were about forty different ways to bathe or be bathed, including douches, douche-massages, and electric applications. In Rotorua's baths one can be treated for rheumatism, sciatica, dyspepsia, gout, liver complaints, skin diseases, or other ills.

MAIN BATH HOUSE, ROTORUA

The sanatorium grounds form the loveliest spot in a valley not devoid of beautiful scenery. West and south rise low, brown, fern-covered hills that meet higher wooded hills, some of which attain the dignity of mountains. Chief of these in Rotorua's neighborhood is Ngongotaha, 2554 feet above the sea. At the base of these heights, near Rotorua, are plains clothed with bracken fern and tea-tree, brightened by a few green meadows. On the immediate west is Lake Rotorua, with brown-topped Mokoia, island of sweet romance, in its centre.

The sanatorium area is a weird place, despite its cultivated beauty. For a first lesson in thermology it is a capital school. There on a moderate scale I saw illustrated some of the greater wonders of the district. There were agitated waters covered with bubbles as large as hens' eggs; pools with contents boiling like syrup in a kettle; others colored, some with surfaces of ever-changing patterns of shifting oil; effervescing gas bubbles in the lake; and splashing and rumbling in steaming fissures.

Not the least interesting of my discoveries were the bits of pumice on the lake shore. They had the appearance of stone, but they were only the froth of stone, bits of lava scum that overran volcanoes ages ago. They were so light that they floated. In the North Island millions of tons of pumice have been discharged from volcanoes, and on the Kaingaroa Plains fully ten thousand square miles have been covered with it. Once believed to be valueless, pumice soil has been found suitable for agriculture, and the settlement of pumice wastes promises to become general in New Zealand.

Rotorua is the greatest picnic ground of a truly picnic land. Every day of the year it has picnics and excursions, "weather and other circumstances permitting," as Australasian steamship agents say. Rotorua is a place of early "calls" and early breakfasts; then away, in whirling clouds of dust, in horse and motor coaches, to Whakarewarewa's geysers, to the infernos of Tikitere, to buried Wairoa, to steaming Rotomohana and suffocated Waimangu; or away to sparkling Hamurana or the bosoms of trout-infested lakes. Every morning for a fortnight there is something different to see; then ho! for the geysers of distant Taupo and Wairakei or to restful Te Aroha and its wooded mountain.

Steam heat, boiling mud, and baths are not the only attractions Rotorua offers its visitors. At the time of my visit there it had in addition the Tuhourangi troupe of Maori entertainers, which, I was informed, had been patronized by Lord Kitchener and Madame Melba, in a recent tour of Australia. I went to the Assembly Hall to see "the Maori at home" and to be stirred by the defiant haka and charmed by the rhythmic, pacific poi.

The entertainment opened with a scene depicting Maoris in olden days, and the reception of distinguished visitors. The hosts were a chief of mighty bulk and a number of barefooted women wearing white waists, and red skirts beneath stringy flax petticoats that rattled with every move of their bodies. Several of them had tattooed chins; some wore ties with high stiff collars, and large greenstone tikis, that distorted image of the human form so popular among Maoris; and each had two poi balls, light spheres of bulrush with short flax strings attached.

Following felicitous exchanges between them and the visitors, a lanky chief and a company of girls, came an exhibition of the so-called poi dance, which is more nearly a motion song. The participants were a dozen women, and as is usual in most poi dances, the players stood while acting. Between their thumbs and forefingers they held the balls, one in each hand.

The dance began with a movement of the hips. As the movements became more rapid there was a close resemblance to the hula-hula of the Hawaiians and the otea of the Tahitians, but the contortions were not so violent. Sometimes knees were bent; at other times hand motions were prominent. In poi games, however,—they were so called on the programme,—there is great variety, and the shouts and stampings of one game may be superseded by singing or silence in another. Seldom, though, are the poi balls idle at any stage of the game. They are played from side to side on hands and wrists, around head and shoulders, and on other parts of the body, to an accordion or harmonica accompaniment and with rhythm in every move of ball and rattle of flax string. The whole is so bewildering and fascinating that usually the beholder is eager to see another performance "straight away," as they say in Australasia.

The hakas this evening were given by a company of magnificent-looking men. They were bare from waist line to shoulders and from knees down. All wore light knee trousers, over which were flax kilts, and each carried a taiaha, a wooden sword something like a narrow-bladed paddle. They were men of sinewy limbs and strong lungs; they leaped as if they were on springs, and their cries, if delivered by an army of warriors, would be deafening. From their performance the spectators gained a good idea of the manner and pitch to which Maoris roused themselves before engaging in a battle. They leaped high into the air, their kilts spreading like parachutes as they rose and fell; they slapped their chests, arms, legs, and hands; yelled and hissed; knelt briefly on one knee; then rose to renew their ferocious poses, striking in front of themselves as if they intended to go bodily through a foe, and nearly all the while fiercely grimacing and exhibiting that Maori symbol of defiance — an extended tongue.

POI DANCE

Much more interesting than Rotorua, in some particulars, is the native village of Ohinemutu, adjoining the State town, just beyond the old fort-hill of Pukeroa. Despite its misfortune in losing a part of itself in an earthquake many years ago—a disaster impressed on its visitors by its leaning church tower—Ohinemutu is progressive; huts it has, but they are patterned after the pakeha's houses, and in keeping therewith many of them support a big galvanized iron or tin chimney on the outside. To me chimneys seemed out of place in this pa, until I was told that they are for use in cold weather, and for those families who have no convenient cooking-hole.

A cooking-hole! Ohinemutu has, of a truth, little need of chimneys since it is an outdoor kitchen. It prepares its meals in fireless cookers—in hot pools and steam holes. Enter its gates, and you shall see meat, fish, and vegetables nicely cooked without cost. In this village nobody growls about burnt food, and fuel bills are light.

Ohinemutu is no embattled pa surrounded by ditches and stout fences and defended by carnivorous warriors, as of old. It is true that on a few gables and other conspicuous elevations unfriendly eyes glared at me, tongues lolled a menace, and grinning teeth seemed eager to close on me; but they were lifeless carvings. Ohinemutu's gates, or rather the open spaces and passageways that take their places, are never closed.

Throughout Ohinemutu I encountered steam. It rose from pools where children swam—along the margin of the lake, along the paths that served as streets, and in front and back yards. Some of these children asked me to throw pennies into the pools, that they might dive for them. Diving for tourists' pennies is a daily pursuit of Maori boys and girls in the Rotorua district. Many pools are too hot for diving, and sometimes people accidentally fall into them, and are scalded to death. I read of one or two men who were fatally scalded in a bath in the manuka wastes back of Pukeroa Hill, and at Tokaanu I heard of a tourist who stumbled into a hotwater hole one night and was so severely burned before he scrambled out that he was in a hospital for months. In the same village when I was in New Zealand, a young Maori wife committed suicide by leaping into a boiling spring, and not a vestige of her body could be found by her husband.

How fortunate are the cooks of Ohinemutu. In that blissful retreat of steam the housewife has no kitchen fire to build, no cooking-stove to polish, and the small boy's play-hours are never disturbed by that world-familiar maternal command, "Bring in some wood." My first view of an Ohinemutu fireless cooker was beside a public path. It was a wooden box, inset in the ground, with a steaming gunny-sack over it, and it had an unpleasant smell. Close by were others like it; in other places I saw these fibrous stove-lids flat on the ground. In one a woman was placing two kettles, and she thrust them in quickly to avoid getting burnt fingers. To another steamer a woman was carrying a large piece of pork; by a hot pool another housewife was plucking feathers from a fowl; and in a yard beside the Tauranga road a white man secreted a pot of potatoes as a miser buries his gold. Ohinemutu was cooking its Sunday dinner.

A mile and a half from Rotorua is the Maori village of Whakarewarewa, or Whaka, as it is often called to save time and conserve the lungs. The main entrance to Whaka is a little bridge with red railings spanning Puarenga Stream, a cold creek between steaming banks. Approaching it, I saw the right side lined by men and women, all gazing below. What was the attraction?

"Penny, penny! Throw a penny!"

That was the answer, given in eager, childish voices. Boys and girls were diving in and into the creek for pennies. Frequently a boy or a girl came up to leap from the platform or railing. Each had a graduated scale of prices. From the platform they dived for a penny, but charges increased rapidly with altitude, and for a leap from the railing, less than five feet above, the rate was thrice the other.

"A haka for a penny."

That is another entertainment to be had for a copper at this same bridge. Whaka's youthful tamas and tamahines were industrious; all appeared to be actors or actresses, and divers. When they were not splashing in Puarenga or were not in school, they were dancing, grimacing, and contorting for a penny apiece. When I asked my guide to arrange a haka for me, it was late in the day and few performers were abroad. My "company" was composed of five small lads and a girl. They gave a sort of modernized haka. In true Maori fashion, they thrust out their tongues as far as possible, rolled their eyes, and stamped their bare feet. That I was prepared for, but I was amazed to hear them sing snatches of "Yankee Doodle," and "Every Ship has a Harbor." From these mites "Yankee Doodle" seemed as unnatural as did "John Brown" from the lips of some of my boy guides in the Cook Islands. These children had been listening to phonographs.

Whaka is another open-air kitchen. In its native reserve it cooks its food. Whaka is, in truth, one big steamer. There nearly a dozen geysers play, hot springs abound, and tossing mud and clay are seen throughout the vale.

One of the most interesting of Whaka's attractions is the soaping of geysers in the Government Reserve. With hundreds of others I went there one day to see Wairoa Geyser soaped for the benefit of moving-picture men. My guide was Georgiana, a Maori with tattooed lips and chin. She was bareheaded, but not barefooted; Georgiana wore a pair of high-heeled shoes.

Soaping Wairoa is always an important event in Whaka, for not often does the Government permit it, because excessive soaping weakens geysers. Wairoa never plays until it is soaped, and sometimes it won't respond even then. At the hour set for the ceremony this day the terrace of Wairoa, the flat adjacent, and the shelter houses and the slopes below it were crowded with spectators.

All the while the geyser Waikorihihi was sending forth clouds of steam and sprinkling with drifting spray the people between it and Wairoa, as if to say: "Watch me. I work nearly all the time, and I don't have to be coaxed with soap either."

THE DUCAL HAKA, ROTORUA

There was a stir in the crowd. It was caused by Kathleen, smiling, small, and supple. She was brilliant in a flax mat completely covered with kaka, kiwi, and pigeon feathers. She tripped to the geyser's mouth; for this pleasant, popular Maori guide, was to coax Wairoa with soap and smiles.

The caretaker approached her with a big white bag in hand. It was half full of yellow soap cut into small cubes.

"Are you ready, Kathleen?" he asked.

"Yes," she promptly answered.

Taking out two or three handfuls of soap, the caretaker threw them into Wairoa's deep throat, and then handed the bag to Kathleen. Grasping the string handle at the bottom of the bag, she opened the mouth, and out poured a saponaceous stream.

"How long must we wait to see Wairoa play?" I inquired of Georgiana.

"Ten minutes, usually," she replied.

The minutes passed, but there was only a slight increase in the volume of steam at Wairoa's mouth, and there were no subterranean signs of an imminent eruption. Fifteen, twenty minutes passed, with very little change.

When thirty minutes had gone there was a rumble, then a splash of water. The people near the geyser backed away. Two or three more splashes followed, and each was higher than its predecessor. Then came a hoarse roar, a rush of steam, and up past a low, sulphur-dyed sinter wall flashed a column of water carrying clouds of steam. Soap, just common washing-soap, had conquered Wairoa and forced it from its lair. Up it continued to go—fifty, sixty, eighty, one hundred and twenty feet.

"Wairoa would have gone higher if it had n't been for the wind," the caretaker told me. "It has been known to go one hundred and eighty feet."

While Wairoa played it played magnificently. In its shaft it rumbled, it flung its hot breath upon the venturesome, and for more than one hundred feet around it shook the ground until the earth trembled. For ten minutes it rose and fell. Then down it went, like a thermometer on a frosty night, until it was a mere splasher.

Kathleen, Wairoa's tempter, wore shoes at the soaping ceremony; but where were they now, after the people had dispersed? She was barefooted as she and other guides wended their way to the village square.

"Where are your shoes, Kathleen?" asked Georgiana.

"Oh, I left them at the geyser," was the reply, in a tone that indicated its communicator would not have cared much if her shoes had been tossed into Wairoa and boiled to bits.

The Government Reserve at Whaka is one of the most active and absorbing spots of the thermal zone. On geyser-built sinter terraces I counted eight geysers and a boiling caldron. Near them were deep, silent pools of clear, scalding blue; deep and shallow pools of hot, soapy-looking water; basins of boiling mud, blue, gray, creamy, black; "porridge-pots" and "paint-pots"; hot springs that simmered and boiled; steaming earth-banks, siliceous walls and rubbish heaps. Excepting the geysers, all was hidden by the low manuka and the lower fern. In this wilderness of shrub the stranger never knows what he will see or hear next. He hears the turmoil of waters and sees jets and blankets of steam, but their sources are hidden, and to reach them the wise step warily.

The geysers of this inclosure lie close together, none being more than a few hundred feet from its farthest neighbor, and several being within a few yards of each other. The majority play frequently, but not with the regularity characterizing Wairakei's geysers. The most active of the strongest is Waikorihihi. Its best endurance test, according to official records, is two hundred and twenty-nine days without a day's stop. Its usual height is from twenty to forty feet. Of about the same strength is the Caldron, a deep basin of blue hot water. When this spouter plays, Pohutu, a few feet away, generally follows suit, and always does so when the Caldron throws water into its cavity. Tossing a column of water from fifty to sixty feet high, Pohutu plays from one to four times a week, and in some months oftener.

Close to Pohutu, but not dependent on it for activity, is the Prince of Wales Feathers. It throws two small sprays and always plays when Pohutu does, as well as at other times. The terrace from which these two geysers shoot simmers in one place like a frying-pan. At the lower end of the terrace, overlooking Puarenga Creek, is Kereru, "The Pigeon," so named because of the slaty color of its mineral discharges, which form a hard mineral coating in a short time. Kereru is usually most active in the afternoon, and after it has been quiescent three hours it plays from seventy-five to ninety feet high.

In the creek, just below Kereru, is the Torpedo, a phenomenon caused by hot mud coming into contact with cold water. When I saw the Torpedo eleven years ago it was very active, but on my last visit to New Zealand it seldom played. When at its best it lifted, to a height of from one to three feet, a circle of inky black water about ten feet in diameter, the circle rising with unbroken surface until it reached its maximum height, when it exploded with a subdued report. The Torpedo may become just as active again, for it is not more erratic than other phenomena of the district.

Waikite, the twin geyser, for instance, was inactive for a period of thirteen years and four months. It stopped playing when the railroad to Rotorua was opened. Possibly it did not like the innovation, nor the rivalry of a steam locomotive. Finally it seems to have become reconciled to the new order, for occasionally it ejects water to a height of fifty or sixty feet.

Some of the sights in New Zealand's thermal wonderland are scarcely more impressive than their names. Those most frequently heard are appellations commonly applied to nether worlds. For example, the Devil appears to have had a lot to do with the creation of the weird and the marvelous. His name is associated with mudhole and blowhole, fire and steam. An idle brain is not more "the Devil's workshop" than New Zealand appears to be. An example of this fondness for Satanic titles is furnished by the Devil's Reception, a basin of boiling mud about fifty yards in circumference. Dotted with mounds of mud from one to five feet high and with sloppy, oily pools, it constantly flings its blackness with cracking, explosive reports. So much like hopping frogs do its ejections seem to the spectator that it often is called the Frog Pond.

Of the fireless cookers I saw in this reserve the one of the most historical interest was the Brain Pot, a shallow silica basin beside the main footpath. Once it had steamed like a boiling kettle; now only slight activity was visible. The Brain Pot has a tragic history. In it were cooked the brains of Chief Te Tukutuku, whose tribe had killed more than three hundred members of another iwi, Georgiana told me. After this slaughter Tukutuku fled with a slave, and for three years the two hid themselves in two caves in the reserve. In front of these caves were, as there are to-day, two warm pools. In one the chief took his daily bath; in the other his food was cooked. One day the slave was seen by some of the affronted tribesmen when he was searching for fern root. He was followed, and the chief was captured. Tukutuku's head was cut off, and his brains were served as a delicacy to his enemies.

Maoris have always been communists, and to a large extent they still are. In Whaka they have a community kitchen. It is not used for cooking only, however. This roofless, fireless cookhouse produces a revenue from curious tourists, and this income, like the kitchen, is communal. Other kitchens in Whaka one may enter without payment of a fee, but not the one in its native reserve. If the visitor does not adhere strictly to the regulations posted before it, he is liable to prosecution. After detailing the sights therein, including a "boiling caldron in which a man lost his life," the notice informs the public that "visitors are strictly requested to pay one shilling each time."

When I started through the tea-tree pole alley leading to the reserve it was noon. I took no guide, believing there would be one in the "kitchen." The only person in sight was an old, bent man carrying a kit of food and a kettle. Apparently he was about to leave the premises, but on seeing me, he quickly deposited his burden in a convenient cooking-box, and with beckoning arms and grunts made for me and the shilling. He wore a white felt hat, a gray sweater, overalls, and white canvas shoes, and in his mouth was a pipe. He was bowed low under the weight of years, yet his step was springy. And why should n't it be? Was not he to get a fourth of that shilling?

So far as I was concerned, my impromptu guide might as well have been speechless. I could n't understand a word he said; in truth, there were very few words he did speak after he found I was n't a Maori scholar. Instead, he became little more than a dumb show, with arm touches as his signals, and grunted "ughs" as his explanations and exclamation points.

His first grunt referred to a hot blue pool inclosed with an iron fence. Into it a native had fallen years before, and had been boiled to death. In explanation of this tragedy, my guide made a wry face, flapped his arms and shrugged his shoulders, then led me to three cooking-boxes, covered with gunny-sacks. Each was thirty inches long and two feet wide, and was filled with food in pots and flax kits. In this same reserve were several other cooking-boxes for the villagers' use, and in either of them a meal could be well cooked in twenty-five minutes, I had been assured by Georgiana.

From one hot spring in the inclosure ran a number of small ditches, connecting with a shallow pool and a row of large open boxes. What were these? The guide tried his best to tell me, but though he flourished his arms and grunted more than before, I could not understand him. A windmill, which he somewhat resembled, would have been just as useful to me. Possibly the old man thought so, too, for with a final volley of grunts he threw out his arms and pointed to the exit, as if to say, "Clear out."

I did not want to "clear out," for I was still little wiser than when I entered the reserve. Fortunately I soon found a Maori able to speak English, and from him I learned that the open boxes were the remains of a bathhouse annex. The bathhouse had been built by Whaka's hotel for the use of its guests, and its water was taken from the ditch-drained hot spring a few yards above. On these baths the hotel paid a rental. In this the villagers as a whole were entitled to share; but months passed without the declaration of a dividend. At last a Maori committee called on the hotel keeper for an explanation. He told it he had been paying the money in good faith to two native men. This so angered the committee and the villagers generally that they threatened to demolish the bathhouse.

"You have no right to do so," the hotel proprietor told them.

"You wait and see," replied the exasperated Maoris.

"Then," said guide number two to me, "all the people come and tear down the house, and they say, 'We will no let the white man come in here again to wash.'"

As for the shallow pool shown me, it was the town washtub. Round this tepid basin, on Blue Monday or its equivalent in Whaka, washerwomen flock like crows in a cornfield.

Over all the "hot lakes" country are astonishing contrasts. There is beauty beside ugliness, purity close to contamination, heat and cold separated by narrow walls, and clear depths near opaque turbulent pits and shallows. Of these opposites none is more pronounced than the difference between Hamurana Spring and Tikitere. The first is a flood of cold, crystal water bursting forth in arborescent wilds several miles from Tikitere; the second, reached by coach through earthquake fissures, is an inferno of boiling black mud set in a sterile bed.

Hamurana is the most wonderful cold-water spring in New Zealand. It is, in fact, an underground stream, and its daily expulsion has been estimated to be from four to five million gallons of water, which it discharges into Lake Rotorua. Although Hamurana is not a tossing marvel, it seems strong enough to lift tons. Its strength other tourists and I illustrated in an amusing way. As we watched it from a rowboat we, following the example of thousands before us, threw pennies into it, to see them flung about and forced into the crevices of the wall. The coins were never able to sink more than a few feet. After we had gone Maoris went to the spring to collect the submerged coppers. As it was impossible for one man to get them unaided, the natives worked in pairs. One man remained above, holding a pole jammed into a crevice, while his comrade, keeping a firm grasp on the support to withstand the spring's buffetings, descended and gathered the coins.

In crossing Lake Rotorua to Hamurana one passes Mokoia Island, whither Hinemoa, '"the young lady in love," fled to the arms of Tutanekai, her lover. The romance of these two is the most celebrated of Maori love stories. Hinemoa, the beautiful daughter of Chief Umukaria, lived, say Arawas, in Owhata, a village on Rotorua's eastern shore. On Mokoia, a sacred isle of gods and graven images and industrious, prosperous worshipers, lived the chief Tutanekai, and "Lady Moa" loved him. Tutanekai loved the maiden also, and the two planned a meeting on the island, "and the signal of it was the playing every night of Tutanekai (on his flute) and his bosom friend Tiki's flute."

Hinemoa's relatives were opposed to her union with the young chief, and on learning of the lovers' plan, they dragged ashore all the boats. This misfortune did not dissuade the girl from her purpose, and one dark night she set out to swim to the island, two miles from her home. She reached Mokoia exhausted, and in a warm spring, where she stopped to rest, the musical Tutanekai found her. The two were married, and from them many of the Arawas trace their descent.

Tikitere is an extraordinary attraction in a very ordinary place, ten miles from Rotorua. Its immediate approaches from Rotorua are low brown hills covered with tea-tree and common fern. Until within a few hundred yards of Tikitere nothing phenomenal is visible; nor, unless previously informed, would one look for any strange or uncommon works of nature in such a region. Yet it is one of the busiest corners of the whole thermal district. It is not nearly so conspicuous as some other calorific surfaces; it is like a big kitchen stove set in a hollow, a stove with many pots, and all those pots perpetually boiling.

The first evidence of underground heat that I saw here was at a turn of the coach road. From a yellow bank on a hillside columns of steam floated lazily away. On the side of one of these hills was a big white patch of silicated rock heaped into a ghostly mound; in it was a large steaming cavity. Next clouds of vapor rose near the road; they came from the pulsing heart of Tikitere.

Tikitere impressed me as the most dismal of all the thermal areas of the North Island; certainly I found none more nauseating. Its silica mounds and banks had a sepulchral appearance, and were thrown up like drifts of snow. In sunlight their whiteness was dazzling. Their surface was stained with sulphur, and from their mud-spattered basins poured suffocating masses of steam charged with sulphuretted hydrogen and sulphuric acid.

THE INFERNO, TIKITERE

These obnoxious, odorous blankets were worst at Hell's Gate, the real entrance to Tikitere. There they enveloped me so thickly that I had to gasp for breath as I halted for a view, and I was soon glad to escape to a clearer atmosphere. Hell's Gate was a thick ledge of silica, overlooking to right and left a large boiling muddy pool. These pools were almost as large as ponds, and over all their surface there was terrific activity. Both were covered with countless bubbles, and in one I heard the water simmer; and no wonder, for Hell's Gate has a temperature of two hundred and thirty-two degrees.

Hell's Gate looked bad enough, but the Inferno was more ferocious still. To reach it I crossed Frying-Pan Creek, a tiny stream running for a short distance over a perforated, seething floor. The Inferno was one of the ugliest and most violent thermal products imaginable. It was a long, irregular basin of splashing mud and ill-smelling steam; its walls, varying in height from a few inches to six or seven feet, were stained with a mixture of mud and oil; its convulsions were so furious that I heard its splashings yards from its rim.

Almost as fearful in appearance, but smaller, was Satan's Glory. It was very noisy and busy, and strewn with large bubbles and broken by splashers. Near it the ground trembled. Close by was the Mouth of Hades, an opening in a silica ledge, below which was a dark, splashing basin of mud; and from the floor of the aperture alum oozed. Connected with Satan's Glory was the Porridge-Pot, containing a boiling mixture of oil and fuller's-earth. In the same reserve and in other parts of the Hot Lakes district are similar deposits of clay.

Tikitere is more than a weird spectacle. It is also a sombre sanatorium. In its springs and mud baths people are cured of rheumatism, lumbago, skin diseases, muscular ailments, paralysis, and other diseases. One of the strongest properties of its medicated waters is sulphuric acid.

In this district sulphur deposits are extensive, and a short distance from the main attractions is an old sulphur mine. Years ago sulphur blocks were to be seen stacked like wood, but at last the percentage of pure sulphur has become too low to insure a profit, and the workings have been abandoned. The principal sulphur mine in Tikitere's vicinity now is the steaming crater of Ruahine.

Sulphur is believed to be responsible for much of the thermal activity in New Zealand. Dr. A. S. Wohlmann, Government balneologist at Rotorua, informed me that he had little doubt that "the chemical action of sulphuric acid on water is one of the causes of heat in the acid waters."

It is refreshing, after being steamed in Whaka and Tikitere, to make a tour of the Cold Lakes. These lakes are pretty, but years ago, when forests completely surrounded them, they were more attractive still. Around neither are there high mountains, the most imposing heights being Matawhaura, an ancient cliff-spurred and wooded Maori burial-place, at the eastern end of Lake Rotoiti. On the south side of this lake is the suicide cliff of Motutawa, over which many Maoris hurled themselves long ago.

A noteworthy fact about Rotoiti is its phenomenal, unaccountable rise and fall. Its fall, sometimes amounting to two feet, Maori tradition attributes to a subterranean outlet, but none has been discovered.

Southeast of these lakes, almost midway between Gisborne and the curving shores of beautiful Napier, is Waikaremoana, "Sea of the Rippling Waters," the North Island's most beautiful lake. Eleven miles long and deeply set between precipitous walls and high wooded slopes at the base of the Huiarau Range, its surface is two thousand feet above the sea, and in its most profound parts its bottom is nearly eight hundred and fifty feet below its ripples.

Waikaremoana is famed for the gray walls of Panekiri, two thousand feet high; for the luxuriance and variety of the flora darkening its shores; for its bush-clad islands, waterfalls, white sandy beaches, and for solitudes broken by the bell tones of the tui. Here one sees ancient hillforts, and hears tales of war and cannibal feasts, of taniwhas and fairies, of gods, demons, and ghosts.

Chapter VI

No trip in the thermal wonderland was more interesting to me than the Round Trip. This tour leads into a buried country, through mud-imprisoned Wairoa, past entombed Te Ariki and MouraMoura,—New Zealand's Pompeii and Herculaneum,—over volcanic Rotomahana Lake and its steaming cliffs to Waimangu, a sand-choked water volcano, and to the gaping summit of fissured Tarawera, which threw red-hot stones and ashes upon the land nearly thirty years ago.

As a volcano, Tarawera was born on the night of June 10, 1886. Assisted by its neighbors, Wahanga and Ruawahia, it darkened the country for many miles with scoria stones, ashes, and dust. For four hours Tarawera rained stone and mud, and with such strength did it burst forth that its explosions were heard as far as Christchurch, five hundred miles away, while flashes of the electrical storm that broke over it were seen in Auckland, one hundred and twenty miles distant. No lava overflowed, but lava walls were formed. Miles away huge earth cracks were made, and Lake Rotorua, fifteen miles beyond, rose several inches. In Tarawera itself and in its vicinity a series of vents formed a fissure nearly nine miles long, from three hundred to fourteen hundred feet deep, and with a maximum width of one and a half miles.

Soon after Tarawera erupted, Lake Rotomahana, two thousand feet below Tarawera's summit, became active. At that time it was a warm body of water, with a thermal, swampy margin, one hundred and eighty-five acres in area, and it discharged into Lake Tarawera, a mile distant. Now Rotomahana is thirty times larger, and its outlet to Tarawera is blocked. Rotomahana is still, as it was then, a discolored lake, and it is completely surrounded with dreary looking mud cliffs, the barrenness of which is relieved only by the waving plumes of the toitoi (pampas grass).

It was not always thus. Under these cliffs lie the White and Pink Terraces, the most beautiful objects of New Zealand's thermal regions before the lake they had overlooked buried them. There they are to-day, shattered and irrecoverable, according to some investigators; entire and little damaged, according to others who are more hopeful than positive. These terraces were high, wide rippled stairways of sinter, smooth and hard. In places they swelled out as umbrella buttresses. In their floors were warm baths, into which tourists and resident Maoris delighted to plunge; over them hung clouds of steam, and under them raged a heat that I found still strongly evident on the site of Pink Terrace.

The White Terrace had a fountain of azure-blue hot water ninety feet in diameter, which sometimes spouted ten or fifteen feet high. When the south wind blew briskly it could be safely entered to a depth of thirty feet, its beautifully encrusted crater meanwhile remaining empty until the wind changed. Then, roaring all the while, it filled at the rate of three or four feet an hour, and when within a few inches of the rim often shot a column of water to a height of sixty feet.

PINK TERRACE

Will Tarawera burst out again with fiery stone? No one knows. Its energy may be exhausted, but it is impossible to overlook its recent birth as a volcano and the fact that it has given but one exhibition of its powers. In New Zealand nothing is more uncertain than speculation regarding volcanic outbursts and earthquakes. New Zealanders, more particularly North Islanders, never know when a town or village in the thermal zone may sink or be showered with burning ashes, or when they may lose a stretch of coast or find it elevated. In both islands earth tremors are frequent.

In Rotorua, where I have been startled by their rending reports, earthquakes are a diversion. They rattle dishes and alarm visitors strolling or playing in the sanatorium grounds; but they are not severe or uncommon enough to frighten the two thousand residents.

Some day Tarawera may be equaled or outdone by Ngauruhoe, or another volcano may appear; but these things do not trouble New Zealanders. There are so many safety-valves in their country that they believe themselves to be reasonably secure from volcanic disturbances. There are thousands of these steam valves from the tiny, noiseless fumarole to the gaping, roaring blowhole and the smoking craters of Ngauruhoe, Ruapehu, and White Island.

The Round Trip is as instructive as it is interesting; to me, visiting Waimangu was like going to school. There I learned theories of thermal and volcanic activity, and I saw them illustrated. The illustrator and teacher was "Bob" (R. H.) Ingle, who often has had more than one hundred pupils in his two daily classes. On this school day, as usual, one class reached Waimangu via Wairoa, the other via the Rotorua-Taupo road. In the creviced wilderness of mud between Waimangu and Lake Rotomahana the two classes met, and the guides exchanged pupils.

In approaching Waimangu via Wairoa, Waimangu's steaming flats and cavities were hidden by mud banks and the walls of the Tarawera fissure. On the commanding elevation where the Government accommodation house stood, a comprehensive view was obtainable, however. Eastward in the distance was the blue line of the Huiarau Range; to the far right, the mountains and hills of Lake Taupo district; and a few miles away, in the same direction. Rainbow Mountain, a variegated mass of rock and clay with steaming cliffs and canyons. Running to the base of all these heights were the desolate Kaingaroa Plains. They looked to be, as they probably are, the remains of a plateau, and they were marked everywhere with isolated, flat-topped bits of land. It was as if a capricious river had cut the plains into thousands of winding channels.

Between Waimangu House and Tarawera stretched enormous deposits of mud. Those running toward Tarawera had been cut by rains into innumerable gravelly furrows, of which many were from ten to twenty feet deep. They were fashioned into sharp ridges and peaks, and thousands of the gray pinnacles were topped by a big bunch of toitoi.

In following Guide Ingle from Waimangu House, we descended almost immediately into Tarawera's fissure. It soon widened into a circle, and in this rose clouds of steam and, from a yellow-white surface stained with iron and sulphur and encrusted with alum, sounds of boiling and sputtering. This was Frying-Pan Flat, and it was well named. In places its surface was so hot that it simmered and bubbled; in other places it was warm; nowhere was it cold. In such a spot it was best to step carefully. The timid among us needed no cautioning, but the rash and careless did. To right and to left were notices reading, "Trespassers on this side of the fence will be prosecuted"; and frequently the guide voiced a warning, and sometimes a command. A young man started off on a little exploration of his own. Ingle saw him, and instantly shouted: "Here, sir; you must not go there. I told you to be careful where you go."

Coming back, the disobedient one stepped on a broken surface, and sunk to his shoe-tops in fuller's-earth.

"Wash it off in that stream," directed Ingle; "it has acid in it." Next a woman ventured alone toward the crumbling verge of Waimangu Basin.

"Hey!" shouted Bob; "come away from there, confound it!"

Frying-Pan Flat was the playground of thousands of small, hot bubbles that rose and broke with a roar every minute of the day and at a very rapid rate. They varied in diameter from a quarter of an inch to an inch, and many threw up tiny drops of clear water from one inch to four inches high. One of these sputtering areas was called the Gridiron. Across its surface were several cracks, caused by an overflow of water from a cold creek in the fissure, and all along these fractures were hot bubbles. The greatest activity on this broken silica crust was at the foot of Gibraltar, a rhyolite cliff one hundred feet high. In miniature it had a rough resemblance to England's fortified Rock; but not in form only was this similarity traceable. The cliff's face was perforated with steaming vents that reminded me of belching cannon.

Into this agitated area we hesitatingly ventured. Stifling steam clouds that filled our lungs with sulphurous fumes enveloped us and caused us to gasp for breath. It was worse than Tikitere, and two or three of the pupils started to retreat.

"Come on," shouted Ingle. "Follow me and you will be all right."

We all dived through, and getting to windward of the vapor, we reached the verge of the "frying" boiler.

"Now," began our instructor, "you are standing in an old crater, one of seventeen that were blown out between here and Tarawera, two of them in 1886. Until Waimangu erupted, this crater was a cold-water lagoon, and, as you see, part of the lagoon remains. Come over here and I will prove to you that the earth did not have to cool before it grew vegetation. The green growth on this rock is algæ, thriving in a temperature of one hundred and fifty degrees. Ten more degrees would kill it. These black pebbles are rhyolite bits coated on the upper side with iron pyrites, and on the lower side with oxidized iron."

Retracing, Ingle led us to where it was clearer, and instructed us in geyser and volcanic action.

"Here is how geysers are formed," he explained. "The cold water constantly running into this hot pool is immediately expelled. And here is the Sponge Cake. The rock beneath its crust has been softened by condensing steam."

Near the Sponge Cake was Ngauruhoe Junior, a small deposit of steaming sand. When Ingle made holes in it with a stick, sand and pebbles were thrown out, and where he pressed it with his foot, a small shower of sand was tossed up a few inches as soon as the pressure was removed.

As we listened to our thermal lecturer, our attention was drawn at intervals to a hoarse roar issuing from a rocky face near Gibraltar. It sounded like an ocean liner letting off steam, and it was emitted by Waimangu Blowhole, a regulator that expelled great quantities of steam more than one hundred feet high. For three minutes it blew steadily, and then was quiet for four minutes. Like the tides, it flowed and ebbed; and, we were astonished to hear, its activity is indeed partly due to the tides, though they are thirty miles away at the nearest point!

Near the blowhole was ample evidence that any day this reserve may suddenly become shifting sand and flying stone. Waimangu Basin, an area of two and a half acres, affords a good illustration of the instability of the earth's crust in New Zealand's thermal regions. Until a few years ago this depression did not exist, and then the cold waters of the creek caused a change. They penetrated to heated depths, and in 1901 there was a terrific explosion in the stream's bed. At that instant Waimangu, the greatest geyser New Zealand, and perhaps the world, has ever known, was born. The basin is still there, but Waimangu plays no more. On October 26, 1903, it made its last shot, unless, as Mr. Ingle predicts, it is born again. Now its vents are choked with sand, and where there was fifty feet of water there is now very nearly that depth of earth.

WAIMANGU GEYSER

When Waimangu played, it sent an enormous quantity of water, sand, and stones from fifty to twelve hundred feet high, and once it threw a boulder weighing one hundred and fifty pounds a quarter of a mile. The black body it lifted was half the area of its basin. It had three vents, and when their expulsions met, the united eruption was vertical; but when they missed connection, there were side shots. One of these killed four New Zealanders, two being women, a few weeks before the geyser ceased playing. This ill-fated party had gone near the pit to take photographs. Suddenly Waimangu shot sideways, directly at them. All were knocked into the creek down which the geyser always poured its flood, and their scalded bodies were carried a considerable distance.

Waimangu's basin is still slightly active. In its alum-sprinkled, sulphur-dyed surface are simmering holes and small spouters and a large muddy pool. These evidences of activity, and a belief that the sand is the main, if not the sole, cause of Waimangu's cessation, have persuaded many theorists that, with assistance, the geyser can be enabled to play again. Acting on this theory the New Zealand Government dynamited the hollow, but without encouraging result.

Adjoining Waimangu Basin was the Inferno, a large pool of hot, blue water at the base of the high cliff on which the abandoned Waimangu shelter shed stood. It was covered with steam, and occasionally muffled "torpedo" explosions disturbed it. When Waimangu was active, the Inferno never failed to rise about fourteen seconds before each outburst of the geyser, but no furious turmoil accompanied the elevations. The Inferno's overflow formed a hot creek, which flowed into Lake Rotomahana, about two miles distant. The channel through which it ran is a dismal place, a rain-sluiced cleft banked high with volcanic mud. In many of these mud crevices, while exploring without a guide, I came suddenly and unexpectedly upon steam vents, and in the creek bed itself I saw two hot-water splashers that mingled their waters with those of the creek.

Rotomahana is one of the so-called hot lakes. There, in a Government launch, I steamed in a hot "sea." Only a small part of the lake was heated, but enough of it was thermal to provide a novel experience. Before the vari-colored cliffs where the Pink Terrace lies buried, the launch ran where geysers vainly tried to lift the water beneath its keel, and where hot springs played and fumaroles hissed and roared. Here the guide drew a pail of water from the lake.

"Put in your hands," said he.
"Oh!"
"Ouch!"
"How hot it is!"

It was a fervent chorus from the class in thermology.

Ashore rose clouds of steam. At the water's edge there was simmering and sputtering, and on the slopes above hot streams ran, broken surfaces sang, small openings steamed like boiling kettles, and the hot breath of shifting, enwrapping vapor caused me to ponder flight.

A few miles south of Rotomahana lies Waiotapu Valley, guarded by steaming mountains. So many sights are there in this vale that it would require days to see them all. Over its scrubby surface run hot-water creeks, and in its siliceous depths are hot baths, colored pools, geysers, sulphur pits and caves, alum cliffs, and a beautiful sinter terrace. The most conspicuous of its wonders is Rainbow Mountain, twenty-five hundred feet high, and composed largely of red and white clay with shades of pink, purple, yellow, and gray, produced by hydro-thermal action. In its slopes are crater hollows with warm springs in their bottoms, and high on its cliffs are steaming funnels. West of it is noisy Mount Maungaongaonga and its powerful blowhole. When very active, this steam outlet can be heard for half a mile. South of Maungaongaonga is Paeroa, another mountain with a heated base; below it is a boiling fountain and a hot stream.

Waiotapu is seen at its best in the early morning, and especially on a frosty one. Steam columns ascend in every part of the vale. There appear to be hundreds of them, lazily rising like fog on a swamp. It is as if a thousand subterranean boilers were discharging their steam through innumerable surface valves.

To the midday traveler the only object of particular interest on nearing the valley's hotel is the Giant Porridge-Pot, a huge mound of splashing mud. It is the largest mud "volcano" in the thermal district, its height above the road being ten or twelve feet, and its active part, from which mud is often hurled several yards, about twenty feet in diameter.

The valley's most interesting part is the Maori Reserve, a white, barren spot opposite to the hotel. The first object shown me here was a deep sulphur pit, a recent collapse that revealed the dangerous nature of the surface. Near this were the Twin Craters, immense cavities formed by sinking. The peculiar action of steam at the bottom of one had gained for it the name of the Paddle Wheel. Close at hand were heated sulphur beds, perforated by steaming apertures with sulphur-discolored mouths. Early in the morning volumes of steam poured from them, but during the day the emissions were small.

Just beyond the Devil's Bridge, a shelf of silica spanning steaming cavities, were the sinter terraces of Champagne Pool, which are rivaled only by the terraces of Orakei-Korako. Of unknown depth, this pool is the largest basin of water of its kind in New Zealand, being, to quote a native guide, "two acres around." Its mineralized waters had formed a white and grayish-white rippled slope several hundred feet long and containing basins of yellow water holding solutions of sulphur and selenium. The precipitations of the pool had for many years added an inch to the surface of the terrace every twelvemonth. In all that time the pool had been covered with steam, and its waters, disturbed probably by gas, had never been quiet. The shores were encircled by a hard, narrow sinter rim built by its ebullitions, which, when combined with a stiff breeze, made the contents look like a choppy sea.

To amuse me my guide, Kiritapu, threw a shovelful of sand into the pool, and almost immediately it began to simmer. This was followed by bubbles which increased in number so rapidly that soon there were thousands of them. Scores of them began traveling round the shores.

"They will go right around," said Kiritapu. And they did.

In a sunken basin near Champagne Pool was Echo Lake, its gray walls lapped with cold, gray-blue water, but in its centre a hot spring or a gas-disturbed area. At one point was a small beach strewn with mud-discolored sulphur beads, produced at the lake's bottom by hot water, and ejected by gas.

The Government Reserve at Waiotapu covers a large area. Through it runs the Waiotapu River, here a small stream, between steaming banks. In deep basins with shattered walls, half hidden by tea-trees, are hot, quiet pools; in other places are gaping depths, long inactive, or showing only whiffs of vapor.

In the midst of this interesting dreariness, concealing its beauty from the ugliness about it, is a fairy-like sulphur cave. Its gray rock roof, softened by condensing steam, is encrusted with sulphur crystals and studded thickly with clear drops of water. The combination looks wonderfully like a yellow frost in which diamonds have been lavishly scattered.

Another unique object in this reserve is Lady Knox, an obliging geyser. This geyser will play for anybody who soaps it; and it will do more—it will blow soap-bubbles. No clay pipe in the mouth of the most zealous soap-blower in the world could produce such a profusion of bubbles as Lady Knox tossed out for me. But it took a bagful of soap-bars to start her.

I had not long to wait for the suds, however. Up they came through the cone-shaped opening, a school of bubbles, each trying to be the first away. The majority broke at the start; others soared away to a height of fifteen or twenty feet, and one floated twenty-five yards before breaking. Some were from two to four inches in diameter. This was well enough for bubble-blowing, but the geyser played only ten feet high, a third as high as it should have gone. The guide investigated.

"Somebody has put a stump into the geyser," said he, in a tone that indicated that he considered it a personal affront.

Chapter VII

Thirty miles south of Waiotapu is Wairakei, in some respects the most active place in the wonderland district. There geysers are always playing, and there Karapiti, New Zealand's greatest blowhole, roars every second of the day.

Wairakei is an astounding region in an uninteresting expanse of manuka and low hills. Those who go there expecting to see evidence of thermal activity from hotel veranda or window will be disappointed. From the hotel not a trace of steam is visible. Yet only a short distance away are more geysers than are found in any other part of the country. Everything is hidden behind the manuka-capped hills.

Geyser Valley, only a half-mile from the hostelry, proved to be a veritable nest of geysers. There were more than in the Government Reserve at Whaka, and, like them, they were within a small compass. Wairakei exhibited nothing matching the strength of Wairoa Geyser, but the remarkable industry of its geysers more than counterbalanced the superior powers of Whaka's chief spouters.

The most active feature in the valley was Champagne Pool, a fascinating, fearful splasher at the base of a rocky wall. It was constantly boiling furiously, and it often burst into fountains from two to six feet high, and sometimes ten or twelve feet high. The pool was deep and beautifully clear, and probably it would be a powerful geyser were its opening smaller.

The show geyser of the vale was the Great Wairakei, shooting from the base of steaming cliffs reddened by oxidized iron. The Great Wairakei is one of the hot-water regulators of Maoriland. It always plays from one minute to two minutes at intervals of nine or ten minutes; and, so the guide told me, "if your watch is not keeping correct time, you can almost regulate it by the Great Wairakei."

The mouth of the geyser was so large that we could see its waters rising. When they had risen three or four feet above their extreme ebb, the gusher burst into action and played from twenty-five to thirty feet high. Like all geysers, it had built a terrace with its siliceous sediment, and had formed its own peculiar crystals.

At the mouth of the Great Wairakei we left a record of our visit. In the smooth spaces between the ripples of the terrace we wrote our names in lead, and we were assured that they would be visible for a year or two before a siliceous coating obliterated them.

There are not many geysers one would care to enter just for the novelty of the venture. In Wairakei, however, the regularity of the majority of the geysers enables such an act to be done with reasonable safety. At the Dragon's Mouth the guide, according to custom, asked me, "Do you want to get inside?" I replied, "Yes," but not until I had been told that the geyser plays so regularly that entering it is not at all foolhardy.

CHAMPAGNE CALDRON

"The Dragon's Mouth plays from one to eight minutes at intervals of eight minutes," said the guide.

"That may be," I thought, "but how do I know that it won't work overtime while I am within its jaws?" Nevertheless, I ventured within the projections that look so much like a dragon's mouth that one woman declared she could see its teeth. The Dragon's Mouth bursts from a soft oxidized wall, which it has beautifully encrusted with sinter. Its beauty, however, was lost on me as I got within range of the Dragon's "teeth." My mind immediately became occupied with stern realities and nerve-racking possibilities. While I enjoyed the novelty, I felt no desire for leisurely exploration. My feet did not lag nor my eyes musingly survey the hot throat; instead I made a very close neighbor of my guide, and was glad the jaws were no wider. I judged the mouth to be an excellent place for a steam bath, but it was too warm for comfort; yet scarcely less comfortable was it than my state of mind as I wondered whether I would get safely through between the shots.

Thermal heat is required to produce geysers, but other causes have been known to precipitate one. Many years ago a packhorse fell into a hole in Geyser Valley, and shortly thereafter an eruption shook and shattered that place—and behold! the Packhorse Mud Geyser was born. For several days it played; then it ceased, and it has not performed worthily since. But how could a horse start a geyser? With its own fat!

"I have a theory," my guide explained, "that the fat of the horse had the same effect on the hot water as soap would have had."

In a clump of tea-trees was the Eagle's Nest Geyser. No eagle ever sat on it, but it looked much like an eagle's nest just the same. It was surrounded by a pile of sticks coated with sinter. Originally there were only a few sticks around the geyser's mouth; the others were placed there by one of the owners of the valley. Through its two openings the Eagle's

Nest played briefly every twenty minutes to a height of ten feet.

Below the Eagle's Nest was the Prince of Wales Feathers, which we forced to play by damming a rivulet and at the same time removing a dam from an adjoining stream. For twenty-five minutes its two plumes, leaping from small openings in the side of a terrace, played from twenty-five to thirty feet high. Below it was an indicating splasher which always erupted a few minutes before the Feathers began throwing.

One of the most remarkable geysers of the valley was the Twins, two gushers that played from the same pool. The stronger one burst up with an explosive sound every four and one-half minutes; the other played every fifteen minutes with a sound like a paddle-wheel.

Another astonishing geyser was the Steam Hammer, a boiling marvel in a large cold-water basin. Rods before we reached it, we heard it pounding beneath its heavy weight, and just as we arrived at the basin's edge we heard a cracking noise. A San Francisco woman turned round quickly and looked at me.

"Oh, I thought you had broken your stick," said she.

"That is the Steam Hammer," said the guide.

Snap, snap! The Hammer was at it again, almost under our feet this time.

"They are cutting kindling wood down there," remarked another tourist. It certainly sounded something like it.

As we gazed at the pool there was a commotion in its centre. "That is unusual," declared the guide. "This is only the sixth time I have seen the water stirred like that. The Hammer never plays higher than that because of the great weight of water above it. Once it did not play for six years."

As we passed up the slope, the ground shook. The tremors seemed to be far beneath our feet. The Steam Hammer was at work again.

Of all the remarkable sights at Wairakei, the most amazing is the Karapiti Blowhole, or the Devil's Trumpet. It has been called the greatest safety-valve in New Zealand, and one scientist went so far as to estimate its pressure to be one hundred and eighty pounds to the square inch. In its continual action it is unlike other blowholes of New Zealand, which are intermittent. Just what would occur if Karapiti's roaring throat were blocked, no man could foretell, but a tremendous explosion or increased activity in other places surely would result.

Karapiti is muffled behind hills three miles from Wairakei's hotel, and issues from a low, sandy wall in a little hollow. At a sharp angle it shoots up with fearful speed through an irregular mouth having a maximum width of about one foot. As long as the Maoris can remember, Karapiti has been trumpeting; in the hundreds of years that possibly have elapsed since it first broke its bounds, it must have expelled enough steam to run the machinery of worlds.

Powerful as Karapiti is, tourists are sometimes too much for him. He can fling back into their faces tin cans, boards, and their own hats, but he cannot hurl back long, heavy sticks nor beer bottles. So, because the bottles are too heavy and because he cannot get enough surface pressure on the sticks, these obstacles half fill his throat. Light boards, hats, and pieces of tin are thrown back with surprising suddenness to a distance of from ten to twenty feet.

I threw in boards of heavy wood eighteen inches long, four inches wide, and a half-inch thick. Several inches from his mouth Karapiti caught them, and held one at a sharp angle on the verge of his upper lip. There the board remained, swaying constantly, until I knocked it down with a stick. It was then blown out seven or eight feet. A five-gallon oil-can was driven back to the top of an incline, where it rocked like a cradle until removed.

Six miles south of Wairakei is Taupo, one of those places where a fisherman can catch trout in a river and cook them in a hot spring on that river's banks. There the Waikato, New Zealand's longest river, famed for its Huka Fall and Aratiatia Rapids, passes within a few yards of boiling pools, and almost within its reach are geysers that mingle their waters with its cold eddies. On its right bank are four geysers; splashers clear and cloudy; steaming earth terraces and mud flats; and the Paint-Pots. When Taupo's residents want paint, they need not go to a paint shop; they have one of their own. From the Paint-Pots, one of them told me, they can get a dozen colors and tints. "Mixed with oil," said he, "their ingredients have been used to paint fence palings."

LAKE TAUPO FROM MOTUTERE

Taupo's best known thermal possession is the Crow's Nest Geyser. It is only twenty feet from the Waikato, and it has built around itself a big lump of silica that looks like a cream puff. This singular object is seven or eight feet high and stands conspicuously isolated. In its base is an opening through which hot water constantly flows to the river. At intervals of from one hour and forty-five minutes to three hours, the geyser plays from ten to thirty-five minutes and at least once daily. Its average height is seventy-five or eighty feet, and its maximum one hundred and twenty feet.

A Taupo geyser that plays infrequently is Waitikirangi, usually to a height of one hundred feet. The Tamati Geyser throws from four to five feet high for one minute at five-minute intervals. The Ioline Geyser is like a spoiled child; before it will play it must be soaped and then covered with a gunny-sack. Even then it plays only thirty seconds, to an average height of fifteen feet.

Among other Taupo wonders are the gulping Satan's Glory Hole, a hot, agitated phenomenon with a red, rocky facing that looks like the stokehole of a furnace; and the Witches' Caldron, a steam-enshrouded, clear pool at the base of a wall that is bright with colors in sunlight. At the edge of this caldron my guide lighted a fire, and at once steam rushed toward the cavity opposite.

Beyond Lake Taupo rise the smoking mountains of Tongariro National Park. Once it was necessary to skirt the shores of this largest of New Zealand lakes, but now the lake can be crossed by steamer. In crossing Taupo there is novelty of a kind not often enjoyed by travelers. Taupo, like many other New Zealand lakes, is believed to be the bed of an ancient crater or of several craters that have lost their walls by erosion.

There are also to be heard on Taupo tales of taniwhas which terrified Maoris in more superstitious days when they navigated it. Even to-day Maoris who have not conquered their supernatural fears take care not to provoke the wrath of the reptile Horomatangi and his supposed attendant, the man-spirit Atiamuri. The traditional home of this monster is near Motutaiko, an island near the centre of the lake. The Maoris of old New Zealand were always careful to avoid this part of the lake, and even now natives dislike to pass between this island and the dreaded spot. "When we get near this place," the Tongariro's engineer told me, "we can't get a word out of our Maori passengers."

Taupo is by far the largest lake in New Zealand, having an area of about two hundred and forty square miles and an extreme length of twenty-five miles. Its surface is twelve hundred feet above the sea; its greatest depth is five hundred and thirty-four feet. On the east and the north it laves pumice cliffs which in one place are three hundred feet high; on the west it beats against lofty cliffs of lava and agglomerate in alternate layers. The greatest of these are the gray bluffs of Karangahape, rising eleven hundred feet above the lake and extending four hundred feet beneath its surface. The lake is a popular fishing-ground, and at Taupo Wharf I saw many large trout swimming far below in the clear depths near its outlet, the Waikato River.

At the lake's southern end is Tokaanu, a pakeha-Maori village in the midst of hot springs and warm baths. Tokaanu's baths are needed by the traveler from the south, for the village is the northern terminus of one of the dustiest coaching-routes in Maoriland.

It is not often that a park can be classed as an inferno; yet, to a great extent, such is Tongariro National Park, a gift of burning mountains. This large scenic reserve was given to New Zealand by Chief Te Heuheu Tukino, and at any moment it may be swept by molten lava, as in other days. In this recreation ground are ice-bound Ruapehu, lashing into fury a hot lake in a frozen funnel; the gas-swept summit of Ngauruhoe; and the steaming craters of Tongariro. Here mountains have been welded together, as in a Pluton furnace. Here can be seen the celestial blue of glacier's rift to-day and the infernal glow of lava pits to-morrow.

Chief of the mountains in this park is Ruapehu, the North Island's highest elevation. The highest of its three main peaks is 9175 feet. At all times glaciers cover its upper slopes, but for three months each year it is scaled by parties of New Zealanders with comparative ease. Although Ruapehu is known to the Maoris as the Snow Mountain, it has within its snow-fields a spouting crater lake which at times is very active. This lake is five hundred feet in diameter and lies three hundred feet below the crater lip, between icy cliffs that can be descended only with the aid of ropes. Years ago an eruption of this slaty-colored tarn caused the formation of hot springs on its shores. In 1911 black and yellow mud poured into it from a vent in its walls, and later there was an eruption of red earth in the lake's centre, and at the same time black ash dust was thrown from the crater.

Ngauruhoe, Ruapehu's poisonous neighbor, is the youngest and lustiest of New Zealand's volcanoes. It has a symmetrical, corrugated cone of scoria ash, stones, and mud, 7515 feet high, and it is always discharging sulphuric acid fumes, which render dangerous a near approach to its summit.

For a decade Ngauruhoe has been getting more active every year. Twelve years ago its crater could be safely entered, but recently there have been frequent emissions of steam and dust. In 1909 the volcano discharged scoria ash; in 1911, Dr. Marshall, of the Otago University, saw glowing lava in its red inferno and heard gas escape from it with violence. Later visitors heard what they believed to be "the roar of churned waters," and the crashing of boulders in one of the two active craters. From a precipice overlooking a hot lake long streamers of steam issued, and from crateral depths came nauseous odors.

A third party found the ground so hot at the top that it was uncomfortable to stand long in one spot, and the noise of escaping steam was so great that it was impossible to converse. Still others, from the plains miles below, say they saw shooting flames, fire-balls, lightning, and clouds of black smoke. The leaping flames, however, may have been merely the reflections of burning lava on clouds.

In its spasmodic action, Ngauruhoe resembles Vesuvius, Mont Pêlée, and Karakatoa; and it is also similar to these mountains in its rock compositions.

NGAURUHOE IN ACTION

A very active mountain is Tongariro, which has been united to Ngauruhoe, more than a thousand feet higher than it, by lava overflows. Tongariro's active craters, Te Mari and the Red Crater, incessantly expel steam, often with noisy force. In places Tongariro's slopes are riddled with fumaroles, in scoria cavities are hot pools, and more than four thousand feet above the sea are the steam-canopied Ketetahi Springs.

The *Ultima Thule*, or, according to legend, the portal, of New Zealand's thermal wonderland, is White Island, twenty-seven miles off the coast of the Bay of Plenty. White Island is a queer place. It is a sulphur pit, an acid tank. On it sulphur boils like treacle, and from a warm lake acidulous waters pour into the sea.

On White Island one must tread carefully, and test the treacherous ground as one goes. This quaking pile of rock and clay is a sibilant, roaring pandemonium of steam. Add to this the harsh screams of thousands of sea-birds, and the imaginative visitor can readily fancy himself at the entrance of an abysmal, fiendish world where ghoulish vultures wait to strike and tear.

Seldom does White Island have visitors, for its terrifying shores are inhospitable and difficult of approach. "Keep off! We do not want you here," its threatening fumaroles seem to say. Its rocks provide no sheltering harbor in time of storm, and landing places are few. In one place only can even a small steamer put passengers ashore, and often this is impossible. Once each year an Auckland steamship company advertises an excursion to White Island, usually in February, but for four consecutive years it was unable to land passengers there. Occasionally launch parties reach the island, but they frequently have to wait weeks for a favorable sea. Years ago a Tauranga sulphur company operated a sulphur mine on the island, but it finally abandoned the work because its boats could not make landings often enough to keep its factory supplied with sulphur. In 1912 another company ventured to exploit the island's sulphur, but with what success I have not learned.

The only life on White Island, aside from scrubby vegetation, is that of birds, chiefly gannets and mutton birds. By the Maoris the young mutton bird is regarded as a delicacy, and every year parties of natives go to the island to capture these creatures in their underground nests. Thrusting a stick into a bird's burrow, the Maori bird-catcher twists it about in the bird's down until it is firmly fixed, and then pulls the titi out.

White Island is a volcano in the solfatara stage, and so active is it that on clear days its steam clouds can be seen fifty miles or farther. From the mainland its lofty pillar of steam looked to me like the outpourings of a great factory chimney. Although the island usually is noisy,—so much so that one must shout to converse near its roaring vents,—there are days when it is comparatively quiet. In its worst mood it is so alarming that sulphur miners once fled from it in affright.

One of the most remarkable things about this top of a submarine mountain is its acidified crater lake. Lying between high rocky walls, this lake has an area of about fifteen acres, and its surface is only a few feet above the sea. At times it rises and falls from two to three feet, but there is no connection between it and the tides, for, I was told, it has been high at low tide. Its waters have a temperature of one hundred and ten degrees, and they contain hydrochloric and pentathionic acids and boron.

The strength of these waters was once singularly shown by the collapse of a boat that had been left on the lake. As strange, too, are the eroding effects of the acids present in crevices and holes around the lake's shores, and apparently permeating the atmosphere. An iron tramway used by sulphur miners long ago became streaks of rust, and a metal bucket left outside a camp building was reduced to a heap of ruins by the same uncanny agencies. Strange tales told me of acid-eaten shoes and clothing also testify to the presence of acid in unexpected places.

White Island shows its hostility to its visitors in peculiar ways. It does more than awe them—it plays tricks on them. When the wise embark for the volcano, they wear old clothes and shoes. The more like tramps they look, the better for their wardrobes. On White Island a man sits down in an innocent-looking spot to rest. The next day he may need another pair of trousers. Or perhaps he plants a foot in an equally harmless-appearing place. Before he leaves the island he may need the services of a cobbler.

"I have seen tourists returning from White Island with heels and soles clattering," said an Opotiki man to me.

"A friend of mine," another man informed me, "told me he was going to the island, and I advised him to wear old boots.

"'Oh,' said he, 'the boots I have on will do.'

"'Be careful, or you'll lose them,' I warned him.

"The very next day the soles of that man's boots fell off as he walked along the street, and where he touched his clothing in acid-soaked spots it crumbled. Another man accidentally stepped into a pool of water, and though he at once stepped out, all the clothing on one leg was eaten away to the flesh and the leg was blackened."

White Island is not the only active island in New Zealand waters. There are four other sea-girt "steamers," three of them in the Bay of Plenty; Rurima, Whale, and Mayor Islands. The other island is the Great Barrier, nearly one hundred and fifty miles north, which has a few hot springs. On Rurima are fumaroles; on Whale Island are hot springs and a stretch of hot sandy beach; and on Mayor Island are hot springs and a glistening crater of black obsidian five miles in circumference and nearly thirteen hundred feet high.

Chapter VIII

The thermal wonderland is not the only weird district in New Zealand. In Waitomo there is weirdness too, for it is celebrated for its caves, lying in a volcanic, limestone area one hundred miles south of Auckland. They are reached by the Main Trunk, New Zealand's longest railway, running between Auckland and Wellington four hundred and twenty-six miles long.

The Main Trunk passes within sight of the mountains of Tongariro National Park and through districts that until a comparatively few years ago were inhabited only by Maoris. Some of the construction features of this line are high steel viaducts and the Raurimu Spiral, which enables trains to ascend about seven hundred feet in two miles. At its highest part the railway is half a mile above the sea, and for more than two hundred miles the cost of construction exceeded seventy thousand dollars a mile.

Compared with Kentucky's Mammoth Cave, Waitomo's caverns are small; but they are remarkably formed. Aranui, for example, has formations resembling lace and fresh snow; it has "shawls" and "blankets," "marble" and "wax," and it is the only New Zealand cave yet discovered that has "water-lilies."

Of the principal caves Waitomo and Ruakuri have been known to the Maoris for generations; but not by them were the caves explored. They ventured to bury some of their dead in recesses near the entrance to Ruakuri, but into Ruakuri's blackness they no more than peered.

As for us who came after, doubly fortified with candle and magnesium wire to search this abode of ghostliness, vengeful sprites and spirits troubled us not, and the forbidding darkness glowed and flashed with beauty. At its entrance Ruakuri, a series of fissures and grottoes with a maximum length of three fourths of a mile, was narrow, dismal, and commonplace. A few hundred yards from its mouth the crevice widened, and here the magnesium light flared upon the "cauliflowers" and "mushrooms" and "Queen Alexandra's Drawing-Room." Just beyond these I heard splashing water; somewhere in the blackness was a hidden waterfall.

ARANUI CAVES

Retracing, and proceeding up another fissure, I saw, well ahead, a sparkle. It looked like a star in a black sky; but soon I saw another like it, then a half-dozen, a score, fifty, a hundred.

"What are they?" the guide was asked.

"They may be diamonds," he replied, with a grin.

Of course they were not; they were glowworms, of which more later.

In the Throne Room, in Rouen Cathedral, in the Coral Cave, and before the Wedding Cake, we saw stalactites and stalagmites of wonderful construction. Here were long, slender tubes that looked like glass, forming, I was told, at the rate of one inch in ninety years. Here were formations, pure white and varicolored, more delicately wrought than coral; and brown, yellow, and white shapes resembling carrots and parsnips.

In one respect Waitomo was the reverse of Ruakuri. Waitomo was beautiful at the beginning and weird at the end. As soon as Waitomo's door was opened, a white grotto, encrusted, and fit for the chamber of a fairy princess, was revealed.

For my visit to Waitomo I had chosen the most impressive hour, nightfall. At that hour there was awesome and mysterious suggestiveness in the preparations and in the approach to the cave's mouth. As the cave-seekers neared Waitomo in single file beneath the trees that darkened the entrance, moonshiners, night-riders, and ghosts were suggested in the low voices, the crouching figures, the cautious tread, and the gloom of shadows.

The supreme architectural feature of this cave was the Cathedral, which had a ceiling sixty feet high. Both ceiling and walls were elaborately decorated, and in the main room a fair-sized congregation could have assembled for worship.

In Waitomo, too, were the Organ and the Jew's-Harp, each possessing stalactites that, when struck, produced music something like that of a steam calliope.

In the Court-Room fancy had formed from limestone a judge, jury, counsel, and prisoners. Near here, sitting on the cold stone floor, was the lone figure of the Monkey.

Perhaps the most amazing sight in Waitomo was Glowworm Grotto, at the rear of the Cathedral. As we approached it in the darkness, for effect, we saw what looked like a roof of gems. These "gems" were the steady gleam of thousands of glowworms, shedding day and night a dim light suited only to goblin worlds. On this scene the guide flashed a magnesium light. The result was startling. Hanging closely together from the roof were countless tiny pendants resembling fine wire strands and weighted with millions of drops of moisture. The whole formed one glistening, gently swaying screen across the damp ceiling. These filaments were the threads of glowworms. Looking down, we saw the glittering canopy reflected in a dark expanse of water.

Retracing our steps, we followed the guide to the top of a wooden stairway. Here the lanterns were extinguished, leaving us in the flickerings of one candle. After a few rods of stumbling, we halted. Something dimly white was ahead, and it was moving. What was it? An uncanny inhabitant of these dripping silences? No—a boat, and tens of thousands of glowworms! We were on the banks of an underground stream, a stream as dark as the river of death; and here were a boat and a boatman as ghostly in appearance as flitting forms of a spirit world.

By the light of a candle half the party boarded the boat and were pushed off. Slowly they glided away, into the intense gloom beyond. Yet there was no sound of an oar; not a splash nor a dip was heard. Even spirits, to whom this silent navigation seemed most fitting, could not have moved more inaudibly. How was the boat navigated? By wire. Standing in the craft the guide grasped a single wire and easily piloted his passengers downstream to the exit.

As the boat left the landing the candle was extinguished, leaving for illumination only the light of the glowworms. At first it was so dark that we on shore could not see face or hand six inches from our eyes. In a few minutes we could see vaguely our own outlines and the cavern walls opposite to us. But the silence did not decrease; excepting when broken at intervals by drops of water falling loudly into the stream, it was as the silence of a tomb.

At last it was my turn for a ride, and a wonderful ride it was. The current carried me under a Milky Way of glowworms, under constellations, satellites, and isolated planets. In fancy the black roof and walls were the sky and the gleaming lights the stars. But the glint of glowworms was not everywhere visible; it was mainly on the roof. There were broad spaces without even one "star," and shortly before I emerged into the moonlight I passed stalactites and stalagmites unlighted by a single ray.

Chapter IX

A beautiful river is one of man's most cherished possessions. The German is proud of the castellated Rhine; the Frenchman's eyes sparkle at mention of the historic Seine; the Englishman grows poetical over the upper Thames; the American points to the palisaded Hudson; and the New Zealander says, "Behold the Wanganui!"

The Wanganui is Maoriland's finest scenic river. It has other rivers that in some respects rival and surpass it, but it has none that totally eclipses it as a beautiful whole. From the mountains to the sea the Wanganui offers a voyage that lures thousands of tourists every year. In gliding down its rapid, canyon-walled stream, no one derives more pleasure than the dusty traveler from Tokaanu. From swirling sand clouds of the Rangipo Desert to the clear, refreshing Wanganui overnight was to me a most luxurious change.

The river has its source near the base of Tongariro, and for the greater part of its length flows through a deep gorge with lichen-draped cliffs and higher, forested slopes. Between Taumarunui and the mouth, one hundred and fifty miles, the river falls five hundred feet; in its steepest part the fall is fifteen feet in twelve chains. There are many rapids, and in passing through these the voyager has exciting moments.

Taumarunui is not much to look at, but it is one of the greatest tourist gateways of New Zealand. It is at the head of navigation on the Wanganui, and is one of the principal stations on the Main Trunk Railway. In this busy hotel town, when you seek the tourist steamer office, it is only necessary to follow the crowd.

"Where shall I find the steamer office?" I asked my landlady on the morning of my trip down the river.

"Oh, it is easy to find," said she. "You'll see plenty of people going there."

So I did. There was a string of them ahead of me, and they looked like picnickers on the march.

At the foot of a stairway, beside a willow-lined bank, I boarded the launch Waireka. It was hard to decide whether this craft looked more like a torpedo boat or a canoe with decks. It had a steel hull more than sixty feet long and less than a sixth as wide, and its draught was—ten inches! Near it were smaller vessels, called canoes, equipped with gasoline engines; these also belonged to "Hatrick's fleet." When we were all aboard the pilot came aft.

"Please move forward," said he; "there is shallow water here."

Then, mounting to his wheel, he gave the starting signal. First we passed rocky bars and were warned off by netting; then came big boulders; next a roar of waters, and — *splash!* We were in the rapids, and showered with flying foam.

For a brief time we twisted and rolled in a narrow, boisterous channel, our eyes on the rapidly shifting scene and the pilot, his eyes on banks and trees that were his aids in navigation. Then came stretches of steep but placid water, and many turns, each with a different vista. Soon the scenery became more interesting. Over shrub and tree rambled the white clematis, toitoi bowed to tree fern, and high up on pine trees climbed the tenacious kiekie and nestled the aerial astelia. Next came high stratified bluffs running back to forested steeps. Farther down were heavier forests, broken here and there by scrub and fern-grown clearings.

"It is n't safe here; please move over."

It was a member of the crew warning two passengers away from the port gunwale aft. Another rapid was just ahead. And there was something else just ahead, also. A slow bell clanged near a sharp turn, and a big dugout canoe waiting near the shore slid alongside the launch with a bump. Maori hands grasped our gunwale, and canoe and launch moved downstream together. Into brown hands a package of letters was thrust by one of our crew. The dugout was a mail boat, manned by a crew of two. "R.M.S." could not be applied to it, but to the Maori settlement across the river it was just as important as is a Royal Mail Steamer to the pakeha of large cities.

WANGANUI RIVER

With the distance traveled the scenery continued to improve. The hills became higher and more thickly wooded, and water-courses, carrying with them the cool breath of moist and shaded banks, flowed into the Wanganui through narrow clefts. Near one of these streams stood, one of the most unique buildings in the world. It resembled a mushroom with a half-dozen stems. It was merely a small thatched cone resting on fern posts, and having as its centre support a live tree fern, which projected above the roof and shaded it.

At one point sandstone cliffs from two hundred to four hundred feet high rose almost vertically. Their bases were hollowed by the river, and in one place so fantastically as to resemble the stump of an immense tree.

Bump! Two and one half hours out of port, in a narrow, very rocky channel, the Waireka struck bottom. A deckhand hurried to starboard with a pole, and in a minute we were off again. Anchored to the right bank, a few hundred yards below this, was a little two-deck steamer. To it we were immediately transferred, and continued the voyage. But we had not gone far before we were bumped again.

"Too much weight on the starboard side," shouted the pilot.

Three or four passengers shifted to port, and the steamer was lifted clear.

"I am getting hungry," said somebody.

"You'll soon eat; we are near the houseboat," was the encouraging assurance.

So we were. The steamer whistled, and there, round a bend, was a long, narrow building that looked much like a river steamer minus smokestack and pilot house. It had two decks, the lower one being divided into staterooms and the upper reserved as a dining-room. Here we sat down to lunch, twenty-four miles from Taumarunui, and we were to eat dinner in Pipiriki, sixty miles below us.

Below the houseboat the scenery became more beautiful with every passing mile, until, miles from our day's destination, we were in the heart of Wanganui's grandeur. The hills were clothed with a denser, more luxurious growth of ornate bush and flowering tree. Most brilliant of all was the crimson rata, greatest of New Zealand's forest parasites. Thousands of tall tree ferns bent over lofty cliffs, and ran in straggling rows up steep slopes or spread into thick groves. At infrequent intervals a nikau palm thrust up its latticed fronds in shaded nooks. Everywhere the kiekie clambered and the long pointed leaves of the astelia rustled, weighting the trunks of tree and fern and clinging to perpendicular walls. With them, struggling for possession of bole and limb, were the wiry mangemange, the cable-like supplejack, and many other climbers and parasites. For miles the short mountain flax clung to the face of cliffs, and in wide bands sword ferns from three to four feet long hid the sandstone mile after mile. From the river's edge spread mossy carpets inlaid with fragile fern and tiny creeper.

Water in diversified form completed this composite picture of grace and ruggedness. The banks dripped with it, they shed it in oozing drops and trickling streams, and they were divided by it. All along the way were small waterfalls, and into the river flowed clear creeks deeply set in narrow channels that presented entrancing mural scenes and created in me a longing to explore.

But, after all, what was the journey through this rippling, rustling fairy gorge but one long, delightful exploration? Every minute there were a turn and a different view. "What next?" was my constant thought. Would it be another cliff formation; a narrow lateral canyon looking like a big crack; a massive hill; a great tree standing out in solitary grandeur above its fellows; a rocky cavity roofed with ferns; another cobblestone bar; or a rapid?

In this world business and pleasure are seldom far apart. Our steamer was primarily a pleasure boat, but it also carried freight, and making port and landing cargo proved to be a most interesting proceeding. The usual landing place was the river bank, and to make a landing it was only necessary to bury the steamer's "nose" in a sandy shelf, throw a rope round a tree, and, when passengers were going ashore, run out a plank. At other times the steamer merely swung close to the bank, and the freight, if unbreakable, was thrown ashore. Likewise cargo for the boat occasionally hurtled through the air, and once the pilot skirted the shore to get a letter thrust out on the end of a pole by a settler.

At a Maori settlement we stopped for our first cargo. Six bales of wool awaited the steamer, and they were surrounded by native men, women, and children, who seemed glad to see us. That wool was placed aboard by one of the most amazing looking stevedoring crews I had ever seen, — five Maori youths. Three wore soiled, white knee-trousers, between which and their stockings were several inches of bare leg. One lad wore only one stocking, and another matched blue overalls with a green headdress somewhat resembling a polar explorer's cap. It looked like a sack, with a hole in one side for the face. Four of the Maoris wore coats while working, though their task was hot and heavy.

Later in the afternoon, shortly after we had passed the Drop Scene, — high cliffs near Pipiriki, — we reached the end of the first stage of our voyage, Pipiriki. This haven looked more like a port than any other settlement we had seen that day. There was a wharf and two steamers were alongside. Maoris were there to welcome us, but there was no cab, moving stairway, or "angels' flight" to carry us in ease to the hotel high on the slope of a range. Instead we had to climb a long stairway, but at its top we received a pleasant surprise; we found a large modern hotel in a wilderness.

On the last stage of the Wanganui trip we started on a larger steamer at half-past five the following morning. Passengers were to be landed at Aramoho Junction, nearly sixty miles away, to connect with the New Plymouth-Wellington mail train. Again we passed lofty cliffs, forested hills, rapids, and beautiful bends. It soon became clear, however, that this part of the river was incomparable with the reaches between Pipiriki and the houseboat. Here were more clearings, more settlements, and more ports.

We were not long out from Pipiriki until we rammed the left bank. A score of Maoris, bright with many colors of dress, shawl, and handkerchief, awaited the onslaught. A plank was put out, and a dozen steerage passengers came aboard. As the steamer moved downstream, they shouted and waved their hands to their comrades ashore, and their farewells were responded to with similar demonstrations. This was the largest number of passengers we had yet received, and it betokened the presence of a village near the river. But from the landing no village was visible.

"What port is this?" I inquired of a fellow voyager.

"Jerusalem," he replied. "It is quite a settlement."

It was quite a name for a Maori kainga, too. To the Maoris it was known as Hiruharama, their name for the Holy City.

After a short run we rammed the left bank again, and took aboard three bales of wool.

"What place is this?" I asked again.

"London," I was told, to my still greater surprise.

Near this wilderness navigation became very exciting. The steamer entered one place too narrow for turning, and it became necessary to back it down a stretch of rapids with the aid of a wire cable. It was a difficult performance, but the pilot-captain, continually shouting orders as he divided his attention between the wheel and the crew, accomplished it without mishap.

Below these rapids we drew up near a dugout beside a narrow beach. On the beach were several Maori children, one of whom was a boy who looked like a Chinese mandarin in miniature. He wore faded, loose pink trousers, a sky-blue shirt large enough for his father, and a sweater with black and red stripes. His shirt-sleeves dangled like those of a scarecrow and his trousers bellied with each passing breeze. But these things did not trouble him; and why should they? He had plenty of room and a variety of color. What more did he need?

At this landing the plank was put out for a big Maori woman wearing a black dress and a white motor-veil. In her hand she carried her "going-out" shoes. The broad shoes she wore were good enough for Corinth, but they were not fancy enough for Aramoho Junction or Wanganui. Yes, this was Corinth. And not far away were Damascus, Galatia, Laodicea, and Athens! Such were some of the names given Maori villages in the old missionary days.

The distance between life and death is often an inch, a hair's breadth, or a second, but seldom is it accurately measured. On the Wanganui it was definitely known. It was the width of a totem pole. This pole stands within a small picket fence on the lower Wanganui. To me it was in its isolation a strong reminder of the far-famed totem pole of Seattle's Pioneer Square. To the New Zealander versed in Taranaki's history it recalled the days when, from lofty heights, from sandspit and from canoe, Maoris challenged the European to deadly combat.

This pole was a demarkation point between war and peace. From it ran imaginary lines dividing native and European lands, and it was a point past which no white man was allowed to ascend the river. One man named Moffatt did so, and Maoris shot him. The pole was erected by Major Kemp (Kepa te Rangihiwinui), a Maori chief who fought with the whites against the fanatical Hauhaus. One of the battle-grounds of this sect and their Maori opponents was the poplar-shaded Moutoa Island, near the river village Tawhitinui. Here the brown allies of the pakeha defeated the Hauhaus with rifle and tomahawk, and thereby prevented an attack on Wanganui.

Wanganui is one of the most important towns in New Zealand; and likewise it is one of the best advertising mediums the country has ever had. In the days when it sometimes took steamers several weeks to get up and down the river, because they had too much draught, Wanganui was not of much relative consequence; now it is celebrated for a number of things. It established the first municipal theatre in New Zealand; it once had the champion brass band of Australasia; it has the only eight-oared aquatic event in the Dominion; and it is the alpha of one of the most obliging railroads man ever operated anywhere.

MOUNT EGMONT FROM HAWERA

Of this railroad—a short private line—it is said that one day, after having waited ten minutes for some of its regular passengers, "it had no sooner started than a loud whistle was heard, and a man was observed, some considerable distance back, making fast time to the station. The train very obligingly backed to the platform and waited for him, finally getting away twenty minutes late."

North of Wanganui, in Taranaki, the land of butter and cheese and iron sands, is Mount Egmont, the most beautiful volcanic cone in New Zealand. Egmont, known to the Maoris as "Taranaki," is isolated on a plain far from other mountains. It rises 8260 feet above the sea, and its cone, the culmination of long, gracefully sweeping slopes, is forest-clad to the snow-line.

The isolation of a mountain so high as Egmont is one of the most remarkable characteristics of New Zealand mountains. The ancient Maoris, who gave voice and being to mountains and to many other inanimate objects, account for this detachment in a charming way. They say that this disjunction was due to Taranaki's affectionate regard for Pihanga, an extinct volcano south of Lake Taupo. In the days when love messages were carried by wind, mists, and clouds, Taranaki stood between Tongariro and Ruapehu, seventy-five miles east of his present location. In those times mountains were gods, and they sometimes had mountains for wives. Pihanga was the wife of Tongariro, which in legendary accounts generally included Ngauruhoe.

Taranaki made love to Pihanga, and for his amorous advances he paid dearly. Tongariro and Ngauruhoe assaulted him with lava and fire. Against these Taranaki battled until he could withstand them no more; then, jerking himself from his foundation with a noise like a rending world, he fled to the western sea. As he went he plowed the deep furrow through which the Wanganui flows, and he did not stop to rest until he planted himself where he stands to-day.

On this mountain, which is ascended by hundreds of persons every year, there is no smoking vent, for Taranaki's heart is now cold. The volcanic soil that it shed on its lower slopes and for miles over the connecting plains is green with leaf and blade, but above its scrub and moss is only a waste of loose scoria and lava.

Chapter X

The world has many cities built on hills. New Zealand has one that to a great extent is set against hills. This is Wellington, the third and present capital of the Dominion, and, in tonnage entered, its chief port.

A little more than seventy years ago, when the city was founded by the New Zealand Company, Wellington's cramped quarters did not cause it much concern. As the largest colony that up to that time had settled in New Zealand, it was more concerned in building modest homes and disputing land titles with obstinate Maoris. The colonists had just removed to Wellington, after sojourning briefly in Britannia, an unsuitable site for settlement on the opposite side of Port Nicholson, and they had no thought of tunnels and regrades. Later settlers, however, realizing that an increasing population would soon demand access to the hills, filled in a strip along the water front to give them room to swing in while they generated steam for the ascent. Now the most valuable part of the city stands where tides ebbed and flowed, and Wellington is still climbing.

The city reminded me of Seattle. Like the Washington city, the Lambton Harbor port has tunnels, deep cuttings, and steep grades; and some tunnels and more regrades are yet to come. In one respect, that of lofty homes, Wellington surpasses Seattle and closely approaches San Francisco. Some of its residences are nearly seven hundred feet above the sea, and back of the city proper are many unoccupied building sites on higher elevations.

On its gorse- and broom-sprinkled hills of yellow clay and soft brown rock, Wellington's residential quarter occupies a commanding position, yet not from any one point is the whole of it, or of the city, visible. Much of it is hidden in canyons and narrow valleys and by curving hills. Although the city has a certain shut-in appearance, its hills have a charm peculiarly their own. They afford a grandeur of outlook which, though limited, is inspiring. Rising at every point of the compass, they form a mighty amphitheatre, of which the sea is the floor. On their slopes, in city and in pretty suburbs, are many exclusive homes, some standing in new, exposed grounds, others half revealing themselves behind imported trees. The whole effect is brightened with hundreds of red roofs.

In the lower part of the city. Government buildings and massive fronts of banks and hotels make an imposing appearance in an architectural way. With the exception of a part of Lambton Quay, the main business streets are narrow. Indeed, it is this very narrowness which lends impressiveness to many of the principal buildings. These thoroughfares are paved with blocks surfaced with tar and sand or shingle. The residential streets, which on maps look like fluttering ribbons, so rambling are they, are macadamized. If an earthquake should bring ruin to Wellington,—which, judging by past experiences, is not an improbability,—the people in these straitened commercial streets would have to be very agile to escape falling walls.

In addition to being forced to climb hills every day, and knowing, if he accepts prophecy, that they may fall upon him at any hour, the Wellingtonian frequently has to brace himself against a strong wind. Astonishing to say, the encircling hills give him little protection from gales off the coast.

"I hear that Wellington is a windy place," I said to a man who had lived thirty years in the capital.

"Oh," he replied, "it can blow. I have seen it blow a horse and cart along."

But winds and earthquakes are not enough to quench the spirit of Wellington. It still has the enthusiasm which actuated it in the days of its youth, and which, after many disappointing years, largely enabled it to become the capital in 1864. Because it had a larger European population than any other settlement in the colony, Wellington believed it was entitled to be the seat of the first government of New Zealand. Governor Hobson thought otherwise, and established the capital at Russell, whence, after a short time, he removed it to Auckland, which retained it for more than twenty years.

For convenience the exasperated Port Nicholson settlers established a temporary government of their own in Wellington; but when the sovereignty of Queen Victoria was proclaimed, May 21, 1840, under the Treaty of Waitangi, Governor Hobson by proclamation prohibited the Wellington settlers from conducting any government unrecognized by the Queen. The Wellington residents were not precipitate in complying with the order, and after its publication the captain of a ship was summoned by the colonists' court to answer for an alleged breach of charter. Declining to recognize the court, the mariner was arrested; but he escaped and complained to the Governor.

Immediately a lieutenant and thirty soldiers were dispatched to Wellington with instructions summarily to put down the settlers' government. The lieutenant's task was easy. He was welcomed with cheers, and the settlers, history tells us, "gladly abandoned their own temporary government now that a properly appointed authority was planted among them."

As the seat of government, Wellington contains a large number of public buildings of wood, brick, and stone. Of the Government buildings the most conspicuous are the General Post-Office; the structures separately occupied by the Life Insurance Offices, Printing-Office, Railway Department, Government Departments, Customs Department, and Houses of Parliament; and Government House, the residence of the Governor. The Government Departments Building is said to be the largest wooden structure in the Southern Hemisphere. To these buildings are to be added new houses of Parliament, to replace those destroyed by fire in 1907. All the present State buildings, with the exception of Government House, face on Lambton Quay or adjacent streets; consequently soon after detraining at Thorndon or Lambton, the visitor feels the dominating influence of established authority.

Of the municipal buildings the chief is the town hall, a massive pile with columnar front on Cuba Street. In this building Wellington has one of the finest pipe-organs in Australasia. Some critics say that it surpasses Sydney's more costly municipal organ.

Near the town hall is the public library. Architecturally, it is not particularly impressive, but to Americans it should be an interesting object, for here, in 1911, American literature won the approval of the capital's juvenile readers. American works had for some time been popular with adult patrons of the library, but youthful subscribers were prejudiced against them. Anything American, it seemed, was thought by them to be fustian. At last came a change, and now, to quote a Wellington newspaper, "The cold shoulder and the disdainful eye are no longer turned upon American volumes. A solid inquiry has set in for American literature, and the army of the curious grows daily. The children of Wellington have 'discovered' the Americans, and like them."

Wellington also has an art gallery, but apparently many of its residents had never heard of it when I inquired for it.

"It is a little beyond the library," my first informant assured me.

I went a little beyond that distance, but I saw nothing resembling an art gallery.

"Can you tell me where the art gallery is?" I asked another man.

"No, I'll be blowed if I can," he replied.

I repeated the question to a third man.

"Blest if I can," said he. "I did n't know we had an art gallery."

Then I went to the public library, and appealed to a young woman assistant.

"It is hard to direct you," she laughingly answered. "It is so small; it is a little red brick building with some trees around it."

Finally I found this secluded building, after inquiring the way again of a group of four men, only one of whom was able to direct me. The gallery building was of modest proportions, as I had been told, and the collection was small. But the name was entirely satisfactory. Over the gallery's portals were these words: "New Zealand Academy of Fine Arts."

In Wellington's commercial district are many large buildings, those of four and five stories being common. The most imposing of these, as a whole, are the banks and hotels. Their frontal appearances, however, are not altogether suited to their surroundings. With some of the city's public buildings, they caused me to conclude that Wellington has a heavy face, a face unduly weighted with adornments of architecture. In narrow streets the aspect of such buildings, particularly those with gloomy fronts, was not cheerful, and after being in their shade a while I was glad to escape to more open country.

TOWN HALL, WELLINGTON

Notwithstanding its cramped quarters, Wellington has a number of recreation grounds and parks of fair size. One of these is Newtown Park, which has the best zoo in New Zealand. On Tinakori Road, a short distance back of the business district, are the Botanical Gardens, where an extensive view of the city is obtainable. Here are wooded dells refreshing in their wild floral profusion, and cool, murmuring waters that sing in forest shades and ripple past flower gardens that delight with their variety.

In Wellington I rode in street-cars owned and operated by its people. On its thirty miles of tram-lines, built at a cost of three million dollars, the city carries more than twenty million passengers annually and realizes a fair interest on the invested capital.

A feature of the Wellington street-car system is the civility of its employees. The most obliging ticket inspector I met in the Dominion was a Wellington tramway employee, and not yet have I encountered a conductor so polite as the one who opened the door of the compartment in which I was sitting, and saying, "Thank you," shut it without having entered, or collected a fare. What did that "Thank you" mean? No one had given its speaker anything or done him a service. On inquiry, I learned that he was merely looking for unpaid fares, and that his thanks meant he was satisfied everybody in the compartment had paid!

As in its pioneer days, Wellington is the chief immigration port of New Zealand. In its fine harbor large steamships frequently anchor with from five hundred to six hundred immigrants from Great Britain, many of whom are "nominated" and "assisted." Since 1904 residents of New Zealand have had the privilege of nominating domestic servants and agriculturists for reduced passages from England to the Dominion. All persons granted such passages are booked to leave London in time to reach New Zealand in the spring or summer. Under this system passengers get a reduction of from ten to fifty-five dollars each in fares. The most favored of all such immigrants are female domestic servants. In six-berth cabins these have to pay only fourteen dollars for this voyage of twelve thousand miles.

Nominations are accepted by the New Zealand Government only on the understanding that residents or relatives will be responsible for the nominee on arrival in New Zealand. Since 1904 more than twenty thousand immigrants have been assisted.

These arrivals find a welcome in New Zealand, but there are other arrivals who do not. Between the ruddy farmhands and domestics of the United Kingdom and the yellow men of China there is a wide difference. One class is practically paid to enter New Zealand; the other must pay, and pay heavily, for that privilege. Once Chinese were permitted to enter the country for fifty dollars per head; since 1896 they have had to pay five hundred dollars each. And since late in 1908 each Chinese immigrant has been required to read a printed passage of not less than one hundred English words.

In New Zealand's capital one of the most impressive objects is the lofty monument raised to the memory of Richard John Seddon, who did so much to elevate the Dominion to its present position. The memorial is a granite shaft surmounted by a bronze female figure typifying political fame. It is dedicated to the dead statesman by Parliament and the people of New Zealand, and on it is written:—

"In him the most lofty qualities of an eminent Imperial statesman were united with wide human sympathies and warm affections of the heart."

For thirteen years "Digger Dick," once from the goldfields of Westland, was Prime Minister of "God's Own Country," as he loved to call it. He died in Australian waters on June 10, 1906, his end being hastened by overwork.

Mr. Seddon rose from humble ranks to the highest political position it was possible for him to win in New Zealand, yet never at any time or at any place was he ashamed to acknowledge his lowliest friends.

"I saw Dick walk up the street with a man that even I would have been ashamed to be seen with," said a Wellington laboring-man to me. "The bloke did n't have a decent pair of boots on; but that did n't make any difference to Seddon."

"Ah, when we lost Seddon we lost the father of our country," lamented the secretary of a labor union to me. "We laboring-men depended upon Dick Seddon. He made his mistakes and he had his faults: but when he did make mistakes, we said: 'Oh, well, Seddon has our welfare at heart.'"

Chapter XI

Southwesterly, across stormy Cook Strait, stretches the five-hundred-mile length of Te Wai-o-Pounamu, "The Sea of the Greenstone,"—The New Munster of early colonial days, the South Island of to-day. Here, in 1770, Captain Cook took possession of New Zealand in the name of King George III. Here Abel Tasman, long before, was deterred from landing by hostile Maoris, and sailed away, leaving behind him a territory that would have made a rich prize for Holland.

In old Maahunui are fertile grain-fields, wide and dreary tussock plains, and mountainous chaos. Here, wearing away the beds in which they lie, are the remnants of an ancient icecap that deeply grooved the mountains and piled their debris in drifts from one hundred to a thousand feet deep. Here also are glacier-gouged basins filled by sea and torrential streams where one can sail on mirroring waters from five hundred to more than a thousand feet in depth. In this land are enchanting gorges; alluring forests; unnumbered waterfalls; swift, clear rivers that flow in profound, narrow canyons; and silt-laden rivers that ramble over wide beds of glacial wreckage.

In traveling from Wellington to Lyttelton, the first of the chief ports of the South Island, going south from the North Island, I voyaged on one of the longest railway ferries in the world. It is a trip of one hundred and seventy-two miles, and it connects with the express trains of the two islands.

En route to Lyttelton I had an excellent view of the Kaikoura Mountains, comprising the Inland Kaikouras, with a maximum height of 9462 feet, and the Seaward or Lookers-on Kaikouras, with an extreme elevation of 8562 feet. The Lookers-on range was so called by Captain Cook, because opposite to them a large number of Maoris in double canoes approached within a few rods of the Endeavour and, stopping there, gazed at the ship in amazement.

When a navigator charts land as he sails past it he is likely to make a mistake. Captain Cook did so when he charted Banks Peninsula as an island. Another and more serious mistake was made near this same peninsula by a Captain Taylor, who mistook a cliff for a harbor entrance and unintentionally rammed it. His vessel was wrecked, and the place of its destruction is called "Taylor's Mistake" to-day.

No mistake was made, however, when Canterbury's first settlers chose for their homes Banks Peninsula and the plains beyond. To-day the peninsula is famed for its cocksfoot harvests, and Canterbury Plains are rich in houses and lands, in wheat and wool and mutton. On the peninsula, overlooking the beautiful harbor of Akaroa, British sovereignty was proclaimed in the South Island for the third time, and French possession, perhaps, was thereby forestalled by a few hours. In Akaroa today are seen landmarks of the first French settlers in this island.

On the plains the Canterbury Association, headed by a bishop, founded Christchurch, the second largest city in New Zealand. It was the association's aim to establish settlements limited to members of the Church of England, but an influx of people of other faiths prevented its realization. "The most English city of New Zealand" is set behind the high hills of Lyttelton, its port. From Lyttelton it is reached by a million-dollar tunnel more than a mile and a half long. Some day, if the dream becomes a reality, the city will be connected with the sea, seven miles distant, by a ten-million-dollar canal.

Fresh as I was from the cramped quarters of Wellington, my first view of the outlook of Christchurch was relaxing. Here were long vistas of clean, well-paved streets, and many open spaces. Here were the meadows, gardens, and recreation grounds of Hagley Park, the grassy, willow-shaded banks of the tortuous Avon, and Cathedral Square, the traffic heart of the city. From the Cathedral's tower I saw the entire city embowered in its trees and hedges and fanned by its numerous windmills.

The Christchurch of early days stood wholly on the plains; the Christchurch of to-day does not. The original site—a chessboard-like area a mile square with streets bearing ecclesiastical names—long ago became too limited for the city's growth, and in addition to filling suburbs on flat ground it is slowly climbing the Cashmere Hills, part of the coast ranges.

The city has a number of buildings worthy of more than passing notice. The Roman Catholic Basilica is a $300,000 church two hundred and ten feet long and one hundred and six feet wide. The front portico, supported by four Corinthian stone columns forty-five feet high, is flanked by two dome-shaped towers one hundred and eight feet high. Over the portico, midway between these towers, are the kneeling figures of two angels at the foot of a massive cross. Canterbury College, which has an enrollment of about five hundred students, is a pile of ornate stone buildings. The Museum is the best institution of its kind in New Zealand, and very well equipped in its natural history departments. The Cathedral is an attractive edifice with a spire that has been twice damaged by earthquake. It looks down upon Cathedral Square, where the street railways centre, the newspapers have their offices, and some of the leading hotels are to be found.

While the city has more miles of street railway than Auckland, Wellington, or Dunedin, its passenger traffic is considerably less, due to the fact that Christchurch has more bicycles than any other city in the country. There are thousands of them, and they have become a factor in the transportation problem of the city.

The Avon River—named for a stream in Lanarkshire, Scotland—flows through both the business and the residential sections of Christchurch, and the stranger is surprised at the number of times he comes upon this pretty but shallow stream. It divides Hagley Park, a beautiful tract of four hundred acres not far from the business district, and which includes recreation grounds and botanical gardens.

Perhaps more popular than this park, however, is Riccarton Racecourse, five miles out from the centre of the city. Horse-racing is a national sport, and this is the best equipped track in the Dominion, offering every November a $10,000 stake. Within the last twenty-five years, here and elsewhere, $125,000,000 has passed through the "tote," legalized and taxed by the State, of which sum the Government has received considerably more than $2,000,000. Into "the machine" the people pour their earnings until, after big race-meetings, even the milkman cannot collect when he presents his weekly bill at the kitchen door.

The day after a race-meeting at Takapuna, an Auckland trans-bay suburb, an Auckland butcher sent his delivery boy on a collecting tour. The accounts of his customers totaled about four hundred dollars. At night the lad returned.

"How much did you get?" his master asked him.

"Four and six (one dollar and eight cents)," was the stunning reply.

In horse-racing in New Zealand millions of dollars are invested by the two hundred thousand habitués of the racecourse. According to Sir George Clifford, if racing were stopped in that country, $5,000,000 would be withdrawn from circulation annually. The extent of the totalizator investments is astonishing. At Riccarton, where the annual attendance is about eighty thousand, the totalizator receipts for eleven days' racing in a recent year exceeded $900,000; and with bookmakers, whose occupation became illegal throughout New Zealand in 1911, the investments were many thousands more. At Ellerslie, Auckland's racecourse, in a later year, the totalizator returns were more than a million dollars.

It is a wonder, after such betting, that New Zealand racetrack habitués have any money left for other gambling. But they have; thousands of them always speculate in "Tatts." And what is "Tatts"? The greatest lottery concern in Australasia. Not officially. No, no! Officially it is Adams's Tattersall's monster cash prize consultation. "Tattersall's," says Tattersall's of itself, "are the only genuine successful consultations in Australasia, conducted under license from the Tasmanian Government, and drawn under special supervision of a representative of Government, and in the presence of the public and members of the press, also the police." Every year "the trustees of the late Mr. George Adams's estate . . . conduct the Sweep Business," says Tattersall's.

It certainly is a sweeping business, all around. From the public millions of dollars are swept by Tattersall's—which, however, retains only ten per cent of the whole—and the Tasmanian Government sweeps in about a quarter of a million dollars a year in stamp duty and a dividend tax on prizes.

The "fixtures" on which Tattersall's yearly promotes "consultations" — what an agreeable word this is! — are eighteen different race-meets in Australia and Tasmania, representing a grand total of nearly two million tickets, exclusive of oversubscriptions, which sometimes are very large. The chief drawing is on the Melbourne Cup, for which 300,000 tickets, one third being ten-shilling subscriptions, are originally issued. In the ten-shilling issues the first horse draws $50,000, or twice as much as the highest prize allotted to the most fortunate holder of a five-shilling ticket.

In New Zealand, Tattersall's does an enormous business, despite the New Zealand Post-Office Department's refusal to forward any mail addressed to Tattersall's or to any addressee known by the department to represent it. How then does Tattersall's get the money sent to it from the Dominion? By bank drafts, through the aid of friends in Tasmania, and through men in New Zealand who for a small fee forward the subscriptions to Hobart. Tattersall's clients are cautioned not to send post-office money orders, and they are advised to send their letters to "any friend in Hobart, who will have no difficulty in seeing that the letter reaches the proper hands." There are many "friends" in Hobart.

Playing the races and taking chances with Tattersall's are by no means the only forms of gambling in New Zealand. In that country the gaming instinct is very pronounced. Gambling is countenanced by the State, is indulged in by churches, and is widespread among the people. The Government, it is true, frowns upon lotteries, prohibits raffles, betting on cricket, football, and other sports, and forbids the publication of racing tips and dividends outside racing-grounds. But it legalizes the totalizator. O inconsistent Government!

With gambling are associated intemperance and prohibition, both very live questions in Maoriland. There the prohibitionists have the brewers and publicans on the jump. In many towns public-houses have been closed; "ten o'clock closing" has been made universal; barmaids, of whom there were more than barmen in 1911, have been restricted in number, their registration since June of that year being prohibited; and in the elections of that year national prohibition was an issue for the first time, but it failed to secure the required three-fifths majority.

An interesting result of the drink traffic in New Zealand has been the establishment of drunkards' homes by the Salvation Army. On two islands near Auckland the Army has quarters for considerably more than two hundred patients. The patients are required to work a certain number of hours each day, and on leaving the institution are given cash gratuities of from five to fifteen dollars. Toward the support of the committed men and women the State gives a capitation; the voluntary patients pay for their accommodation.

Chapter XII

Two hundred and thirty miles southwest of Christchurch is Dunedin, the fourth city in population in New Zealand and the chief gateway to Fiordland and the Cold Lakes. It is reached by one of the most interesting railway routes in the country. For a large part of the way its sea vistas rival those of the Southern Pacific's Coast Line in California, and for many miles the train passes through meadows and wheatfields divided by gorse-hedges. On this route, also, are Timaru, a well-built town with the prettiest beach in New Zealand, and Oamaru, the stone city where a brick chimney is an uncommon sight.

Dunedin is noted for its Scotch characteristics. It was founded by Scots, and it is said to have more Scottish residents than any other New Zealand city. Proof of Scotch individuality I saw there on every hand; in the Octagon, where one side of the street is graced by a monument to Robert Burns, and the other side by a memorial to the Reverend Thomas Burns, the first Presbyterian minister in Otago; in handsome Presbyterian churches; in Caledonian and Burns societies; in marching pipers, in reels, flings, and hornpipes; and yet again in the railway station immediately on my arrival.

To its handsome tower I was quickly attracted, for at its top were four lions guarding the British royal arms. Each lion had a scholarly pose, and looked as if he were delivering a valedictory.

Dunedin is situated at the end of Otago Harbor, an inlet about sixteen miles long. It lies in a very hilly district, and both on the north and the south the immediate approach to the city by rail is through tunnels. Like Christchurch, it has a seaport,—Port Chalmers, eight miles distant,—but recent dredgings have made it unnecessary for it to depend entirely upon its port for ocean shipping.

Of New Zealand cities, Dunedin, next to Auckland, presents the finest views. It has not an encircling panorama equal to Auckland's, but within its own limits it does surpass Auckland in beauty and general attractiveness. Greater segregation of land and water and conspicuous isolations give Auckland a superior magnificent whole, but Dunedin, borrowing more from nature, has screened its more exclusive parts with native bush, and in addition has provided itself with many open spaces, such as the Botanical Gardens, the Oval and Market Reserves, the parked Octagon, Jubilee Park, and Victoria Gardens.

Despite its hills, Dunedin is not seriously cramped for room in its business district. On the landward side of Princes and George Streets, the main commercial thoroughfares, business cannot go far without climbing steep hills, but seaward are other long paralleling highways, and more room is being made by filling in shallow harbor areas.

DUNEDIN

To climb its steep hills the city employs cable cars, the city's electric tramway system being confined mainly to flat ground. There are two private cable lines and one owned and operated by the Borough of Mornington. On the steepest part of the municipal line the grade is about thirty per cent. These cable systems figure that it is worth more to a man to be carried uphill than downhill, and they charge accordingly.

Dunedin has an aspect of solidity. Its streets are well paved, its principal buildings are substantial, and many of them are ornate as well. The majority of the business blocks are built of stone, brick, and concrete. The highest of them is the seven-story reinforced concrete structure built for the New Zealand Express Company, at a cost of $225,000.

The architecture of the public buildings is pleasing. The town hall, overlooking the Octagon, has not been weathered into blackness like Wellington's municipal hall, and it is more pleasantly situated. By some critics it is considered to have the most musical clock chimes in the country. Near the town hall, and built with a donation of $50,000 from Andrew Carnegie, is the best Carnegie library in the two islands. Other important buildings are the Law Courts; the Boys' High School, noted for its large swimming-bath; and the University of Otago, housed in a group of buildings of the domestic Gothic style, and having attached to it thirty professors and lecturers. By this institution, more than forty years ago, university education was first established in New Zealand.

It is one of four affiliated with the University of New Zealand, the other three being Canterbury College, Christchurch; Victoria College, Wellington; and Auckland University College. The University of New Zealand was established in 1870, and is an examining body only. Its senate of twenty-four members awards degrees on the results of examinations conducted by examiners appointed in Great Britain. According to the University's Royal Charter, these degrees are entitled to "rank, precedence, and consideration throughout the British Empire as fully as if the said degrees had been conferred by any university of the United Kingdom."

The best place from which to view Dunedin is Flagstaff Hill, a few miles west of Princes Street. Flagstaff Hill is a hill without a flagstaff. On its summit I found only an iron support for one. When I inquired about the staff, a Dunedin man said: "There was a flagstaff there, but the larrikins took it."

Another man told me there never had been a staff on the hill; but if there had been, perhaps larrikins would have removed it. For larrikinism is one of the evils of New Zealand. Everywhere there one hears of the larrikin, or young hoodlum. Larrikins are an unorganized, mischievous fraternity. They are always despoiling or marring public or private property or making people the butt of coarse jokes and jeers. If something is stolen, "the larrikins took it"; if windows or park seats are broken, "the larrikins did it."

THE BOYS' HIGH SCHOOL, DUNEDIN

On Flagstaff Hill one can see the whole of Dunedin, excepting small parts hidden by bush and brows of hills. From its summit, in a wilderness of tussocks and black boulders, the eye beholds beauty and grandeur.

The visitor to Dunedin should not fail to climb Flagstaff's top, but as he goes, let him beware of Ben Rudd. The top of the hill is neutral territory, but not entirely so are its slopes. On New Zealand railways it is "Look out for the engine"; on Flagstaff Hill, when I reached its foot, it was "Look out for Ben Rudd." Externally, Ben Rudd, judging by an account of him I received, is a sort of miscellaneous man, like Hawthorne's Uncle Venner, but without that patriarch's geniality. I first heard of him when I stopped at a farmhouse to inquire the way to Flagstaff's summit.

"There are several ways," said the pleasant, chatty woman who answered my knock. "But look out for old Ben Rudd."

"Who is Ben Rudd?" I asked.

"Oh! have you never heard of Ben Rudd?" cried she, throwing up her hands in amazement. "He is a hermit living at the foot of Flagstaff Hill. If you try to get through his rabbit-proof fence, he will shoot you. If you meet a small, crouching old man with a little black beard and fingers interlocked under his chin, and who says to you, 'Mister, what may you be wanting here?' that's Ben Rudd. His clothes are all patches; he must have a million patches."

"Is he dangerous?" I inquired.

"Well," she answered, "if, in answer to his question, you tell him to 'Go to Halifax,' he will stone you. Instead say real cheerfully, 'Good-morning, Mr. Rudd! What a fine morning it is! I have lost my way. Can you direct me?' If you do that, Ben will treat you all right."

As I had no desire to be stoned, I asked the woman, "Where am I likely to meet Ben? If I take that short cut you mentioned, won't I miss him?"

"Oh, yes, you may," she replied; "but you never know where you'll meet Ben Rudd."

I continued on my way, thankful that the weather was fine, so that I could use it as a password, as advised. But I did not meet Mr. Rudd, and heard no whizzing stones.

The panorama of Flagstaff Hill proved well worth the trip. Eastward, rolling in unbroken from a remote, unobstructed horizon, the ocean broke against the pretty, billowy Otago Peninsula, swept up the white beach between Lawyer's Head and St. Clair, hurled itself against the cliffs between St. Clair and Green Island Beach, and lapped the shallow shores of South Dunedin, once a part of the sea bed and later still a swamp. Between the peninsula and the hill were the city and its harbor. In the foreground were the heights of Mornington, Roslyn, and Maori Hill, where beautiful homes have been built from three hundred to seven hundred feet above the sea. Below them ran the leafy fringe known as the Town Belt, divided by sinuous Queen's Drive, a name that suggested what it did not signify—a broad and well-paved driveway. On each side of this drive were many delightful bowers. There, clustering thickly together, were fuschia and other low growth, canopied and weighted heavily with clematis, lawyer, and other creepers; and there the manuka, white with scentless blossoms, exhaled its strong aroma of leaf and limb.

On Maori Hill were revealed the lake-like city reservoir and the shady retreats of Ross Creek, its chief feeder. Below Maori Hill meandered the Valley of the Leith, a charming dale running toward Mount Cargill between leaf-screened cliffs.

West of Flagstaff ran the gorge of the Taieri River, and in the distance, over hill and vale, rose the Lammerlaws, the Rock and Pillar Range, and, dimly outlined, Mount Ida and Mount St. Bathans, overlooking the Central Otago goldfields.

Southward stretched the hedge-bordered paddocks of Taieri Plain, which with its varied colors produced by cut and uncut grain, and hayfields and groves of trees, looked like a crazy quilt. On the eastern side of this plain is the largest glacial drift in New Zealand. Forming a range of hills more than twenty-five miles long, it is from a half-mile to three miles wide and about a thousand feet deep.

In all this panorama nothing is so fascinating as the wild seacoast. In front of Dunedin and for miles to its right and left the ocean beats against high, rocky cliffs, rolls ceaselessly through caves, and sweeps up short, yellow beaches. One of the most absorbing spots is the convenient cliff profile, Lawyer's Head, the northern terminus of St. Kilda beach. Here, on a coast of half-submerged rocks, and sand-dunes held in place by a tangle of wiry grasses and shrubs, the sea constantly floods and drains a weird and cavernous playground. Here brown seaweed scourges, from twenty to thirty feet long, unceasingly flay the rocks that give their tenacious roots support. One moment they dive to their roots; the next instant, struggling like coiling snakes or sweeping in gracefully on a breaker, they furiously assail their dripping, adamantean home.

Almost at the southern extremity of the South Island, one hundred and thirty-nine miles from Dunedin, is Invercargill, the roomiest town in New Zealand and the most southern town of its population in the world. The founders of Invercargill must have been advocates of the broad-gauge principle; for the town's two main business streets, Dee and Tay, are each one hundred and thirty-two feet wide. To a Wellington man they probably look nearly wide enough for a cross-country run.

In Invercargill five railways centre, and it ranks next to Dunedin as a gateway to the Cold Lakes and the western sounds. In oversea shipping, Invercargill's port, the Bluff, seventeen miles distant, is the third entry and clearance point in the Dominion.

At the Bluff concentrates New Zealand's largest oyster fleet. In Foveaux Strait, separating the South Island and Stewart Island, is one of the most extensive oyster beds in the world. The deep-sea oyster beds in New Zealand are exploited wholly by private enterprise, but the rock oyster industry is controlled by the State, which took it in charge because of injury to the beds by irresponsible pickers.

INVERCARGILL

Through the Bluff passes the tourist traffic to Stewart Island, the Rakiura of the southern Maoris. This island, situated about twenty miles south of the Bluff, somewhat resembles South America in miniature, with Paterson Inlet occupying about the same relative position as the mouth of the Amazon.

Stewart Island is one of the most beautiful and romantic islands of the world. Here, a century ago, in picturesque harbors and coves haunted by cannibals, anchored venturesome English, American, and Australasian whalers and sealers. To-day, all around Rakiura's boulder coasts, are names reminiscent of wild and perilous escapades, in which more than one whaler and sealer were slain and eaten by Maoris. In those days vessels lay at anchor in the island's harbors with loaded cannon and with sentinels on duty; to-day the chugging of pleasure boats is heard where carronades then barked, and the merry laugh of delighted campers has replaced the murderous cry of savages.

No longer is the Strait a famous whaling-ground, and the seals, slaughtered by the thousand for many years, have been so nearly exterminated that they are protected by legislation. Yet Stewart Island is still a great rendezvous for fishermen, as it is for tourists. In its bays are trumpeter, blue cod, flounders, groper, trevalli, and other fish, and into some of its rivers trout have been introduced.

Mountainous and densely wooded, Stewart Island has an area of six hundred and sixty-five square miles, with an extreme length of thirty-nine miles and a maximum breadth of twenty miles. Its highest elevation is Mount Anglem (3200 feet), an extinct volcano with a lake near its crest. On all sides the ocean breaks against a rocky shore, and rolls against many neighboring islets infested by tens of thousands of mutton birds, which afford Maoris an annual hunting, feasting, and preserving expedition of several weeks' duration.

To those seeking the finest scenery of Stewart Island, the easily accessible Paterson Inlet appeals most strongly. This sea-arm is about ten miles long, and its shores are covered to the water's edge with a variety of trees; yet everywhere, excepting where short, yellow beaches interpose, the sea washes against rocky faces and boulders. The inlet's smallest islands are capped with bush and splashed with the rata's crimson.

The islands form one of the inlet's main attractions, its bosom being dotted with them. There are Faith, Hope, and Charity; the oval Iona; and Ulva, where one can mail, as one would mail an ordinary postcard, a puharitaiko leaf letter. On the broad and silvery under-surface of this leaf messages in ink can be written as easily as on a leather card. South of Paterson Inlet little of Stewart Island is known to the average tourist, because as yet that part cannot be conveniently reached.

Chapter XIII

In the southwestern part of the South Island, over the tussocky hills and plains of Otago and Southland, is New Zealand's grandest lake region; its magnificent sounds that rival the fiords of Norway; river canyons with cloud-swept rims; and sea-cliffs rising thousands of feet above the tides. Here lakes and sounds, dividing the land among themselves, ramble irregularly over the country, cutting into the heart of mountain ranges, forming islands, peninsulas and promontories, and receiving the waters of innumerable crystal streams. So remarkably indented and isolated is the land between Lakes Te Anau and Manapouri and the Tasman Sea, that from the head of Doubtful Sound to Milford Sound, one hundred miles north, one huge island is almost formed.

The principal sounds are great straggling arms of the sea that run far inland, exploring the hills with long lateral inlets, and here and there almost meeting a large lake or a connecting chain of small lakes. Some of the odd and awkward shapes of these fiords are like gigantic jaws extended to excavate the mountains which bar their further progress.

For one hundred and forty miles the granite coast of the Fiordland National Park is indented by fourteen sounds from six to twenty-two miles long. The chief of these, from a scenic viewpoint, is Milford, ten miles in length and running between the handsomely proportioned Lion Rock and the bold, spiring Mitre Peak, which forms one of the world's most striking mountain pictures. Only eight of these sounds are usually visited, the others not being especially attractive. South of Milford the popular fiords are George, Thompson, Doubtful, Breaksea, and Dusky Sounds, and Chalky and Preservation Inlets.

LAKE MANAPOURI AND CATHEDRAL PEAKS

All these sounds fill deep hollows excavated by glaciers, and so sheer are their walls that in many places vessels can anchor to trees at the water's edge. In them the depth of water is greater than at any other part of the New Zealand coast, Milford Sound, for example, having a maximum depth of 1270 feet. As yachting and camping grounds. New Zealand's fiords, with their densely forested shores, rising from 1000 to 6000 feet high, and their sylvan isles, are unsurpassed by similar retreats in either hemisphere.

Beautiful New Zealand is not all beautiful, even in the South Island, its most beautiful part, so many of its scenic wonders lie beyond dreary tussock plains and hills. Across such lonely grass expanses I went to reach the Cold Lakes, the sounds, and the Southern Alps. My ways to all these wonders and to the coast of gold and greenstone beyond were over hills of glacial deposits, through valleys of alluvial drift, within sight of crumbling mountains, and over great estates where millions of sheep and rabbits grazed.

Over stretches like these, where I sometimes journeyed from ten to twenty miles before meeting a human being, the traveler is transported mainly by horse-coach or motor-car;

for of all these attractions the only one reached directly by railroad is Lake Wakatipu. Te Anau and Manapouri, the most southern of the largest lakes, are forty miles from the nearest railway station; but the coaching trip begins at Lumsden, fifty-two miles distant, where there is more frequent train service. These two lakes are one hundred and eighty-eight miles from Dunedin, and are on the route to Milford Sound.

All the way from Lumsden the coach-road ran across what was practically one great sheep range. In places the road was barred with gates to confine the sheep that here fed on tussocks from one foot to three feet high. Here, as throughout the eastern part of the South Island, tussock grass was as common as tea-tree in the North Island. It was not so prolific, though, as it had been before certain destroying agents—fire, drouth, sheep, and rabbits—had attacked it.

In New Zealand rabbits are a curse; and yet, as I shall show, they also are a blessing. I have seen their burrows in hill, plain, and river bank, and their skeletons, stripped of their fur by trappers, bleaching on many a fence beside public roads. The rabbit pest in New Zealand is by no means so serious as it is in vast areas of Australia, but legislation has been passed, and exists to-day, to combat it.

To the owners of grazing-stations the rabbit is a marauding rodent; to trappers, freezing works, and skin exporters it is a treasure trove on feet. In a single night trappers catch from fifty to two hundred rabbits, daily freezing works handle thousands of them, and every year exporters ship between 7,000,000 and 8,000,000 rabbit skins. In the last twenty years more than 120,000,000 rabbit skins have been exported from New Zealand.

A feature of the route to the Cold Lakes is the pronounced evidence of glaciation. There are deep and wide channels that apparently are the beds of ancient ice streams, and dry basins that once probably were lakes. Many persons believe that Manapouri and Te Anau are but the remains of an immense inland sea. That these lakes have been much higher is certain;

the regularly formed banks rising well above high water mark on their eastern shores clearly indicate it.

Of these two lakes Manapouri, the smaller, is the most beautiful sheet of fresh water in New Zealand. It lies between mountains from three thousand to five thousand feet high. Its clear blue waters mirror dense forests; its long arms are like fiords; and it is dotted with thirty-five wooded islands. Manapouri's surface is five hundred and ninety-seven feet above the sea, and its deepest part is eight hundred and sixty feet below mean tide. Its area is fifty-six square miles, its extreme length about twenty miles. It is connected with Te Anau, thirteen miles distant by road, by the beautiful Waiau River.

Once the shores of Manapouri were peopled by Maoris; now, excepting the tourists at the hotel, their only inhabitants are birds. Some of these birds are friendly, too. At the lake's head our launch was sometimes met by a pair of wekas, or native wood hens, and they were so tame that they almost permitted the passengers to pick them up.

As I approached Manapouri from Lumsden it was visible for the first time over the top of fern-covered benches. By these the attractiveness of the eastern shore was lessened, but elsewhere were no detracting features. On the northern shore, in the near distance, shimmered the mile heights of Cathedral Peaks; west of them towered the Spire of the Keplers; on the south, at the head of Hope Arm, was the quaint-looking Monument; beyond it the barrenness of Titiroa's singular summit; and west of it were the crags and peaks of the Hunter Mountains, the appalling steeps of Precipice Peak, and the ice-armored heights of the western sea.

On clear days Manapouri presented one of the most superb vistas of the world. Yet there are many who prefer to see it veiled by the mists of stormy hours. On cloudless days the glistening snowfields, the deep blue of distant mountains, the green and purple shades of forests, interspersed with the bright-red blossoms of the rata, formed one sublime, unobstructed panorama.

All this was alluring, but it was not mystifying, nor did it excite the curiosity so deeply as did the perspective of gloomy days.

SAFE OR HAPPY COVE, HEAD OF LAKE TE ANAU

On misty days all was not seen with one sweep of the eye; always there was something reserved. Then one saw ghostly forms of mountains behind shrouds that were constantly lifting, lowering, thickening, or dispersing. Peaks appeared to sink in the beds of mist, mountains were belted and blanketed by mist, and waterfalls and tumbling streams seemed to pour from the clouds.

At all times waterfalls form one of the chief charms of Manapouri. On rainy days they are so numerous that a score can be seen at one time from more than one point on the lake. Everywhere the precipitous slopes shed water in streams that dash madly through causeways of rimu, rata, and beech; over luxuriant beds of moss that form a continuous growth running far down mountain sides like strips of velvety carpet; and through the face of moss-covered cliffs.

Manapouri's most charming parts are its arms, narrow reaches from three to six miles long. Indeed, Manapouri is little else than arms. In them all are delightful nooks—rivers and brooks terminating at little beaches, sheltered coves that are invisible until one is abreast of them, and cool sylvan retreats beneath frowning rock ramparts.

Te Anau, New Zealand's second largest lake, looks like an enormous hammer-headed monster with three crooked legs. These fancied legs are deep, enchanting fiords that thrust themselves far into four high, rugged mountain ranges. On the east the coast is comparatively regular, and for about twenty miles is uninteresting. On this monotonous stretch of fern-matted benches all excursions on the lake begin, and here halt for a night all travelers to Milford Sound via Milford Track, which begins at the lake's head.

Te Anau lies in the bed of a glacier that extended from the lake's southern extremity to the head of the Clinton River, a distance of more than fifty miles. It is about forty miles long and nine hundred feet deep, and its surface is seven hundred feet above the sea. Although only from one mile to six miles wide, Te Anau has a coast-line two hundred and fifty miles long. Hundreds of years ago its southeastern shores were peopled by Maoris, but late in the eighteenth century they mysteriously disappeared. Now this, the only inhabited part of the lake, is mainly a sheep run.

In the beauty of its fiords Te Anau worthily compares with Manapouri. These are from eleven to sixteen miles long, and the entrance to each is set with wooded islands. South Fiord, the longest, is almost half as long as the lake's main body. It lies between the wild, broken ridges and peaks of the Kepler and Murchison Mountains, and it is remarkable for the chain of small lakes that drain into it. There are more than a dozen, and one lies within two miles of Gear Arm, Thompson Sound. The Middle Fiord, widest of the arms, has two branches and an extreme length of thirteen miles. North Fiord, lying between the Stuart and Franklin ranges, looks like a river in a canyon.

En route to Te Anau's head there is only one regular port of call, a large sheep station where our steamer stopped to transfer mail and freight to a gasoline schooner. Thereafter the scenery was rugged. There were long vistas between canyon-like walls; unbroken expanses of beech forests, hung with beard-like lichens that at a distance looked like white flowers, stretched as far as the eye could see to the crags, cliffs, and peaks of the snow-line; and water-falls, half hidden by trees, plunged from lofty heights. On the east were the perpendicular precipices of Eglinton, on the west the white bluffs of Tower Mountain and the tilted, slab-like Mount Kane.

The upper part of the lake was itself like a fiord. Nowhere was it more than about a mile and a half or two miles wide, excepting at its head, where, on the west, it widened into Worsley Arm and, on the east, curved to meet the Clinton River. Here peaks rose from five thousand to six thousand feet high, mighty uplifts of granite torn, grooved, and mitred by glaciers that melted into torrents thousands of years ago.

In the midst of these we reached Te Anau's head.

"Now just look up Clinton Canyon," said the captain of our steamer proudly, as we headed for the wharf.

It was a scene that enraptured. Straight ahead, flanking Clinton Canyon on the right, loomed Mackenzie, a great bump of a mountain sprinkled with ice and snow. On its right were the bold outlines of Te Anau's frigid heights, and near at hand were Skelmorlie and Largs Peaks, each terminating more than a mile above the sea. In the left foreground a mountain thrust up an immense knob similar to the neck of a short, thick bottle.

Then my eyes rested on a clear, silent river flowing into the lake. It was the Clinton, which later, in a deep canyon dripping with waterfalls and heaped and strewn with mountain wreckage from frozen snowbanks, I was to see turbulently cutting away its banks, dashing madly against great boulders, and finally dwindling to a mere creek beneath the shadows of Mount Hart and Balloon Peak. Down this river an appalling rush of water sometimes comes, and the same is true of creeks discharging into the lake. It was one of these which, changing its course, isolated the old wharf at the lake's head and made it necessary to build another.

"At three o'clock on that day," the captain told me, "I could walk across it without getting my feet wet; but at four it was a torrent."

At the edge of Te Anau's head starts Milford Track, ending at Milford Sound, about thirty-three miles distant. The first stage is a level stretch half a mile long ending at the Glade House, a State hotel on the left bank of the Clinton. From this point and for miles up the canyon, is one of the most beautiful forest walks in the world. The trees wear bouquets. The path is shaded by beech trees, and many of them are decked with the parasitical mistletoe. Fastening itself on trunk or limb, the plant blossoms into a great bunch of scarlet, forming one of the finest forest effects imaginable. For miles along the track the mistletoe bedecks the trees and its fallen petals emblazon the ground.

Milford Track, the Tourist Department assures the traveler, is "the finest walk in the world." From a scenic viewpoint, it unquestionably is one of the most extraordinary walks on earth; but the Government, which controls the track and keeps it in repair, is not referring to the construction when it says "the finest." This is evident to all who follow its winding course. To many persons the track is a trying place, but this often is largely so because of their unreasonable haste. A good walker can cover the entire distance in one day, but if the majority of pedestrians tried to do so they would be indisposed for a week.

Milford Track is not a racecourse. It is a place to study nature, to hear the music of waterfalls leaping from granite walls thousands of feet high; to see, within a small radius, rocky ruggedness and the refreshing beauty of tree, fern, flower, and moss.

For this trip it is best to take three days. On the first day Pompolona Huts, ten miles from the Glade House, can be comfortably reached. The second day can be well spent walking to Quintin Huts, nine miles distant, including the ascent and descent of McKinnon's Pass, which has an altitude of thirty-four hundred feet. On the afternoon of the third day Milford Sound is reached.

Life on Milford Track would furnish a fit subject for a comedy. Here one sees the lame and the halt, the footsore and weary; here cripples, limping to and about the huts and Glade House, tread as cautiously as if stalking game.

At the huts are great quantities of tinned goods, and big appetites. The married couple in charge of each hut never know when a hungry walker will seat himself or herself on a bench before the long wooden table and call for canned soup, fish, beef, or sausage. As a famishing New Plymouth solicitor said to me, " It does not matter much what it is, so long as it is something."

The huts are conducted by the Tourist Department from November 1 to April 30, the only part of the year when the track is free from snow. They are rough wooden buildings with galvanized iron roofs, and on the outside each has a large chimney of the lean-to kind so common in New Zealand's "back-blocks." In these way-places the dining-room also is the kitchen. Likewise it serves as a cheerful, informal social hall, where, before a wide fireplace hung with pots and kettles, the walkers talk of the day's happenings while, if a wet day, their damp clothing dries in the heat of four-foot logs. At these places meals and beds (bunks furnished with blankets) are paid for with coupons obtained at Glade House, the charge being fifty cents for either meals or beds. All tourist patrons must have a track ticket also, which costs eighty-four cents.

Another convenience on Milford Track is a telephone service. The telephone line runs the whole length of the walk, but the service does not. For a brief time it was in operation between Glade House and the sound, but keeping the line in place over the pass became too troublesome, and it is now serviceable only from Glade House to Pompolona Huts. Another telephone line is in operation between Sand-Fly Point, Milford Sound, and Sutherland's accommodation house, where all visitors to the sound are lodged. When this system is not in working order it is customary to use dynamite to summon Captain Sutherland's launch, two miles distant. But even when the telephone is efficient it sometimes takes a long while to get results.

A Government guide-book says that "in answer to the ring, Milford's pioneer launch will shortly be seen rounding the point." Not always. The party I was with waited two hours for its appearance, and we were told that a delay of that length was not unusual at Sand-Fly Point. The first reply we received was, "He [Captain Sutherland] won't be long"; at the second ring it was, "He'll be over in half an hour"; at the third call this was reduced to fifteen minutes; and when we were all desperate and felt like dynamiting the point and thereby killing some of the sand-flies that were pestering us, we were relieved to hear, "He is on the way."

In its itinerary of travel, the Tourist Department gives valuable suggestions regarding dress and equipment for Milford Track walkers, but it does not say anything about sand-flies. According to maps there is a Sand-Fly Point at each end of the track, but these do not show all the sand-fly points. There are sand-fly points all along the track, and every time the walker halts, from one to a score of these points are thrust into him. The sand-flies of Milford Track are especially fond of tourists, and the only way to baffle them is to wear gloves and veils or mosquito-netting; anoint the hands, face, and neck with ointments which the insects do not like; or stay within closed doors. These winged gluttons are acrobats—they stand on their heads when they alight on your hand. But they do not do it to amuse you; they are "going down" for blood.

There was a lure about Milford Track that made me eager to get across the Clinton and disappear into the stately forest it divides. Ahead, blotting out a great expanse of sky, was Mount Mackenzie. Other colossal forms as mighty as it rose to its right and its left. And away ahead, beyond Mackenzie, was formidable Balloon Peak, unsealed until recently; and beyond it and on every side of it, peak succeeded peak from five thousand to nine thousand feet high. These splintered tops of granite ranges overlooked a jagged world that ran northward until it met the greater wilds of the Southern Alps.

As I proceeded, between the straight, shapely trunks of beech trees—from one foot to three feet in diameter—there appeared ever-changing vistas of river, rapid, cascade, and cliff. For about six miles there was an unbroken forest; thereafter the continuity was interrupted by clearings and areas of scrubby growth. In this bush was a wealth of ferns, moss, and lichens. There were coarse, wiry ferns, soft, fragile, and beautifully indented ferns, and there were ferns that climbed trees and crowned moss-covered rocks. Completely covering other rocks beside the track were gray lichens that at a distance resembled masses of coral, and on trunks and limbs of trees light-green lichens hung in streamers and tufts. Throughout the forest mosses formed carpets and cushions and on canyon slopes were acres of brown and green moss saturated by seepage and stream.

Where the forest was most luxuriant it veiled the sternness of the canyon's granite piles to the snow-line, but above that were only shrubs and snow grass to the point where there appeared to be nothing but ice and snow and dripping granite ledges. These ramparts were streaked white with what apparently was powdered débris; and where they could find a resting-place there were huge frozen snowbanks, through which torrents bored large caves and long dark tunnels that were as cool as refrigerators.

After I had been ferried across the Clinton, the walk fairly began. All the way to McKinnon's Pass the track closely followed this stream, which lies in a canyon from one fourth to a half-mile wide. The granite walls are from three thousand to four thousand feet high, and they run upward into mountains with crests from five thousand to seven thousand feet above the sea. Excepting during floods, the Clinton is a clear, placid stream for a considerable distance from its mouth, and for miles flows through a beech forest that reaches across the canyon and climbs precipitous slopes wherever it is possible to obtain sustenance and roothold.

In the Clinton I saw the blue of glaciers, the white of foaming cataracts and shallow gravel beds, and the willow green of calm depths. Over a varied bed it flowed, now hurdling over granite fragments, now tearing savagely at piles of boulders and driftwood, and lastly running smoothly over sand and gravel drifts. All along the Clinton I heard the sound of water; one moment gurgling, murmuring, rippling; then it was splashing or roaring over obstructions, or falling heavily from beetling heights. Only for brief intervals was I out of sight of waterfalls; they were so numerous that, opposite to Pariroa Heights, I counted thirty through one opening in the forest. Some were dropping sheer hundreds of feet, others raced down slopes that were almost vertical. Many leaped from such great heights that they reached the floors of the canyon in the form of mist or fine rain. At the back of Pompolona Huts I saw a cascade dissipated into rain long before it reached the bench below; and I witnessed the same thing in Arthur Canyon, where three falls, fed by Jervois Glacier, became long, wavering playthings of the wind far up the cliffs of Mount Elliott.

As I emerged from the denser portions of the forest between Glade House and Pompolona Huts, I saw, miles ahead, a high wall stretching across the canyon. This was McKinnon's Pass, connecting Mount Hart and Balloon Peak, over which I must go to reach Arthur Canyon, the continuation of the path to Milford Sound. From a distance the wall looked impassable, but its summit I finally gained by a rough and rocky zigzag course.

On this pass, overgrown with coarse mountain grass, dotted with pools of water, and brightened with the white and gold of the Mountain Lily and the snowy blossoms of alpine daisies, was one of the grandest of mountain panoramas. Here was a picture of encircling snow peaks, canyons and rivers, glacier and snowfield, waterfalls and mountain wreckage. Immediately to the right as I faced westward was the remarkable spire of Balloon Peak; to the left were the sheer descents of Mount Hart; more distant were the tremendous precipices of The Castle Mountain and of Mounts Pillans, Edgar, and Elliott. On Mount Elliott there was faintly discernible the blue of ice cliffs on Jervois Glacier hundreds of feet high. This snow-capped icefield had the appearance of a great mass of baking powder or flour breaking apart under its own weight and forming crevices and crumbling heaps.

CLINTON CANYON FROM MCKINNON'S PASS

On one side was the curving Clinton Canyon, on the other side was the more abruptly terminating vista of Arthur Canyon. Both were magnificent beyond words, both had their eyrie cliffs and lofty waterfalls, their roaring and placid reaches of creek and river, their lake and delightful forests. But though Arthur Canyon seemed on the whole to be more wooded, more open and more cheerful, and had the finest waterfalls and the only lake worthy of the name, it was not, from the top of the pass, so suggestive nor so creative of curiosity as the sweeping canyon lines of the Clinton. In the last curves visible from the pass looking down the Clinton there was a suggestion of something interesting beyond, just as there is in the bend of any beautiful river. Away below was Lake Mintaro, a pond receiving the waters of glacial streams; the dark mass of forest; and, as also in Arthur Canyon, areas of grasses and bushes that, at that distance, gave the canyon floor the appearance of green meadows. At times fog overlaid the canyon until it looked like one great river of mist.

The flowers on the pass and its slopes are common in high altitudes throughout this region, and are found in profusion in the Southern Alps. Most beautiful of them all was the *Ranunculus Lyalli*, a buttercup misnamed the Mountain Lily and known also as the Mount Cook Lily and the Shepherd's Lily. With its broad leaves, sometimes exceeding fifteen inches in width, it looked to me like a water-lily stranded on land. Its pure white waxy blossom, centred with yellow, is the most pleasing floral object in New Zealand's alpine regions. Another very common flower on the pass was the celmisia, a daisy from two to three inches in diameter. In New Zealand there are about forty species of this flower, and all but one are endemic.

On the pass, a short distance to the left of the track as one goes toward the sound, is a track-walkers' memorial to Quintin McKinnon, who, after several attempts to find an overland route to Milford Sound, discovered this pass in 1888, four years before he was drowned in a squall on Lake Te Anau. The memorial is a pile of loose stones raised by tourists going over the pass.

The descent of the pass into Arthur Canyon and on to the Quintin Huts, four miles, is the roughest part of the track; likewise the ascent of these four miles is more arduous than the climb on the opposite side. The first part of my descent was beneath the mighty buttresses of Balloon Peak, towering thousands of feet above me. Its perpendicular walls were covered with tufts of snow grass, and its overhanging ledges, caused by slips, looked ominous as I passed almost directly under them. Such ledges were common in both canyons, and they served as explanations of the great quantities of débris seen in some places, notably at the foot of Elliott. Here there was an aspect of mountains falling into ruins. Millions of tons of rock, including boulders of many tons' weight, lay scattered about, forming at alternate times the beds of dry creeks and formidable streams that no man cares to attempt to cross when at their highest.

After getting across this wilderness of stone, which flowers and shrubs helped to render less desolate, the way became easier. Then there was deep satisfaction in looking far above me to the white walls of the pass and away below where the nakedness of granite was hidden by another luxuriant beech forest. Through this forest the track ran a very stony course until it made a forked turn. Here were two tracks, one leading to Milford Sound, the other to Quintin Huts. Among track walkers there is no indecision at this junction as to which is the right road. Hunger decides that. In this case the "right" road was the left road, which led to the huts and another canned meal.

A mile and a quarter from Quintin Huts was Sutherland Falls, "the highest falls in the world," New Zealanders say. This cataract reminded me of Yosemite Falls; for like the California wonder, it descended in three leaps, but its height (1904 feet) was about 700 feet less.

The source of Sutherland Falls is Lake Quill, a glacier-fed tarn lying between Mounts Hart and Pillans. At their broadest points they are only a few rods wide, but they carry a large body of water. The successive leaps are 815, 751, and 338 feet.

The falls are easily approached, but such a strong wind is caused by the last leap that, several hundred feet from it, I was enveloped in flying spray, and the umbrella I held afforded little protection. At that distance grass and shrubs were constantly dripping and water stood in pools or ran in tiny streams. In their first leap the falls dropped upon a ledge of rock and into a pool of water with a sound like the roaring of a powerful steam vent; the second descent was like the spouting of a great flume.

It was a scented path that led from Quintin Huts to Milford Sound. In the more open spaces the way was perfumed by the white, delicately constructed blossom of the ribbonwood, by the pink-tinted veronica's bloom, and the red flower of the fuchsia. In the forests the beech predominated; but there also were the spiked foliage of the totara and the miro, the red blossoms of the rata, the long, narrow leaves of the lancewood, and the shapely fronds of the tree fern.

All along this canyon were cliffs from three thousand to four thousand feet high, and back of them rose mountains from two thousand to three thousand feet higher. The most remarkable cliff scenery was that of the Sheerdown Mountains. In one place on their summits, well back from the canyon, was a continuous line of bluffs at least five hundred feet high and possibly two miles long. Opposite to them, across Lake Ada, were the lofty Terror Peaks, the Devil's Armchair, and Mount Phillips.

Of the lesser attractions in Arthur Canyon a very common object was the weka. In grassy, shrub-grown places this brown, droll-looking fowl frequently crossed the track and dodged into the bush. Its wings were not sufficiently developed to enable it to fly, but it ran surprisingly fast. Wekas allowed me to approach within a few feet of them, but whenever I made any effort to capture them, they instantly fled, worming their duck-like heads through grass and bush with astonishing facility until they were out of sight.

About five miles below Quintin Huts was Arthur River Ferry. At the ferry the river was a clear, placid stream, but in many other places it was a torrent fighting its way over large boulders. So, too, was Mackay's Creek, which flowed near it. Born in the Terror Peaks, this stream furnished one of the wildest scenes in all this untamed granite land. Boulders formed its bed, the bridge spanning it rested upon an enormous one, and from its source to its mouth it was a succession of falls and rapids. Mackay Falls, its most beautiful cataract, plunged from a bower of trees, ferns, and moss and made one of the superior pictures of Fiordland. Another fine cataract fed by glacial streams from the Terror Peaks was the Giant's Gate Fall, which dropped about two hundred feet into a pool of marvelous blue.

A short distance west of Arthur Ferry I skirted shadowy Lake Ada, through which the Arthur River flows on its way to the sound. Whether viewed from boat or from apex of the track cut from the rocky bluffs high above the lake, this mirror of the mountains reflected wonderful shadows of peak, cliff, cloud, and forest. In it I glimpsed the Sheerdowns, which raise a lofty wall along its eastern shore; the jagged form of the Terror Peaks; and the Devil's Armchair, "a sharp and frosty throne perched high in cloudland and cushioned with the never-melting snows." All the lake's lone, uninhabited shores were darkened by the beech, and high up the surrounding mountains its small leaves formed an unbroken evergreen mass.

Two miles beyond the northern boat landing of Lake Ada the track ended at a sign reading: "Closed season for seals." To me, just emerged from dense forests inset with lakes and rivers, this notice seemed strangely out of place, and this impression was sustained by a calm, beautiful sheet of water right ahead which looked like another lake. But it was not a lake. Like General Sherman, I had marched—while others less fortunate had limped—to the sea. Before me was Milford Sound, and ten miles away were the heavy breakers of the Tasman. A great many years ago this sea-arm had been the haunt of sealers; now it was a rendezvous of tourists.

Here Mitre Peak lifted itself more than a mile above the sound and presented a cliff face familiarly known as the "Titan of sea cliffs." Here were the Palisades of Kimberley, shedding waterfalls that expanded into mist long before they reached the sound; here were the graceful Lion; Pembroke Peak and its glacier; and Tutoko Peak (9042 feet), highest of all the mountains of Fiordland National Park; lastly, here, when the sound was calm, were water reflections such as seem impossible for any other part of the world to excel.

And here, at Sand-Fly Point, others and I beat the air in vengeful pursuit of sand-flies more agile than ourselves, and awaited the coming of the launch in command of Captain Donald Sutherland and his hardy crew. Yes, although the Captain was both pilot and engineer and had little need of deckhands, he had a crew aboard. But they did not work; when they were not aviating about the sound, they just sat around and watched their master labor. And they were permitted to do so because they were the Captain's pets—and sea-gulls.

"They have followed me about the sound for years," explained the Captain, "and sometimes they are with me all day at the Heads."

As the launch glided away from the gloom of Mount Phillips and rounded a point, there leaped into view the granite mass so well described by its name—Mitre Peak. Rising 5560 feet above the sea, midway on Milford's southern shore, it is the most remarkable mountain spectacle of Fiordland; and no New Zealand mountain has a more striking contour, or is more widely known. The isolation of its loftier parts accentuates its distinctiveness as a whole, but it would be a very impressive landmark without this separation.

Mitre Peak is seen in its most beautiful form from the upper part of the sound. There it falls abruptly into the sound on one side, and on the opposite side it pitches sharply to the high wall that darkens Sinbad Gully, lying between itself and Mount Phillips. Mitre's barren pinnacle is the culmination of a long ridge, curving gracefully up from a high wooded flank. On it no man has ever trod. Mitre Peak, apparently, was intended for man to admire, not to climb.

On the north side of the sound are the imposing Lion, and Palisades of Mount Kimberley. The Lion is the finest example in New Zealand mountains of a fancied resemblance to a lion. It has a head of sterile granite, its shoulders are perpendicular cliffs with a maximum height of three thousand feet, and its back is dark with trees.

MITRE PEAK, MILFORD SOUND

On this same shore are Stirling and Bowen Falls, chief of the many waterfalls always to be seen on the sound. Stirling Fall, five miles from Bowen Fall, has a straight drop of five hundred feet over the Palisades. Bowen Fall is one of the most unusual cataracts in the country; in striking a ledge in its descent from the Darran Range, it forms a parabola that to me looked like the playing of a great hydraulic hose. As seen from the sound the point of contact resembled the bowl of a spoon. From the deeply worn ledge the fall shot upward about fifty feet and outward much farther. From the apex of the parabola the height of the fall is five hundred and forty feet.

The amount of water that pours into Milford Sound is astonishing. In Freshwater Basin, during heavy rains, the sound's brine is displaced by fresh water for a considerable depth. The same phenomenon has been observed in the sounds south of Milford. In Daggs Sound fresh water to a depth of several feet has been found a cable length from shore after a heavy rain.

Another amazing fact about Milford is its reflective powers. In calm and brilliant weather mountains are outlined in its waters almost as clearly as they appear above the surface. It is as if one were looking into a slightly defective mirror.

In a region of desolate grandeur, where age is deeply written on lofty mountains of mica schist that show the grinding, planing power of glaciers, lies New Zealand's Lucerne, Wakatipu, its longest and third largest lake. About fifty miles long and averaging little more than two miles in width, it looks like an enormous crank handle. For twenty miles it runs north, then turning west for twelve miles, it runs north again for another score of miles. It lies more than a thousand feet above the sea, and it has a maximum depth of twelve hundred and forty feet. Azure blue, cobalt blue, and the blue of coral seas are seen in its waters; and on the highest summits of the practically treeless ranges that wall it in, snow exists at all times of the year.

Above Wakatipu rise rock terraces hundreds of feet long, which lead to peaks from five thousand to nearly eight thousand feet high. Excepting near the lake's head, only isolated groves of trees are seen, and even there is desolation, for the beech forests have been devastated by fire. The tussocks, which look like sprinkled dust as they yellow on the mountains, the bracken fern, the tutu, and the Wild Irishman, can do little to diminish the general aspect of cheerlessness, even when assisted by the white gentian flower, the snowberry, the coprosmas, and veronica.

Geologists say that Wakatipu occupies the bed of a glacier, and that once it was much higher and larger; but according to Maori mythology they are partly wrong. The South Island Maoris have a tradition which says that this lake bed, and other large lake beds of the South Island as well, was dug with a spade about a thousand years ago by Chief Rakaihaitu. If this be true, Rakaihaitu was the greatest navvy New Zealand has ever produced; and had he lived until today he would have been the very man to dig the Panama Canal.

THE LION, MILFORD SOUND

In his reputed excavation of Wakatipu, Rakaihaitu so warmed to his task that he almost forgot to make any islands. At the last moment this oversight seems suddenly to have dawned upon him, and he left four spadefuls of earth in the basin. These are called Pig, Tree, Pigeon, and Gum Tree Islands, but three of them need renaming. The only one honestly entitled to its name is Gum Tree Island, which has several eucalyptus trees on it. On Tree Island I saw not a single tree; on Pig Island there were no pigs; and on Pigeon Island no pigeons; but, a lake resident informed me apologetically, in reference to each of these misnomers, "there used to be."

In Wakatipu district evidence of glacial erosion is very marked. I saw it in ice-worn mountain, in drifted debris, in huge stranded boulders, and, especially in the north arm, in many striking terrace formations. Professor James Park, director of the Otago School of Mines, says there is proof that this region has been covered with a continuous ice sheet of vast depth, and that probably it spread over the greater part of the South Island in the Pleistocene period, when, he declares, "glaciation in New Zealand was not exceeded in magnitude anywhere in the Northern Hemisphere."

In Wakatipu basin there is evidence that the maximum thickness of this icecap exceeded seven thousand feet; and this ice plateau, Professor Park believes, was part of an ice sheet extending to the south polar regions. In his opinion, too, there was a mighty conflict between glaciers of the Von and Greenstone Rivers on one side and glaciers of the Dart and Rees Rivers on the other side, resulting in mountains of ice being driven against the Richardson range, on the eastern shore of the lake. According to indications, these mountains formed part of a sea-bed at the beginning of the tertiary age.

By rail Lake Wakatipu is one hundred and seventy-four miles from Dunedin. The railroad passes through agricultural and pastoral plains that for many miles are from five hundred to one thousand feet above the sea, until near the lake. Here it enters a valley that apparently is the dry bed of an ancient outlet of the lake. The banks of this channel are high and its bed is littered with gravel and boulders. The nearer the railroad approaches to Wakatipu the wilder the aspect of the valley becomes, until finally its whole surface is strewn with boulders.

Here the train makes a long sharp curve, and rushing down grade, stops at the little wharf of Kingston, Wakatipu's port of entry. From the train passengers and baggage are immediately transferred to a small government steamer running to Queenstown, the chief town of Wakatipu district, twenty-five miles north.

The traveler is not sorry to leave Kingston, especially if he reaches it on a gloomy day, as I did. The port and its environs did not afford a cheerful prospect. Kingston itself was only a hamlet, and about the only object of beauty in its neighborhood was the blue of the lake. On the benches and hills above the lake were only dark projecting ledges and boulders, tussock sward, and scrubby growth of leafy plants.

The steamer was not long out, however, until there was an improvement. Up the lake's east side about five miles was a tilted ridge with three rough divisions. It was a peaked outcrop with a history.

"That is the Devil's Staircase," said an old miner to me. "A hundred head of fat cattle rolled off there into the lake forty years ago. They were being driven to Queenstown, when one of them became frightened and plunged over the cliffs, and the others followed."

On the west side of the lake, opposite to the Devil's Staircase, were the broken forms of Mount Dick and the Bay Peaks, both exposing high perpendicular walls terminating in sharp points six thousand feet above the sea. On the same side were the Bayonet Peaks, a collection of high and huge pinnacles that looked like the half-buried ruins of a mighty temple or of a cemetery of prehistoric giants. The dark cliffs, turrets, columns, and splintered crags seemed fit dwelling-places for ghostly tribes.

The most striking spectacle en route to Queenstown were the Remarkables, a range on the eastern shore, beginning at or near the Devil's Staircase and running to the Kawarau River, Wakatipu's outlet. As seen from the lake, the Remarkables' western face was so broken and jagged that, if placed upright, it would have looked like mountain ranges in miniature. On the marred front age appeared to be more deeply written than on any other part of the rugged surface of Wakatipu district.

Compared with the fertility of the mountains of Fiordland, the Remarkables seemed to be practically one lifeless mass. Here, from base to loftiest peak (Double Cone, 7688 feet), were sombre barrenness and fearful solitude. Excepting in rare places on the lower slopes where a beech found roothold and moisture, there was not even one friendly tree. Almost everywhere was black, inhospitable, sterile rock, lessened in its severity on the higher slopes by tussock and snow grasses wherever it was possible for these to obtain sustenance. Lower down there mingled with the tussock the bracken fern, the poisonous tutu, and the thorny Wild Irishman, which is guaranteed to make wild any son of Erin who gets entangled in its spines.

Plowed by glaciers, and scarred by thousands of rivulets born with every rain to scour with the sands of decomposing rock, the mountains have been fashioned into precipices, peaks, crags, "saw teeth," and sharp ridges with many ramifications. On grassy slopes and in all creek beds lie boulders, slabs, and stone splinters and chips; and the steepest parts only the shadows of shifting clouds can scale.

The Remarkables appear most impressive when seen at a distance; a near approach lessens the grandeur suggested from Queenstown and its vicinity. They also are less imposing when viewed from high elevations, as from the top of Ben Lomond. They are seen at their best in winter, when they resemble a roughly surfaced slate marked in white with chalk. Then the gray of crumbling débris, the lighter scourings of water courses, and the yellow of the tussock in streaks and patches, are to the eye displaced by snow, the only dark spots visible being those steeps where snow cannot find a resting place.

Facing this sterile magnificence, on a pile of glacial débris, at the head of rectangular Queenstown Bay, is Queenstown, one of the chief tourist resorts of New Zealand. In "the days of old, the days of gold," Queenstown was a city of tents; now it is a town of hotels. Here, as at Rotorua, I was met by a crowd of hotel runners, who offered the glad hand, smiled benignly, and told me where I could get "superior accommodation." Gold is still found in Wakatipu district, but no gold mine there is quite so good as the one possessed by those catering to the thousands of tourists who throng Queenstown in the summer.

"But in the winter, what does this mob of innkeepers do?" I asked my busy landlord.

"We sit down," replied he complacently, "and count the days that will pass before the tourists come again."

QUEENSTOWN AND THE REMARKABLES

Built largely of small blocks of the soft and brittle mica schist, Queenstown reminded me of a Mexican adobe town. Many of the stone buildings were whitewashed or plastered on their exteriors, suggesting age and aiding the imagination in picturing a Mexican settlement.

Just back of Queenstown is Queenstown Hill (2958 feet); westward are Bob's Peak and Ben Lomond; beyond them the loftier Cecil's Peak and Walter Peak; to the east is Queenstown Park, a narrow peninsula separating Queenstown Bay and Frankton Arm. Both private and public grounds have been beautified with imported trees and flowering plants, and bordering the pretty, narrow bay are willow trees.

Along the shores of this bay is one of the most singular beaches in the world. It is inches deep with stone chips, and these and surrounding cobblestones are tipped and streaked with white quartz and many of them glitter with mica. Intermixed with them are countless worn fragments of red, purple, gray, and green glacial drift, and, on the park side of the bay—corks! Never before on any other beach had I seen so many corks as I noted among the graywacke boulders on the west shore of the peninsula. Apparently bottle parties on Queenstown beaches are as common as keg parties in prohibition districts of New Zealand.

Another interesting feature of Queenstown Bay, the cause of which is not so easily accounted for as these evidences of fraternal cheer, is a strange and slow pulsation of the lake, frequently noticeable. At intervals the bay's surface rises very gradually from three to six inches, and then as slowly settles. Several theories respecting the cause of this phenomenon exist; and probably the most reasonable one is the assumption that the lake's outlet is too small for an uninterrupted discharge of the immense volume of water poured into it by rivers, and that the outflow, piling up at the exit, causes the rise.

All Queenstown visitors seeking superb views of lake and mountains climb Ben Lomond (5747 feet), the summit of which is reached over a five-mile trail that can be comfortably covered in three hours. The top of Ben Lomond is a dark shattered mass; from it thousands of tons of rock have tumbled, and now lie thickly on its slopes. From Lomond's crest more than half a dozen mountain ranges are visible. In winter, as far as the eye can discern there is one undulating field of snow darkened only by jutting peaks; in summer, snow is seen only on the highest ridges. As a whole the panorama is a bewildering succession of broken mountains from five thousand to seven thousand feet high; terraced hills with long, dark expanses; deep gorges; lakes; and streams carrying golden sands.

The most majestic and beautiful scenery of Lake Wakatipu is at its head, thirty miles from Queenstown. En route high mountains are visible all the way, but until rounding White Point, opposite to the Von River, and heading north, all are similar in formation to those around and below Queenstown.

As soon as the Mountaineer had fairly entered the northern arm, there was unrolled to my eye one grand stupendous whole. Straight ahead, away beyond Glenorchy and Kinloch, the heads of navigation, soared a group of lofty, snow-clad mountains. There was the mighty, sprawling mass of Earnslaw (9165 feet), chief of them all; there was the huge bulk of Somnus; the fearful precipices of Mount Knox; and the impressive heights of Cosmos. These and other colossal forms were tumbled about as though dropped indiscriminately from the sky.

Bold Peak, one of them was called; but they were all bold peaks, standing out clearly defined and rising from six thousand to nine thousand feet. From the steamer the two peaks of Earnslaw seemed to rest on a rim half encircling their foundation. This rim was like the wall of a fractured basin, the floor of which was white with snow. Below the snow-line was a dense beech forest, which continued westward to the sea and southward to Fiordland.

Beyond the Crown Range, forty-eight miles northeast of Queenstown, is the river-like Wanaka, by some regarded as

New Zealand's prettiest lake. A few miles from it is the large, rectangular Lake Hawea, famed for its deer stalking. Wanaka is thirty-five miles long, its surface is more than nine hundred feet above the sea, and its maximum depth is about one thousand feet. At its southern end it is so rambling that it resembles a greatly indented interrogation point.

Wanaka is surrounded by mountains from five thousand to nearly eight thousand feet high; and back of these leaps the glistening Aspiring (9975 feet), highest of all New Zealand mountains south of the Southern Alps. On Aspiring great glaciers gleam and form the source of many streams. Until 1909 its icefields and tremendous precipices defeated all attempts to scale it.

Chapter XIV

Switzerland proud as it may well be of its world-lauded mountains, is scarcely prouder of them than is New Zealand of its Southern Alps. For though the world at large has not as yet done so, the Dominion has discovered to its own satisfaction, that its Alps compare worthily with the Alps of Switzerland both in variety and scenic splendor.

But though Maoriland challenges the physical superiority of the Swiss Alps, it unreservedly admits their supremacy as money-making attractions. The Swiss Alps are a mighty source of revenue; the New Zealand Alps are as yet mainly a source of scenery. No hundred thousand tourists annually jab New Zealand's Alps with alpenstocks, as in the Central Alps of Europe. Here, where the first mountaineers were Maoris, no numerous grim tales of tragedy make one shudder, no hundred bleeding corpses annually stain the snows. Here is a mighty field for exploration, a great white solitude with deep silences still unbroken by footfall of man.

Yet time is bringing a change. The stillness is now more often broken, the human tread more frequently is heard. To this argent world, where the eye glimpses sea, lake, and river, richly wooded height, and grassy plain, from one vantage-ground, pleasure-seekers yearly repair in increasing numbers to climb, ramble, glissade, and ski.

New Zealand's Alps are more than three hundred miles long, but their name applies more particularly to their highest portion, in the west central part of the South Island. The loftiest peaks are in the vicinity of Mount Cook (12,349 feet), the "Aorangi the Cloud Piercer" of the Maoris, more than two hundred and fifty miles from Cook Strait, the northern terminal of the chain. Until, as geologists believe, the chain was submerged by sinking, it evidently extended to the North Island. It is equally probable that this subsidence disconnected the main divide of the North Island, and that the high Kaikouras, in the northeastern part of the South Island, were a part of this divide.

The Southern Alpine Range consists chiefly of overturned folds, and judging by its enormous moraines it evidently was higher ages ago. These moraines are much higher than those of the European Alps. On this point. Professor James Park says that "the younger Pleistocene valley moraines of Switzerland are small compared with the vast piles of glacial débris at Pukaki and Tekapo, in the Mount Cook area."

In height the Southern Alps are excelled by the Swiss Alps; but they have a large number of peaks approximating, or more than, ten thousand feet in height, all within a few miles of Aorangi.

In the New Zealand Alps there are hard and dangerous ascents, but to the tourist none is known which in difficulty and peril worthily compares with the Aiguille Grépon, Aiguille Dru, Torres Inglese, or Kleine Zinne. To the average Northern Hemisphere tourist, however, the Southern Alps are unknown, and few professional mountain climbers have made their acquaintance. Some day, when Southern Alpine visitors number thousands instead of hundreds, the great variety of this long white world will be far better known; and precipitous cliff faces, "chimneys," and slabbed height, now ignored or undiscovered, will be sought and conquered by alpenstock and armored foot.

In their accessibility the Southern Alps excel the Swiss Alps. Their glaciers, which are larger than those of Switzerland, are reached with astonishing ease. Furthermore, the snow-line in the New Zealand Alps is much lower than that of Switzerland's Alps. On the west it is so low that, between latitudes forty-three and forty-four degrees, the Fox and Franz Josef Glaciers descend to within slightly less than seven hundred feet of sea-level and into dense forests.

A varied world, in truth, are the Southern Alps and their radiating ranges. On one side are the festooned forests of the Tasman seaboard; on the other side are sparsely inhabited tussock plains. Here stormy elements and great rivers of ice are slowly wearing down mountains; here torrential snow rivers aid and continue the work of destruction by carrying away the eroded silt and with it filling valleys and lakes. Here are great glacial beds filled with white lakes; forest-rimmed blue lakes; and wild streams that are full almost to the top of their banks one week and are dry the next. Here glacial débris is heaped to mountain heights; trees grow where once the ocean rolled; hot springs "ooze from decomposing sulphides in the pressure-heated strata"; and here are gold and greenstone, the koura and pounamu of the Maoris.

The heart of the Southern Alps can be reached via the passes of Westland, but the tourist routes thereto are on the east, chiefly from the railway terminals at Kurow, 120 miles from Dunedin, and at Fairlie, 139 miles from Christchurch. The main route is via Fairlie, which is ninety-six miles from the Hermitage, the State hotel near Mount Cook. From Fairlie the Hermitage is reached in one day by motor-coaches.

From Timaru—where all passengers via Fairlie change trains—to Fairlie the railway passes through a rich wheat district, a flat and rolling country of pleasing appearance and good roads. From the train the passenger may see wheat ripening while snow falls on the Two Thumb Range, northwest of Fairlie, on the lower slopes of which, in winter, votaries of the ski disport.

From Fairlie to the Hermitage it is a devious and, in the main, a dreary road, especially after leaving Burke Pass, which crosses the Two Thumb Range about fourteen miles from Fairlie. Practically all the way the road passes through large sheep ranges, where people are seldom seen, and where, in a distance of seventy miles, there are only three hotels, which are from thirty to forty miles apart. Between Pukaki and the Hermitage the traveler may go twenty miles before meeting a human being; and as for trees, excepting where they have been planted at hotels and sheep stations, there are virtually none; while on the stone-littered Mackenzie Plains even the tussock grass grows poorly.

By this route I obtained my first good view of the Alps near the foot of Burke Pass. Forty miles away, over a yellow tussock sea, stretched a long, undulating line of white above one apparently interminable line of blue. For miles this sublime picture broke the monotony of plain and hill; and finally, after being obscured for some distance by rising ground, it was enhanced by a magnificent view of Aorangi.

Beyond Burke's Pass the first object of interest passed was Tekapo, highest of the principal lakes of New Zealand, which washes the base of the Two Thumb Range twenty-five miles from Fairlie. Tekapo lies more than twenty-three hundred feet above the sea, and its area is thirty-two square miles. Like Pukaki, thirty miles distant by road, it is fed by large and turbulent glacial streams, and these so discolor it that it looks like a basin of water-diluted milk.

Tekapo's grassed slopes are not inviting to lovers of sylvan shades, but much less inviting are the unfruitful benches of Pukaki. On Pukaki's southern shore, where the coach road turned abruptly toward Aorangi's peaks, I saw a desolate region. Here the tussock was less prolific than at Tekapo, and the glacial débris on which it struggled for existence was very extensive. Along the shore large dark boulders were strewn in profusion, and as we neared the hotel beside the Pukaki River, the lake's outlet, outcroppings of broken drift, which here formed hills, were prominent.

Forty miles from Pukaki's hotel is the Hermitage. Of that distance about one third of the road closely follows the western shore of the lake, which is about sixteen hundred feet above sea-level; thereafter, until near the Hermitage, the Tasman River, which flows into the lake, is followed. The Tasman is a river with many divisions, and it receives the waters of numerous glacial streams, including the Hooker River and the discharges from the great Tasman Glacier, its source. For the greater part of its length it flows through gravel beds, spreading about at will over a wide flat.

SECTION OF THE ALPS AND TASMAN GLACIER

The streams flowing into the Tasman are an interesting study. Some of them are mainly conduits for rain, and in the summer these become dry within a few days after a heavy precipitation. I have seen such water-courses clear within three or four days after they were heavily charged with silt.

Down the Tasman there frequently sweeps a terrific Alpine wind. Against its blasts, blown as if through a funnel, it is impossible for pedestrians to keep a straight course, and at times, as I learned by experience, they can scarcely proceed against them at all. In these winds, which commonly continue without intermission for a day, spray from madly-flowing rivers is flung rods from their banks, and drifting clouds of dust which at a distance resemble flying spume, are seen all along the Tasman's shingle flats.

On this road Mount Cook is seldom out of the traveler's sight on clear days. Here, looming up tremendously, nearly eleven thousand feet above him, it appears to far better advantage than when viewed at close range. At a distance it seems more isolated, its three peaks are more conspicuous, and its supremacy is more readily appreciated. It also presents a fine appearance from the Hermitage. As seen from the Tasman Glacier it is displayed mainly as a ridge; miles away, on the south, it is more grouped. While those who prefer the group formation may not be particularly impressed by the Tasman Glacier view, others prefer it.

Long before reaching the Hooker River Valley, up which one turns to get to the Hermitage, there is seen curving at the base of sharp-crested De la Beche and past the barren, pink-flushed walls of the Malte Brun Range, the Tasman Glacier. It looks like a great white river, which it is—a river of frozen snow larger, it is claimed, than any other "outside the circumpolar regions, except the ice-streams of the Himalayas." It is eighteen miles long; its maximum width is two and one fifth miles; its average width is a mile and a quarter; and it is hundreds of feet deep. Like other mountain torrents it has its rapids, or what correspond to them, but they are rapids that move slowly. And with all the terrific pressure they and the mass behind them exert, the glacier's daily flow is only eighteen inches, an inch for every mile of its length.

In the Hooker River Valley, in a cozy retreat beside the terminal moraine of the Mueller Glacier and below the prodigious cliffs of Mount Sefton (10,350 feet), lord of the Moorhouse Range, I was lodged at the Alpine climber's haven. In this well-chosen spot, twenty-five hundred feet above the sea, with a Government as host and Alpine guide, I was made to feel at home, and was provided with all the requisites of mountain climbing. Here, too, I obtained an inspiring view of Aorangi, and along the whole face of Sefton saw ice filling canyons and crowding against cliffs which it slowly was chiseling away. Nearer still, within a few hundred feet of the hotel, were ice blocks, ice walls, and ice caves.

The Hermitage—since considerably enlarged—was a group of one-story, galvanized-iron-clad buildings on a grassy slope near the Hooker River and within sight of the Tasman River. The first exterior view of the Hermitage proved it to be the headquarters of mountain climbers. On clotheslines back of the hotel hung leg cloths, stockings, and garments; and against the "boot shop" and elsewhere alpenstocks and ice-axes leaned.

The boot shop was an indispensable adjunct to the Hermitage. In it was a big stock of armor-plated boots, thick-soled, studded with nails that had tops as large as the heads of spikes, and further protected with metal clinchers. There were many sizes, and, I learned later, even more weights. Every wearer had a different estimate, and often, in the course of a single day, several estimates. But there was one fact about these boots that should have made them feel lighter than they were—great men had worn them, or, at least, a good number of them. And so it still is to-day: although the average visitor to the Hermitage may not by mental ability metaphorically walk in the footsteps of the great, he can walk in the boots they have worn.

In addition to the Hermitage, the Tourist Department conducts several accommodation huts in the Alps. In these the beds are bunks and the cooks are guides or porters. Two of these huts are on the Tasman Glacier route. The majority of climbers via this glacier end their first day's excursion at Ball Hut, fourteen miles from the Hermitage and thirty-four hundred feet above the sea. This hut can be reached on horseback, but not so Malte Brun Hut, nine miles beyond it at an altitude of fifty-seven hundred feet, to which all supplies are carried on porters' backs.

The goal of the majority of visitors to the Hermitage is the Tasman Glacier and the peaks, ridges, and domes that wall it in on the west and north. The Tasman Glacier is the grand parade of the Southern Alps. Into it a half-dozen large ice streams flow, and along it are ranged a score of mountains from nine thousand to eleven thousand feet high. Besides Mount Cook there are Tasman, 11,467 feet; Dampier, 11,291; Silberhorn, 10,796; Roberts, 10,487; Malte Brun, 10,421; Elie de Beaumont, 10,200; Douglas Peak, 10,107; Haidinger, 10.059; and De la Beche, 10,040.

From the hotel to the Tasman Glacier there are two commonly traversed routes. One crosses the Hooker River by a swing bridge and runs along the steep face of the Mount Cook Range to the Tasman Valley; the other route follows the opposite bank of the river to "the cage," a box running on an aerial tramway, in which Alpinists are ferried across the Hooker.

The terminal moraine of the Tasman Glacier would be an excellent place to operate a stone crusher. As I saw it, en route to Ball Hut, it appeared to be one vast rock heap for several miles. Great quantities of this débris had been so finely broken as to be suitable for road-making without further treatment. On this sterile heap, rising far above my head, nothing grew, but in the scrubby growths beside the path were many flowers, the veronica, buttercups, daisies, violets, pimpernels, and the yellow spines of the Wild Spaniard; here also were the totara scrub and its edible red berry.

Trees were scarce, but there was one I shall not forget. This was what might properly be termed the Halfway Tree, for it shaded the Halfway Place between the Hermitage and Ball Hut. The Halfway Place wasn't a hotel, nor even a house. It consisted of a small tree, a table, a galvanized-iron-bound chest containing tea, sugar and cups, and piles of "billies" and bottles. Here my Maori guide and I halted for tea—and gooseberries. Beside the tree was a gooseberry bush, and a very popular bush it was, according to my pilot.

"Everybody has a go at the gooseberries," said he as he helped himself.

We did not stop here to "boil the billy," as we had at first intended; instead we each plucked a Mountain Lily leaf, and dipping it into a cold, swift stream, we quenched our thirst, then pressed on to Ball Hut for supper. When we got within sight and hail of the hut the guide stopped and loudly hallooed. It was a call for "tea," and in answer thereto a porter appeared at the door. When we arrived, we sat down to canned meat and beans, canned milk and fruit, and bread baked at the hotel.

That night only these two men and myself were at the hut, but, nevertheless, ours were not the sole voices there. Other voices there were, and they were loud and harsh. They were the calls of the kea, the mountain parrot, of the South Island, which has a cry that sounds very much like its name. The kea has a strange history. Once it lived on berries and grubs, but years ago it became fond of mutton; and now, according to widely credited accounts, it is very destructive to sheep. Alighting on the back of a sheep, the kea fixes its claws in the wool or flesh and quickly makes an opening with its two-inch beak. Its cries attract other keas, and beneath their combined attack the sheep soon collapses.

The kea is a very inquisitive bird, and it is equally bold. Along the Tasman Glacier keas peck at the nails in one's boots and with their beaks test one's clothing. A guide told me that one had even perched on the toe of his boot.

At Malte Brun Hut one day, I drew four or five keas about me on a large flat-topped rock. At first they were three or four feet away from me, but very gradually and cautiously they approached until the beak of one was within an inch of the metal-headed pencil I held in one hand. Then the bird backed away. Soon a bolder one joined my audience, and, after much meditation and searching scrutiny, actually took the pencil from my hand. But he did not seem to care for it, for he almost immediately dropped it. In front of another kea I held a pocket mirror. Seeing himself reflected in it, he warily peered over the mirror, apparently expecting to find a bird on the other side. When he learned that he had been deceived, he walked away in evident disgust.

On the morrow we resumed our journey up the glacier. The Tasman Glacier is a wonderful spectacle, or, rather, a combination of wonderful spectacles. It has ice canyons and caves; ice shafts from one to two hundred feet deep; waterfalls that pour over icy ledges; streams that flow in icy tunnels; and millions of tons of boulders and broken rock torn from the mountains.

At its terminal moraine, about twenty-five hundred feet above the sea, is an unsightly mass of ice and stone; at its head a mile and a half above the tides, its surface is rounded into great snowbanks and broken into huge blocks that are clear of débris. It has crevasses as numerous and varied as the clefts of rain-washed banks; it has hidden waterfalls that tumble into funnel-shaped pits; it has streams, some of them concealed, that run during the day and are frozen into silence at night; it has still water of delightful blue in oval fissures and round basins of exquisite, fairy-like blue.

My first comprehensive near view of the Tasman Glacier, its connecting ice streams and their lateral moraines, was obtained a short distance from Ball Hut, after climbing the steep path to the top of the Ball Glacier, which flows between Mount Cook and its range. On the crest of the first ridge of the Ball Glacier's lateral moraine my eyes swept over a wild and astounding scene. Over a wide and long expanse were great projecting spurs, pinnacles and banks of snow, and deep cavities. The whole was soiled and weighted with immense quantities of boulders and shattered stone.

It was a treacherous place. Over large areas the ice was thinly surfaced with rock fragments, and what appeared to be nothing more than big stone heaps were in reality ice masses covered with a few inches of debris. On these both guide and guided were forced to proceed cautiously to avoid accident. It was likewise on the long lateral moraine of the Rudolph Glacier, which meets the Tasman at the Fall. Here also were big stone heaps and deep cavities, and isolated rocks of great size moving imperceptibly to wreckage piles that had existed for centuries.

CUTTING STEPS ON ICE FACE, TASMAN GLACIER

Everywhere on the Tasman Glacier were deep and dangerous fissures that looked to be bottomless. Before these some people, I was told, become so terrified by their aspect that they lose sight of beauty in fear of injury or death. On the glacier's ever-changing surface there are no well-defined tracks, as some visitors expect to find. The guides make their tracks as they go, and they have new ones every day.

Of the ice streams flowing into the Tasman Glacier the finest is Hochstetter Ice Fall, a precipitous glacier descending from Mounts Tasman and Cook. It is four thousand feet high, a mile wide, and "a thousand Niagaras frozen into one." The whole is a crumpled, shattered mass of blue, white-capped walls and ridges, and deep crevasses.

The roughest part of the Tasman Glacier is the Fall, where a spur of the Malte Brun Range thrusts itself into the glacier as it swings to meet the Rudolph Glacier. The Fall consists of frozen rapids that have a descent of five hundred feet in one mile. If the glacier could be melted suddenly, there would be created here rapids such as the world perhaps has never known. And with all its rapidity, it would take the melted river a good while to exhaust itself, for in places the glacier is estimated to be one thousand feet deep, and opposite to Malte Brun Hut it is said to be fifteen hundred feet deep.

As we procceded up the Tasman Glacier we heard, nearly every hour of the day, the thunder of avalanches. Many of them we saw as like waterfalls they plunged from ice-quarried ledges and, rolling and leaping, reverberated for the last time in deep hollows or at glacier's edge. Some of them seemed to be not more than a half-mile away, but the rarefied atmosphere was deceptive; they usually were two or three times more distant than they appeared.

On an elevation commanding a view of all the principal elevations and glaciers on the northern and western sides of the Tasman Glacier I enjoyed the simply hospitality of Malte Brun Hut, an anchored inn. Standing three hundred and fifty feet above the glacier, this caravansary was so exposed to the furious winds that sometimes sweep down the valley that it was lashed to a huge boulder at its rear. At Malte Brun was one of the finest purely mountain panoramas of the world. At relatively close range were the domes of Hochstetter and Elie de Beaumont, the peaks of Mount Green and Walter and the Minarets, the walls of Haidinger and Cook, and the varied configuration of other lofty mountains in their vicinity; at the hut's rear, almost bare of snow in summer, were the formidable steeps of Malte Brun. Here, also, 'midst wild flowers and grasses, we saw Alpine climbers crossing the Tasman Glacier and ascending mountains across the valley.

At Malte Brun Hut I learned of a feature of mountaineering that is popular in New Zealand. On rafters above the dining-table were several pairs of skis for the use of visitors. These skis, like the gooseberries below, were in great demand. My Polynesian guide told me so. "Everybody has a go at the skis," said he.

But he did not add, as he truthfully could have done, that the skis frequently have a "go" at tourists. Skis are alike the world over, and their idiosyncrasies are as marked in New Zealand as elsewhere. They have notions of their own about navigation, and very perverse notions they are, too. For carefully laid courses they have naught but contempt; under the feet of the unskilled they are intractable. They start willingly enough, perhaps, but only with malevolent intentions. On them one scarcely launches one's self before trickery begins.

Skis are in accord in only one respect—their determination to throw the skier. In some other things they do seem to agree, but these are mere incidents contributive to the main purpose. Often they act as if they were going to ram each other, but such is not their design. Theirs is more often a hurdling game. They hurdle over each other, and the skier hurdles over them both. At other times the skis, like some married people, agree on a separation almost at the start. In that case they run as far apart as they can, and one's legs, becoming imbued with the same spirit of isolation, do likewise, each faithfully following its ski until the downfall of man is accomplished.

It is safer, if inexperienced, to use skis as toboggans. But even then you will find that when you want to go down they want to go up; and presently you find yourself skidding on the snow, with the skis on top of you, perhaps, in an attitude of "Now we have you."

The slopes of Hochstetter Dome and the smooth upper reaches of the Tasman Glacier are ideal places for the ski. Here one can enjoy the sport for two miles without interruption from broken surfaces. On these slopes I hoped to witness a good exhibition of skiing, and I did, but it was not what I expected.

"Do all guides here know how to ski?" I asked my pilot.

"Oh, yes!" replied he promptly.

As he prepared to illustrate his proficiency to me, I said, "I 'll stay behind, Guide, and watch you go down."

"No," he objected, "you go ahead and you can see me go past. I 'll catch up with you."

He did, finally, but he was so long coming that I looked back to see what he was doing. I was just in time to see him picking himself up. A few seconds later I looked back again. He was still going, but he had turned completely around, and seemed to be trying very hard to ski uphill. When he reached me he had an abrased and bleeding wrist.

"Now you get on," said he, seating himself on the skis.

"Is that the way you go down?" I asked.

"Sometimes," he replied. "The snow is too hard this morning to ski down. This is the way all tourists go down."

We started well, but the skis soon altered our course to suit their own malicious pleasure. The fractious things appeared to be eager to see the world, and the ways they chose lay far apart. Now we were on, now off; now wearing out our clothes on the snow.

From Malte Brun Hut one of the most popular trips is the ascent of Hochstetter Dome (9258 feet). With the most ambitious essayers of this climb it is customary to start anywhere from one to three o'clock in the morning, thereby reaching the summit, six miles distant, in time to see the sun rise over mountain, forest, and sea. When taken by moonlight this is one of the most alluring excursions imaginable.

About these moonlight expeditions there is an air of mystery. In preparation for one of them my guide and I awoke long past midnight. To avoid arousing sleepers we talked in whispers while breakfast was being prepared; and finally, softly closing the door, we stole silently away, out into deep silences unbroken save by an occasional word and the crunching of snow. Above us, enveloping us, was the soft glow of the moon; beneath us was the glistening snow; and in every direction dark mountain masses loomed through mantles of white. It all seemed like a dead and frozen world, a ghostly, goblin-like world.

En route to Hochstetter Dome little more than thirty-five hundred feet of altitude had to be surmounted. The first part of the journey was up easy grades; the latter part was so steep that if we had made a serious slip on one of the Dome's great billows we should have rolled thousands of feet before stopping. Everywhere these benches exhibited appalling grades, and on the two higher ones we found it necessary to cut steps and advisable to use a rope. On these the intense cold so affected my chattering companion that, on nearing the top, he asked me, "Do you think it's any use to go any farther?"

As we reached the Dome's summit the sun was rising. First its pink flush tipped the myriad peaks above and below us; then moving slowly down the mountain slopes it became absorbed in the gloom far beneath. With the descent the greenish hue of the western horizon gradually became darker, until it likewise was lost in the darkness of the nether realm. On the east was a brilliant sky. There the tussocks of Canterbury were brightened by sunbeams while sunshine still climbed the Alps to disperse the shadows of Westland's forests.

It was a wild and fascinating scene on which the sun's rays alighted, a scene of peaks, precipices, canyons, and snowfields interminable to the eye, a scene of forest, river, and sea. To the northeast snow-clad peaks stretched as far as the eye could see; southwest and west ranged the mighty barriers of the Tasman Glacier. In the farther west was the sombreness of wooded hills and valleys; beyond these leafy undulations ran the long white line of the Tasman's surf. On the east the

Alps threw flanking ranges far into tussock land, away across the ice-born Godley and Rangitata Rivers.

One of the most interesting of my ascents in the Alps was up Ball Pass (about 7400 feet), within the shadows of Mount Cook. For diversity this route across the Mount Cook Range would be difficult to surpass. The first part of the climb was steep and hard, through scrubby growth which my brown guide and I had to clutch for support; the second and last part consisted of shattered rocks and snow-fields. All the way to the bare rocks were flowers, the celmisia, the veronica, the Mountain Lily, and several other kinds; and as elsewhere in New Zealand mountains, the prevailing color was white, with yellow at intervals.

As we scrambled upward over bush and boulder and loose and broken rock masses that on the edge of cliffs seemed ever ready to form avalanches at the slightest touch, our view increased until we saw nearly the whole of the Tasman Valley with its glaciers, its moraines, and its river. Flowing into the Tasman River we beheld the Murchison River, born in the Murchison Glacier, eleven miles long. Thirty miles distant shimmered the white surface of Lake Pukaki.

At the top we stood in the shades of Aorangi. Five or six miles westward, across the glacier-filled Hooker Valley, plowed by the Hooker River, rose a massive mountain form weighted with glaciers. It was Sefton, one of the finest appearing mountains of New Zealand. Its two peaks and the black cliffs below them were clear of clouds, and as it thus lifted itself high above its immediate neighbors, Sefton was a worthy rival of Aorangi at its best. From the pass Sefton appeared more effectively isolated than does Mount Cook from any part of the Tasman Glacier, and it is not surprising, therefore, that by some judges Sefton is preferred to Aorangi as a view.

The supreme ambition of quite a number of Southern Alpine climbers has been the ascent of Mount Cook, but comparatively few have scaled it. Aorangi is difficult to climb, and there are times when the guides at the Hermitage will not undertake the ascent owing to dangerous ice conditions. From the hotel the average round-trip length of Mount Cook ascents is from four to five days, but as weather conditions are uncertain a week or two may be required sometimes. From Cook the sublimest view of the Alps is obtained. On clear days even Mount Aspiring, a hundred miles away, is visible.

The Hooker River Valley, into which we were to descend, was dark with glacial accumulations. For the greater part of its length it was partly filled by the Hooker Glacier, seven and one fourth miles long, and to a smaller extent by the Mueller Glacier, eight miles long, which flowed into it at the base of Sefton. The descent into Hooker Valley from Ball Pass was through a forbidding-looking cleft of rocky chaos, down formidable snow steeps, and over wild waters emerging from snow tunnels and caves.

Before beginning the descent, my guide placed a rope around himself and me. This surprised me, for I had been told that we should encounter no ice. I divined the Maori's intentions, however, when he told me to sit on the snow in front of him. We were to toboggan down terrifying slopes on our trousers! The guide was to be my anchor, separated from me by several yards of rope, and his anchor was his ice-axe.

Dubiously I inquired, "Won't the snow wear out my clothes?"

"No; go ahead," replied the native. "Just lie down, and don't dig your heels into the snow."

I tried to comply, but I soon found myself plowing the snow with my heels, which caused us to stop. Another start was about to be made, in a different direction, when I saw "breakers" ahead in the form of a broken surface suggestive of crevasses. As I intimated that I did not want to go that way, the guide reconnoitred, and decided to take another course. It was well he did, for when we got lower down this bulging surface proved to be the top of a cliff.

After that no more obstacles appeared, with the exception of sharp stones which lay half concealed in the snow and caused us to squirm and shift to save our clothes from damage. It was thrilling sport. For half a mile we coursed, alternately stopping and starting and slackening and increasing speed, varied by searching for the most suitable slopes. Sometimes we went at such a rate that it seemed impossible for us to halt until we reached the rocks far below, but the guide always succeeded in fixing his axe in firm snow and pulling up with a sharp jerk.

MOUNT SEFTON AND THE FOOTSTOOL

When our sport was ended, we picked our way on the edges of snow-fields and across steep rock-strewn streams, and thence upon a long snow strip that roofed a creek. On this, leaping over crevasses formed by collapses of the roof, and avoiding thin edges, we continued until we reached the last bit of snow. Several times I stopped to look about me, causing the guide to remonstrate.

"Keep going," commanded he bluntly. "It don't look too good here; there are too many loose stones about."

The route from the foot of Ball Pass to the Hermitage ran near the left bank of the Hooker, but the river was hidden in an icy channel until near the Mueller Glacier. Still more concealed than it were the disappearing creeks and rivulets in the valley. In one place I saw a waterfall tumbling from the Cook Range; the stream of which it was a part discharged into the river; but I was astonished to find that it did not cross the intervening path. Instead it went under the track, through a terminal moraine. In other places, too, glacial streams burst through moraines like springs.

As we traversed the valley my guide apparently was searching for something, first on one side of the track and next on the other side, and he always looked down. Was he seeking a treasure? Yes; and under a boulder he found it. The treasure was a cached "billy," containing sugar, tea, and a cup, and it was to provide us with afternoon tea. Stopping beside a creek, the Maori gathered branches of dry shrubs for firewood, and soon had a fire sufficient to boil the billy, which was done by holding it over the flames on my alpenstock.

In Australasia, boiling the billy is a very common practice, in the bush, in camp, on the tramp, on goldfields and kauri-gum-fields, and in many other places. The billy is a black-faced pail in which water is boiled for tea and in which tea is brewed. The blacker the billy the better, a sable countenance being proof of long and honorable service and lending flavor to the tea.

Not all the superb outings of the Southern Alps are confined to the vicinity of Mount Cook. One of the best of New Zealand's Alpine tours is over the Alps to Westland, to the coast of gold and greenstone, and to the land of Seddon.

From the treeless ranges of the east to the leafy luxuriance of the west is a wonderful transformation. Here frozen sterility meets fertility supporting tree and fern, palm and orchid. Here are swift gold-bearing rivers, the Grey, the

Arahura, the Waiho; here are lakes famed for their shadow pictures, the Kanieri, the Mapourika, the Mahinapua; other lakes deeply set in glacier's bed, and lakes that are shallow and sedge-lined; and here is the blue of foliaged mountains, and the scent of many flowers.

And finally, in a latitude corresponding to that of the central part of New York State, are the beautiful Fox and Franz Josef Glaciers, the first nearly ten miles long, the other a mile and a quarter shorter. Their grooves are deep and abrupt; in their caverns and fissures are the shades of a soft, ethereal blue; and in the forests above them the fiery-hued rata blossom contrasts vividly with the shimmering white below.

Chapter XV

New Zealand has many beautiful river gorges, some that are well known to tourists, others that few travelers have seen. In the South Island are two gorges of which it is particularly proud. These are the Otira, providing an Alpine route between Canterbury and Westland, and the Buller, a gold-bearing stream running through Nelson for more than one hundred miles.

The Otira Gorge is short, lofty, and rugged, and in its best parts narrow. The Buller Gorge also is lofty, but it is not so rugged, and on the whole it is wider. The journey through the Otira is soon ended; through the Buller it is prolonged. Both are magnificent scenic routes, and observers differ as to which is supreme. The Otira is bolder, but the Buller has inspiring outlooks that the Otira lacks. All travelers through the Otira see the best part of the gorge, but not all who have traversed the Buller road are sure they have seen the best part of its foliaged course. A great many persons have not seen half the Buller Gorge, yet some of those whom I questioned did not hesitate to proclaim the superiority of the part they had seen over all the rest of the canyon.

In approaching the Otira Gorge from Christchurch my way led through the pleasant farms of Canterbury, into tussock hills, and high above the Waimakiriri River via the daylight-to-dark railway, which had sixteen tunnels in less than seven miles. Near the terminus of this road, Cass, the yellow dullness of the tussock met the dark-green beauty of the mountain bush.

At Cass the Otira coach road began. For several miles it followed the Waimakiriri Valley, which was flanked with forested mountains from four thousand to six thousand feet high, topped and streaked with slate-colored shingle. As is usual with streams of this character, the Waimakiriri claimed the whole of the valley's wide flat as its own, and having swept away all surface soil, it exposed broad areas of cobblestones and gravel which its waters never laved excepting in times of flood. Just beyond Bealey the Waimakiriri was forded; thereafter to Arthur's Pass, which overlooks the gorge at a height of three thousand feet, the road passed through the Bealey River Valley, bush clad and pretty, and in view of the tunnel then being bored for New Zealand's first trans-Alpine railroad.

OTIRA GORGE, WEST COAST ROAD

The top of Arthur's Pass was not in itself a captivating vantage-point from which to view the Otira's charms, since it was overgrown with flax and tussock and strewn with boulders; but satisfying was its prospect. On its west was Mount Rolleston and its glacier; to the east were other high mountains; to the north, winding between barren-topped ranges, was the gorge. Shortly below the pass, on the north, the hardy flax intermingled with flowering shrubs, forming a tangle discouraging to mountain climbing. Then appeared trees that spread to the snow-line; and above them were unfruitful cliffs.

Now the road became steep and tortuous. Far below it raced the small and noisy Otira River, lashing itself into foam against its rocky obstructions. High above it ran a beautiful mixed forest, blooming with the rata's crimson and sheltering fern and moss and rambling creeper. And for miles, ever at a precipitous pitch, the road ran beside bluffs mantled by flax, fern, and shrub, and past flowering canyon walls blazing with patches of living red.

At Otira the coach-road terminated, and here began the railroad that runs a devious course through Westland to Greymouth, the largest seaport on the South Island's west coast, and northerly to Reefton, a mining town twenty-one miles from the Buller River. In Westland I found civilization in the rough. In this rainy country the train passed through embryonic settlements and vanishing forests, and past the disorder and desertion of old lumber camps and sawmill yards. Here was the primitive,—plodding ox, logs laboriously rolled to saws by hand, roads that were wretched, and comforts and conveniences that were few.

At Reefton I saw an astonishing number of hotels. When I had walked up Broadway, its main street, I was quite satisfied to accept the statement made to me by a Totara Flat minister, that this, the first New Zealand town to be lighted by electricity, was "the greatest town for hotels in the country." This is chiefly so because Reefton caters to the tourists coaching through the Buller Gorge.

From Lake Rotoiti, which is practically its source, to within a few miles of the important coal-exporting town of Westport, the Buller River courses between mountains from three thousand to nearly five thousand feet high. For thirty-three miles from the lake it has an average fall of forty-four feet per mile, and it has so many rapids and shallows that it probably never will be made navigable.

Near its junction with the Inangahua River the Buller's attractiveness, when I saw it, had been lessened by clearings; but the loss of forest was partly compensated for by tree-adorned sandstone cliffs. In places this formation, purple-stained and draped with foliage, rose hundreds of feet near the river; at other points it formed the walls of distant mountains.

Two miles below the Inangahua Junction the river made one of its large bends and left the road well inland. For about four miles it was hidden by a wide, swampy flat; next it appeared in beautiful form at the base of vertical wood bluffs. Here as elsewhere along the Buller, excepting where it had been destroyed, a mixed bush climbed to the tops of the mountains.

Above the Junction the gorge's beauty had been despoiled for long distances by clearings; but there still were many fine scenes, notably near Lyell. To the traveler northward-bound, this dilapidated mining town is the portal to what many persons enthusiastically acclaim to be the finest part of the Buller Gorge. For seven or eight miles beyond Lyell the coach road was hundreds of feet above the river, and for much of this distance it passed through forests.

Here the gorge was seen as from a hill top, and there was an absence of that restricted feeling experienced in narrower canyons. Midst the song of birds and the scent of flowers, here was the cool breath of moss-carpeted creek channels darkened by tree and fern; there were distant views of verdurous mountains and infrequent glimpses of the river, murmuring, roaring, eddying in its rocky prison far below.

In passing through the Buller Gorge the traveler bound for Cook Strait abandons the coach at Kohatu and there entrains for Nelson, the popular resort of Blind Bay. In one respect Nelson is the most celebrated town in New Zealand. It has, I was told, "the prettiest girls in the country," and "seven women to every man." This last claim seemed so improbable that I asked the secretary of Nelson's Chamber of Commerce about it. From him I learned that the census returns furnished me were padded. "There is still a dearth of ladies to go round," said Secretary Hampson, although he admitted that Nelson has a larger proportion of women than many other parts of New Zealand.

About forty miles northeast of Nelson is the remarkable French Pass, navigated by steamers running between Nelson and Wellington. This narrow, picturesque channel lies between the mainland of the South Island and D'Urville Island; and here tidal waters from Cook Strait swirl and eddy as if the ocean were pouring through a fissure into the earth.

BULLER GORGE, HAWK'S CRAG

But it is not this for which the pass is most noted. It owes its celebrity mainly to Pelorus Jack, the "pilot fish." Generations ago Jack disported about the bows of Maori canoes en route from Pelorus Sound to the pass. To-day, as he has been for twenty years, he is the gamboling pilot-companion of steamers en route to and from the pass on the east. Through the pass he does not venture. On these steamers every passenger looks for Risso's dolphin (*Grampus griseus*), and when he does not appear there is keen disappointment aboard.

In New Zealand "Pelorus Jack" are magic words. Everybody who knows Jack's history is interested in him;

everybody likes to read about him. He is often in the public eye, and the public press has given him many a line. Several times he has been reported dead, but obituary notices notwithstanding, he still lives, and he has lived, says one old Maori chief, for fully two hundred and seventy-five years.

Sometimes the dolphin takes a vacation for two or three weeks, and it is then his human friends wonder if the ocean of oblivion has claimed him. Since 1904 Jack and all other animals of his kind in Cook Strait—and he appears to be the only cetacean of his species there—have been protected by an Order in Council. But Death the indiscriminator will not grant him a protective order, and so, some day, on a Marlborough beach, perhaps, there will be washed ashore the inert bulk of a fourteen-foot blue-white grampus, and Pelorus Jack's last obituary will then be written.

When Jack is on duty, he always dives and swims round the prows of steamers as if he were showing them the way or wished to play with them. At these times he is likely to be seen anywhere between the pass and the Chetwode Islands, off the mouth of Pelorus Sound. Sometimes when the tourist traffic is heavy he is off duty for a few hours. Knowing this, we who were on the Pateena, outward-bound from Nelson, could only hope that Jack would act as our pilot on our way to Picton.

For once the steerage deck proved to be a popular place with first-class passengers; for once steerage passengers had an advantage over first-cabin occupants, for on the Pateena steerage quarters were forward, and it was there that Kaikaiawaro could be seen best. Before the steamer was out of the pass the bow rail was crowded with passengers, who were willing to stand in the cold, cutting wind until they were chilled and their eyes watery, just to see a *Grampus griseus*. It was a remarkable tribute to a grampus. At this lookout Jack was almost the sole theme.

"He bounces," explained a woman who had seen him on a previous trip.

"There he is!" excitedly exclaimed another voice.

But it was only a white gull. For a half-hour we discussed Jack, but still he did not appear.

"I am afraid he's turning us down," spoke a woman as we neared Clay Point.

So it seemed. Other white gulls raised our hopes as they rode distant waves, and as quickly dashed them by rising on the wing.

An hour elapsed, and still we shivered, and strained our eyes until they pained us. As we neared the Chetwodes our hopes were lowered like a thermometer in a blizzard; for we were told that if Jack did not appear before we were abreast of them, we should not be likely to see him at all.

"Do show yourself," we thought in unison.

But not a fin was thrust above the sea. The Chetwodes were on our port bow; now they were at our stern; still Jack we did not sight. The passengers abandoned their vigil and returned disappointed to warmer quarters aft—disappointed because a grampus would not come to meet them!

And why wouldn't the dolphin meet them? Probably because he had piloted the Pateena on the morning of this same day as it was en route to Nelson.

Between Nelson and Wellington lies the maze of waterways known as the Marlborough Sounds. Here, where a ragged peninsula thrusts itself well north of the southern extremity of the North Island, is the most broken part of the Dominion. It is a gouged-out land; a land excavated as with giant fingers; a land wonderfully indented with beautiful bays and inlets, coves and narrow channels; a land of many islands and near-islands, of long, slender, and crooked extensions, of sharp points and narrow isthmuses. Here, where inlet succeeds inlet until in places they resemble rows of dock basins, is one of New Zealand's finest and most popular pleasure resorts. Here, with more than five hundred miles of shore-line, are Pelorus and Queen Charlotte Sounds. In them abound fish of many kinds, and they are the rendezvous of scores of pleasure craft.

The Marlborough Sounds are very different from the fiords of Southland. They reflect no lofty snow-clad peaks, no mighty granite parapets, no falls matching those of Milford Sound. Overlooking them primeval beauty has been marred by the destruction of large areas of forest, and the adjoining hills, which reach their highest elevation in Mount Stokes (3951 feet), are largely pastoral runs.

Of the two principal sounds Pelorus is the more beautiful, its waters being bluer, its shores more wooded, less abrupt, and freer of fern. It also is the larger, its length being thirty-four miles and that of its shore-line three hundred and fifty miles.

Queen Charlotte Sound, twenty miles from the mouth of Pelorus, is deeper and darker than Pelorus, and has a more pastoral appearance. As in Pelorus, long before the steamer reaches the sound's head Cook Strait is lost to view; and here, too, as in the western sound, vessels can safely anchor close to the coast in many places. At Picton, twenty-five miles from the sound's entrance, my steamer passed within a few yards of the shore.

Chapter XVI

The voyager to New Zealand who lands first at Auckland, and begins his projected tour of the country by setting a course for the vaunted scenes of the south, leaves behind him one of the most interesting parts of the Dominion — North Auckland. Among oversea visitors to Maoriland, North Auckland is not celebrated as a tourist district, and though in guide-books they may read something of its charms, they are more impressed by descriptions of scenery south of it. Yet until this peninsular extension has been toured New Zealand has not been properly seen.

Deeply indented with beautiful harbors and for miles exhibiting bold rocky coasts, this foot of Aotearoa's boot-like shape stretches northwest from Auckland for more than two hundred miles. More than any other part of New Zealand, this is the land of kauri gum and the home of the vanishing kauri, greatest of Niu Tirani's trees. Under the Treaty of Waitangi the sovereignty of Queen Victoria was here proclaimed; here the pakeha's government was first established; here Christianity was first preached to the Maoris; here lived Hongi, "Napoleon of the Maoris," and friend of the missionaries; and here raged the first war between Maori and white.

Here, also, where whalers were the first white settlers, civilization in New Zealand had its beginning; yet much of North Auckland still comprises "back blocks." While fertile and spacious districts of the south were developed and grew rich, the sparse white population of the neglected north was left to cry for roads and railways. Even yet North Auckland has relatively few miles of railways.

The longest stretch of railroad it possesses is the Helensville Branch, terminating about seventy-five miles from Auckland. The tourist does not usually go farther on this line than Helensville, a health resort on the Kaipara Harbor, thirty-eight miles from Auckland. There are hot mineral springs here, and through this port passes traffic bound for Wairoa River points.

At this town, en route to the Wairoa River, I boarded a small steamer on the muddy Kaipara River, a tidal stream wriggling into Kaipara Harbor and washing the slimy roots of mangrove trees.

The Wairoa — which also flows into Kaipara Harbor — is the most important river in North Auckland. On its murky waters I saw borne the commerce of many sawmill towns and settlements built along its banks. In its lower ports large steamships and a number of sailing vessels were receiving cargoes of timber, and in midstream tugs with log rafts in tow were constantly plying. In the slimy, slippery mud banks exposed by the receding tide logs lay half buried, and when the tide was setting in there was visible the singular spectacle of logs floating up stream from twenty-five to fifty miles above the river's mouth.

Voyaging on the Wairoa was pleasantly informal. No dressy crowd met the steamer when it glided alongside a wharf, but just everyday, work-a-day people. And as for those who caught and made fast the steamer's ropes, they were voluntary wharf-hands or wharf-hands by the captain's request; and sometimes they were obliging officers or deck-hands of lumber carriers, which for a few minutes were used as a connecting link with the wharf beyond.

In these ports the traveler is always welcome, and if he arrives in the late summer, as I did, or in the autumn, he is welcomed with music, not, however, with the outbursts of town bands. In this case the musicians are crickets.

In North Auckland the cricket thrives wonderfully, both on the hearth, or as near as he can get to it, and on the road. Everywhere his cheerful temperament expresses itself in song, now in jubilant solo, again in one grand chorus. Nevertheless, the cricket's chirping performances are not appreciated. Even while filling the earth with melody he has been called hard names; and among other dire visitations threatening him are poisoning and death by turkey's bill.

Yet the cricket is one of the oldest settlers in the country. At least forty years ago he arrived as a stowaway from Tasmania, and no one has done more than he to colonize the land. When he sailed from Tasmania "Eastward ho!" was his cry of progress; now it is "Everywhere ho!" With hop, skip, and jump he and his have spread over the land until even in Auckland's Queen Street and Karangahape Road I have heard him at midday above the roar of traffic.

Eighty-five miles north of Helensville is Dargaville, the chief town on the Wairoa. Here I boarded a small steamer for the up-river voyage, terminating at Tangiteroria, thirty-five miles distant. In a scenic way this part of the river was more interesting than that below, yet even here the Wairoa was essentially a commercial stream. To a great extent the beauty that had made the river celebrated had disappeared with the stroke of axe and rake of saw.

The loss of primeval beauty was somewhat compensated for by the incidents of navigation and port calls. The captain of the Naumai was an all-around man; a busy and a jocular skipper. As we prepared to leave Dargaville at eight o'clock in the morning he helped to load the cargo, and it was he who put out and pulled in the gangway. He also was purser and pilot; in fact, so busy that he ate his dinner of meat and potatoes at the wheel.

As for the cargo, it consisted of boxes and bundles of bread, strings of fresh fish, barrels of beer, about a dozen kerosene cans filled with skid grease, and three pairs of ox yokes. The yokes were discharged at Ounuwahao, the bread and fish were for "all along the line," and the beer was destined for Tangiteroria. As shipping clerk the captain gave such orders as, "Meat, bread, and mail go ashore here"; and "Better put old Tommy's corn ashore, too, I suppose."

The running schedules of the Naumai, it appeared from the remarks of a woman passenger, were somewhat variable.

"You are often undecided," said she to the captain, "whether to tarry for your breakfast or have lunch before you leave home to catch the steamer. It is likely to arrive any time between eight and eleven o'clock."

"Well, isn't that near enough?" asked the jocose captain.

When the traveler reaches Tangiteroria, perhaps he will not recognize it as the head of steamer navigation on the Wairoa. I, at least, did not. At a little landing I was leisurely pacing the deck when the captain approached me and said, "This is your destination." Following the beer barrels, I found that Tangiteroria consisted mainly of a little white wharf, an unpainted store of about the same size, and a hotel where beer and a few other things were available and "dinner now on."

Through Tangiteroria passes the route to the Wairua River Falls, "the Niagara of New Zealand," fifty feet high and about two hundred feet wide. The river which feeds these falls is a very prosaic stream before it plunges over the dark walls of Omiru, flowing sluggishly, excepting when in flood, between low, clay-capped banks bordered by flax, toitoi and cabbage trees, in a district abounding in tea-tree and common fern.

In this part of North Auckland are extinct volcanoes, red volcanic soil, and rock-strewn acres. Where volcanoes have not poured out their rich compositions, or rivers have not deposited prolific soil, the surface is almost wholly clay. Once it was thought these clay lands were comparatively valueless, but they have been found to be suitable for fruit culture.

In favorable localities oranges, lemons, and limes grow, in some districts grape culture is a success, and in the far north the banana ripens. The New Zealand banana will never be a serious competitor of the South Sea banana; probably it will never be a competitor at all.

In one of the chief fruit districts of North Auckland is the pleasantest and largest town in the peninsula. This is Whangarei, about one hundred and twenty miles north of Auckland, at the head of a harbor twenty miles long. At the beautiful entrance of this harbor are the sharp and shattered heights of Manaia, a limestone mountain which the elements have sculptured into giant fantasies, and round which hover strange legendary tales.

Fifty miles north of Whangarei is the broad island-dotted Bay of Islands, the most historical spot in New Zealand. Here the first white settlements in New Zealand were established and the sovereignty of Great Britain proclaimed. On this bay was the Dominion's first capital and the chief rendezvous of Maoriland's whalers. The first war between the colony and its natives was fought here; and on Christmas Day, 1814, Christianity was first preached to the Maoris by the Reverend Samuel Marsden.

WAIRUA FALLS

On the south side of the harbor, between the encircling hills of a small bay, is Russell, once Kororareka, New Zealand's first capital. Now it is "the old town of Russell." The capital is more than five hundred miles away, and for at least ten years the New Zealand Official Year Book has dismissed it with the brief statement that it "has a good hotel, besides having a post and telegraph office." But Russell can always boast of having been for many years the most important port in the land. In early days its harbor was filled with whaling and trading ships, and on one Christmas Day about seventy-five years ago nearly thirty whalers were in the bay, and more than a thousand members of their crews were ashore at one time.

North of the Bay of Islands is the charming harbor of Whangaroa, celebrated for its delightful nooks and striking configurations. Among the best-known of its curious sculpturings are Mushroom Rocks and the Duke of Wellington's Head. This last-named cliff face is well denominated. It has pronounced eyebrows, a hooked nose, and firmly set lips.

As seen from the peaceful little port of Whangaroa the most prominent of the harbor's rock figures are St. Peter's and St. Paul's, each several hundred feet high. Of the two, St. Paul's is by far the more impressive. Seen from afar its dome-like summit is wonderfully attractive, and it appears to be higher than it is. This conglomerate of boulders and cobblestones was once a Maori fort. The fortifications disappeared long ago, but away up near the cupola I found proofs of former occupation. Scattered about there were many pipi shells, which suggested that the hill once formed part of the ocean's bed, but which really proved that when Maoris held it as a citadel they ate shellfish.

Historically, Whangaroa Harbor is one of the most interesting places in New Zealand. Here, in 1809, occurred the massacre of the Boyd's crew, one of the most atrocious deeds ever recorded against the Maoris.

The Boyd, a ship of five hundred tons, called at Whangaroa Harbor for kauri spars while en route with the first direct cargo from Australia to England. On board were seventy white passengers and five Maoris who were working their passage to New Zealand. One of these natives was Tara, son of a Maori chief, or, as one historian says, himself a chief. Giving as his excuse that he was sick, this man refused to work, and the captain flogged him twice. To a Maori this was exceedingly degrading, and only blood would bring satisfaction.

As soon as Tara landed he showed his bruised back to his tribe. Immediately revenge was planned, and obtained by treachery, the opportunity for which came when the captain and some of his crew went ashore to choose the trees to be felled for spars. The natives, cleverly separating them, murdered and ate them. Then, disguising themselves in the clothes of the massacred, Maoris boarded the vessel at night and killed everybody on it, excepting a cabin boy who had shown kindness to Tara, a woman, and two children. The woman and children were saved by hiding themselves.

The attacking party also suffered. Tara's father and several other natives were killed by the explosion of a barrel of powder they carelessly handled. The explosion also set fire to the ship and totally destroyed it. As for Tara, he ever afterward hated Europeans, and in turn he was disliked by his own people, who undertook to revenge his humiliation because, according to Maori custom, an insult to one Maori was an insult to his entire tribe.

If the whalers on the coast had not resolved to have revenge for this massacre, probably no further consequences would have resulted from this imprudent flogging. But the whalers thirsted for utu also, and attacking the chief whom they erroneously believed responsible for the slaughter, they destroyed his village and killed every native In it, excepting the chief, who escaped.

A result of this vengeance was long and murderous strife between the whites and the Maoris. For three years after the massacre, says one historian, "natives took revenge on any pakeha who fell into their power." The whites retaliated, and, says Gudgeon, "very few vessels departed without committing some act of violence."

Nearly two hundred miles north of Auckland, on and at the base of low red hills overlooking a pretty harbor, is the sleepy little town of Mangonui, which some day will be the northern terminus of the North Auckland Main Trunk Railway. Near it are extensive mangrove swamps, slimy nurseries of the sea overrun by tiny crabs. In the swampy districts north of it are some of the richest kauri deposits in New Zealand.

Of all the principal industries of New Zealand the most singular is the kauri-gum industry. Soon after reaching Auckland I heard of gum-stores, gum-merchants, gum-brokers, and of lonely gum-seekers, who pitched their tents in wastes of fern and tea-tree. When I scanned a newspaper I saw paragraphs about gum quotations, and I found gum displayed in many windows. On Customs Street I discovered kauri-gum merchants to be as common as mercers and hatters on Queen Street. Altogether it was quite a gummy place.

Kauri gum exists only in the Auckland Land District, south of which the kauri tree does not grow, and mainly north of Auckland City. In the latter portion of the district so large is the area overturned by gum-diggers that in sections of it which I traversed the whole countryside seemed to have been spaded up. Properly this resinous product is not gum, but it is universally so called in New Zealand. The New Zealand gum is valued chiefly for its varnishing-making properties, although it also is extensively used in the manufacture of linoleum. Since 1847 New Zealand has been exploiting its gum deposits, and to date they have yielded more than $80,000,000, or nearly twice as much as has been realized from coal produced within the Dominion in the same time. They still annually yield about $2,500,000, the greater portion of which is contributed by the United States, the heaviest buyer.

When kauri gum was first marketed it sold for only twenty-five dollars a ton; now the average price is about thirteen times greater. The most valuable gum is transparent, which sells as high as six hundred dollars a ton, and often is used as a substitute for amber.

The first gum marketed was extracted much easier than most of that found to-day; it was either on the surface or barely embedded. Next it was found about a foot below the ground; now much of it lies several feet underground. The gum also is obtained by climbing living trees and tapping them,—a hazardous method that is prohibited on Crown lands,—but by far the greater part is obtained from the ground, where from two to four layers are found, indicating the previous existence of as many forests.

In exuding from the trees the gum has solidified into brittle lumps and undergone so many chemical changes that experts can assort it into a score or more of grades. Many of these lumps weigh from fifty to one hundred pounds, and I learned of one that weighed three hundred and sixty pounds.

In color kauri gum varies from pale yellow to reddish-brown and black. When first taken from the earth its color is obscured by soil, which has to be scraped off before the gum is marketable.

After the industry was fairly started gum digging proved so profitable that it attracted thousands of men. To-day there are five thousand permanent and three thousand casual gum-diggers. The greatest aggregation of diggers are Austrians, who were attracted to New Zealand many years ago by the inspiriting accounts of two sailors and, later, by the success of two Austrian gum-diggers who returned home with $45,000 won by them in a Tattersall's sweep. Usually they work together in gangs of from twenty to thirty, spending the summer in the swamps and the winter on the hills. They work long hours on the fields and spend parts of the mornings and evenings scraping gum in their dilapidated-looking camps.

In his quest for gum the digger works with spear and spade. The spear is a pointed rod from eight to twelve feet long which is thrust into the soil to locate the gum. When a deposit is discovered the spade is used to uncover it. In some places the gum lies so deep that extensive excavations are required, and in very wet swamps hand pumps are employed to draw off the water. In such places digging is very disagreeable.

In good deposits diggers earn from fifteen to twenty-five dollars per week, and for a while sometimes double these sums. At Ahipara a gum-buyer told me that one man had earned two hundred and fifty dollars in six weeks.

GUM DIGGERS AT WORK IN KAURI FOREST

From the fields, after scraping, in which many women join, the gum is taken to gum depots for sale. At these depots some of the gum is graded, as also to some extent on the fields; but the greater part of it is graded in Auckland, the chief gum-buying and exporting port of New Zealand.

Beyond the gum-fields, away north to New Zealand's land's end, is Te Reinga, "a low point jutting out into the sea, with a sandy beach below." At one time a pohutukawa tree stood there, and down one of its roots, say Maoris, spirits descended into the earth to Reinga's portals. Some Maoris, I learned by inquiry among them, still believe spirits enter the future world at this point.

The passage of spirits to Te Reinga is beautifully told in Judge Maning's translation of the Maori poem, "The Spirit Land." The lines describing the spirits' flight are as follows:—

"To the far North, with many a bend, along the rugged shore
That sad road leads, o'er rocks and weeds, whence none returneth more.
The weak, the strong, all pass along—the coward and the brave—
From that dread track none turneth back, none can escape the grave.

"Passing now are the ghosts of the dead;
The winds are hushed, the rude waves hide their head;
And the fount flows silently,
And the breeze forgets to sigh,
And the torrents to moan
O'er rock and stone,
For the dead pass by!
Now on the barren spirit track
Lingering sadly, gazing back,
Slowly moves a ghastly train.
Shades of warriors, brave in vain."

One of the most interesting features of my tour in North Auckland was life in the "back blocks." Of its rural districts one of the most primitive was north of the long, river-like Hokianga Harbor, away in the hills of Broadwood and Herekino and on to the seventy-mile beach of Ahipara. In places rough bush tracks were the only highways, hotels were far apart, and oxen pioneered the way for horses. Here were little farms stocked with a few cows, sheep, and pigs; houses with large exterior chimneys of wood or galvanized iron; blackened clearings, and the smoke of annual forest fires.

In such settlements public amusements are few and infrequent. Therefore when a moving-picture show or a vaudeville company comes to town, it is a great event to the inhabitants, even though the performance be a poor one. It is customary, too, to strengthen the evening's entertainment by following it with a public dance.

Arriving late at Peria one day, I had no sooner sat down in the empty dining room for tea than a young Maori waitress eagerly informed me: "There's going to be a show to-night. I am going to it."

As she spoke her eyes sparkled, she smiled broadly, and in her best dress, new shoes and collar and tie, she made a picture that was bound to impress some brown Peria swain before the night waxed pale.

Although North Auckland's remotest districts are compelled by force of circumstances to deny themselves many amusements, they appeared to me to have plenty to eat, especially in Herekino, a little settlement in timbered mountains of the west coast. This hamlet is just the place for picnics; indeed, if I was correctly informed, Herekino's two boarding-houses set picnic tables every day.

When I sat down at one of their well-laden boards I felt like a boy at a Sunday-School feast. It happened that, being late, I sat alone, and therefore the bounty spread before me was the more impressive. From end to end of the long table were cakes and cookies, but I was most attracted by two large dishes of jam tarts. There were dozens of them. And why such profusion? Was it because the district schoolmaster and his wife and the village doctor boarded there? No, I was assured; it was just a Herekino custom to set a good table.

Jam tarts such as I saw at Herekino are very common in New Zealand, but they and all other pastry tarts are by no means the only kind. In Maoriland there are tarts and tarts.

"The tarts were good," I read in a Queenstown hotel register on the day of my arrival there. The intelligence cheered me, for I interpreted it as a promise of delicious pastry. I was at the hotel several days, yet not in all that time did I see a tart. At last it dawned upon me that the writer was referring to young women; for I had been told that in New Zealand it is "his tart" and "her Johnny."

Tarts are very well in their place, but when an American pie-eater finds them usurping the pie, as in New Zealand, he feels like lodging a protest. In the Dominion they have American-built railway cars and locomotives, American plows and binders, American this and American that, but— they have no American pie. True, they have the word, but beyond its application to meat-pies it is a misnomer. In pastry-cooks' shops I sometimes saw what looked like a pie, but it was advertised as a tart.

At hotels they gave me what the menu said was pie, but no self-respecting American pie would recognize it as such. Aside from the meat variety, it is hard to classify so-called pie in New Zealand. There are so many species. One very common sort sprawls all over its plate. Undeniably it is a half-caste, but whether it is a half-caste pie or a half-caste pudding only an expert classifier could tell. This alleged pie half protrudes from its crusty shell. Another sort often comes entirely out of its shell, while there are others that have no shell at all; but as a rule these latter are sheltered at one side by a flaky square or rectangle.

Many New Zealand pies are served in half-developed soup-dishes, or in dishes that are a cross between a soup-plate and a large saucer. A Dunedin pie, served me in one of these hybrid dishes, was six parts apple and one part crust; in other words, it was a mound of fruit topped by a thin crust less than two inches square. As a bottom crust apparently had not been mentioned in the recipe, none was discernible.

In Wellington an American chanced to see a real pie, under the cognomen of tart, in the window of a tea-room. Marveling greatly, he stopped to stare, and as he gazed fondly on the pie he wished that he was hungry; but as he was not, he finally tore himself away with the resolution to return when he was prepared to eat. He neglected, however, to note the tea-room's location. For two days he searched before he found it; then into it he strode.

"What kinds of tarts have you?" he asked a waitress.

"Apple, cherry, and black currant," she replied.

"I'll have one of each, please," he ordered, and joyously sat down and ate them then and there.

A dozen miles from Herekino is Ahipara, celebrated for its beach, one of the finest and longest in New Zealand. Ahipara also is a Maori stronghold, and has one of the largest native schools in the country. When I was there this school had more than one hundred pupils, who were instructed by a white man and his wife and two Maori assistants. Although it was a native school, eight or ten white children attended it. In New Zealand mixed attendance in Maori districts is not uncommon, and it is marked by little, if any, friction between Maori and white pupils on account of race distinctions.

Maori boys and girls like to attend school, and to do so many of them travel astonishingly long distances. In one school an inspector found that in a single week many children had covered one hundred and twenty miles. Heta Harewi, a lad fifteen years old, walked twenty miles every day to attend school in 1910! Another North Auckland Maori youth had an easier way of getting to school. He rode a young bull to the house of instruction.

At Ahipara I saw several Maori boys and girls hurrying to school after it had been called one morning.

"You are late," said I to a boy. "Are you late every day?"

"Yes," he breathlessly answered to my surprise. "I have to come six and a half miles."

The parents of Maori children also show an interest in education. One father rode ninety miles to be present at the examination at which his two children, who were only in the preparatory class, were presented.

The Maori child is just as apt a pupil as the white child, the Secretary of Education informed me, but he labors under a disadvantage. He must first overcome the language difficulty, and he must learn an alphabet nearly twice as long as his own. Naturally, some of his replies to his teacher's queries are of peculiar construction. In explaining the meaning of "angry foes," one boy said: "Angry foes are friends to fight with." In estimating distances it is common to say: "Good horse, two miles; bad horse, too far."

Just as strange are some of the calculations of youthful Maoris. Once a native boy received notice to go before a Government officer for medical inspection. The journey to the place of examination and return took an entire day, and the youth resolved to be compensated for his time. Accordingly he sent to the Government a bill for two large bags of chaff and an extra meal for his horse, two days' rabbiting, and one meal for himself.

Chapter XVII

The scenic charms of New Zealand are attributable in a large degree to the wonderful wealth of flora with which this land is blest. New Zealand is one of the most remarkable botanical regions of the world; so wonderful, indeed, that in his division of the earth into fourteen botanical districts, one celebrated scientist accords New Zealand twelfth place.

Aotearoa is indeed a prolific land. In it are fourteen hundred different flowering plants, and two thirds of them are found in no other part of the world. Its forests, perpetually green, are massed in many places with brilliant flowers sometimes so nearly the color of trees that they are almost invisible. From tussock plain to Alpine heights beautiful blossoms brighten the traveler's way. Here the fern is so common that it has become an emblem of the country. Here flourish the latticed nikau, southernmost of the palm family, and the greatest of forest parasites, the tree-strangling rata. Here are plants which suggest that New Zealand once extended to Melanesia and was a part of Australia; and there are other plants which suggest an ancient association with South America and sub-Antarctic regions.

New Zealand's forests are among the most beautiful and luxuriant in the world, but to lovers of autumn tints they have one detracting feature. They are everywhere and always green. In them is every shade of green, all suggestive of eternal spring. A few trees shed tinted leaves in winter, but the nearest approach to autumn colors which the average traveler sees is the tints of sword ferns on cliff faces and by mountain roads. But when the forests are in flower the vast expanses of green are brightened with scarlet, crimson, pink, yellow, and white. Then is seen the red of the pohutukawa, the rata, the puriri, and the mistletoe; the red and yellow of the kowhai, the creamy blossoms of the hinau, and the white of the ribbonwood and clematis.

Generally speaking. New Zealand has two classes of forest, mixed bush and beech. The mixed bush is wide-spread in both islands; the beech is found chiefly in the South Island. The first contains such a great variety of plants that as many as forty or fifty species of trees and shrubs have been found on one acre. In both classes of forest the average height of trees is from sixty to eighty feet; the maximum height is one hundred and fifty feet, in the mixed bush.

It is doubtful if forests more beautiful than the palm and fern-graced mixed bush can be found anywhere. In it trees and undergrowth thrive as in a tropical jungle. Beneath the masses of the small-leaved foliage of the larger trees is a dense growth of young trees struggling to force their way up to the sunlight. Under them all is a fairy carpet of delicate moss and moss ferns. In this grow the curious kidney fern, maidenhair ferns, various kinds of sword ferns, and many other kinds of ferns; for New Zealand has about one hundred and fifty varieties of ferns. Up every gully and canyon are groves and groups of tree ferns, and at intervals the trim fronds of the nikau shoot upward.

In all New Zealand there is not, perhaps, a more pleasing forest plant than the gracefully drooping tree fern. In its slender trunk, widely spreading fronds, and leaning propensity, it strongly resembles the cocoanut palm. In forest depths, where it grows best, it commonly attains a height of from twenty to thirty feet, and one that I cut down near Waihi was fifty-two feet long.

A worthy rival of the tree fern is the nikau palm. It is related to the eastern beetle nut, and is New Zealand's only palm. In the North Island it is very plentiful; southward it ranges as far as Dusky Sound. The nikau is from twenty to thirty feet high, and its fronds shoot up at a sharp angle from a trunk so smooth that birds cannot get a foothold on it. When the kaka, or wild parrot, seeks to gorge itself with the scarlet fruit growing in big clusters just beneath the branches, it has to hang head downward from the leaves. By the Maoris these leaves are woven into kits and baskets, and in woodsmen's camps they are often used as roofing.

Still more numerous than tree fern and palm are the parasites,—stranglers, creepers, and aerial marauders. Every tree sustains a climber or a mossy growth. Many of the largest succumb to the attacks of the greatest of them all, the rata (*Metrosideros robusta*), the second largest tree in New Zealand. This strangler grows in the North Island, where it reaches a height of from fifty to one hundred feet and an average diameter of from three to twelve feet. Although known chiefly as an epiphyte, it also grows without support, but in that form its growth is much slower and the matured tree is smaller. Its reddish wood, covered with furrowed, reddish-brown bark, is hard and heavy, and has great strength and durability.

In New Zealand forests there are parasites which completely cover the trunks of trees, but none of them hugs to death and entombs its benefactor as the rata does. The life of this parasite reads like a romance. The rata is not a climber, as many persons believe; it begins its deadly work above the ground. Here, for example, is a leafy lord of the forest that for hundreds of years has successfully resisted decay and the assaults of many tempests. One day a tiny seed, blown by the wind or carried by a bird, finds lodgment high in one of its forks. Germinating in a bed of vegetable mould, the seed produces a sprout. After a time the nourishment of the mould becomes insufficient for its needs, and then it begins to run down the tree. As it descends it throws out lateral tendrils; these in turn develop transverse tendrils, and soon all of them diverge to encircle the tree.

The great tree is doomed; it has been attacked by one greater than itself. It is to be choked, hugged, and smothered to death by the rata. Ultimately the rata itself becomes a large tree, and in time it completely incloses its victim and crushes out and absorbs its life. Then, with this dead and decaying tree as its heart, the rata proudly rears its massive head, even higher, sometimes, than did the one it conquered, and, like it, defies the fiercest tempest.

The lordliest tree in New Zealand forests is the kauri (*Agathis australis*). Yet in one respect the kauri's form does not partake of dignity; it is so thick as compared with its height and proportions of trunk and top that it is somewhat squatty. As a rule, about half the tree consists of top, a canopy of long limbs tipped with small bunches of foliage. The tree's average height is from eighty to one hundred feet, with a maximum of one hundred and fifty feet. The diameter of the gray trunks averages from four to twelve feet, although a maximum diameter of twenty-four feet has been found. The finest specimens are on high ground, and it is doubtful whether the tree ever flourished in swamps, as gum deposits suggest. It is more likely, say some investigators, that the gum swamps are subsided areas.

The kauri's age is unknown, estimates varying from hundreds to thousands of years. One tree five feet in diameter was estimated to be three hundred years old. At this rate many kauris have been growing more than a thousand years.

One of the finest objects in the North Island bush is the pohutukawa, the spray-swept tree. Like the cocoanut palm, it thrives best near the sea, and seldom grows far from water. Bending seaward, the pohutukawa sweeps over until its immense, sprawling top is sometimes almost upside down. In many cases its overhanging branches are sprayed by the surf, and occasionally oysters collect on them. When blossoming, scarlet flowers with numerous slender stamens burst from myriad sheaves. Then for miles on beach and high on cliff, I have seen Maoriland's Christmas tree flaming against landscape and sky.

A GIANT KAURI

A hardy plant that is most common on low and swampy ground is the cabbage tree, or palm lily, which bears a white, sweet-scented flower. In New Zealand it has a wide range, and in places forms forests. Some species are from twenty to twenty-five feet high; others are so dwarfed as to be stemless. The limbs are all at the top of the tree, and at the end of each limb and its branches is a bunch of sword-like leaves resembling the spiky head of the pineapple plant. They are from one foot to three feet long, and in their centre grows a large cluster of white berries, which are relished by pigeons. A peculiarity of the leaves is their phosphorescence when decaying.

Perhaps no New Zealand plant is harder to kill than the cabbage tree, so named because settlers once ate its soft, immature heads as a substitute for cabbage. So tenacious is the soft wood that even its chips have taken root in damp soil. On it fire makes little impression. Pieces cut from living specimens cause little or no injury. And when the tree is cut down it grows again.

Outside its forests one of the most beautiful plants of New Zealand is the toitoi, or toetoe. It is similar to the Argentine pampas grass, and is by far the tallest grass in the Dominion. It grows in large bunches from six to ten feet high, and often its flower stalks are a yard higher. Nodding from each plant are a score or more of feathery-tipped stems, varying from light to dark yellow and brightening the darkest background. The toitoi's drooping plumes I have seen continually waving and bowing along marshy water-courses, in flax swamps, beside rivers, up small gullies where tea-tree and bracken fern divided the land, and on lonely hillsides in solitary clumps.

Chapter XVIII

Zoologically, New Zealand is as remarkable as it is botanically. But this is true mainly in a negative sense. In one case nature has been prodigal, in the other case it has been one-sided and parsimonious.

Within New Zealand's borders Nimrod would have found nothing worthy of his prowess, unless it were the long-extinct moa or an incarnated taniwha. Excepting what has been introduced, its land mammalia is confined to two species of bat. It has no snakes, no land reptiles, barring lizards, and with the exception of the katipo spider there are no poisonous insects.

In its avi-fauna New Zealand has been strangely and bountifully favored. It has land birds that cannot fly and migrating birds that cross oceans, even to remote Siberia. And in the days when some birds were far taller than men, it had gigantic avi-fauna of which single specimens were almost large enough for a tribal feast.

Why has New Zealand been so generously blest with flora and so niggardly supplied with land fauna of the reptilian and mammalian branches? Why, as it seems to have been connected with Australia, has it no kangaroos or wombats, no duck-billed platypus, or any of the many species of snakes found in the island continent? Why, too, has New Zealand none of the animals of South America or of South Africa, if, as extinct land insects, worms, and shells indicate, it was a part of these continents? No man knows.

New Zealand has been especially favored with flightless birds. Now these are comparatively rare, but hundreds of years ago they were plentiful. The greatest of these was the ostrich-like moa (*Dinornithidæ*), evidently the largest creature that ever existed in New Zealand. The moa was absolutely wingless, it apparently was slow and stupid, and some of the eighteen known species were ridiculously squatty. Of the squatty sort was the *Dinornis elphantopus* which, though the heaviest built, was only half as tall as some other species.

The moa's height was from two to eleven feet; the tallest had a leg five and one half feet long. The neck was very long; some of the bones of the largest birds were five or six inches in maximum diameter at the joints; the largest eggs had a lengthwise diameter of nearly a foot; and gizzard stones were from one fourth of an inch to an inch thick. From head to legs—in some species to toes—the bird was covered with short, soft feathers similar to the feathers of the emu and the cassowary, and there are indications that some moas had a tuft of feathers on the head.

The moa existed at least as far back as the Pliocene age. In the Pleistocene period a very large percentage of moas died, possibly as a result of the long, cold winters common to that age; and in large quantities their bones were washed into lakes and swamps or buried in sand-dunes and river alluvium. In Glenmark Swamp, Canterbury, the remains of more than a thousand have been found, and in Southland fully four hundred skeletons were discovered within a radius of twenty-five feet.

Following the Pleistocene age the moas increased as the climate became more equable, and when the Maoris arrived they were plentiful in both islands. In vague Maori legends the moa's extinction is ascribed to fire and earthquake, but it is generally believed by authorities that the Maoris themselves exterminated the bird, probably three or four hundred years ago.

Of living birds New Zealand has a great variety. The land birds, which are far outnumbered by water and shore birds, are noted for their difference from the land birds of all other countries. Three of them—the kiwi, weka and kakapo—cannot fly, and the fern bird, now seldom seen, flies weakly.

The most singular of these birds is the kiwi (*Apteryx*), a long-billed bush bird that sleeps during the day. The kiwi, of which there are brown and gray species, has a peculiar shape. It has no tail, and in appearance is a cross between a football and a gourd. The bird nests in holes and hollow logs, and close observers say that apparently its eyesight is defective and that it is guided almost wholly by smell. In its egg-laying capacity the kiwi is, perhaps, the most unusual bird in the world. Although only as large as an ordinary domestic fowl, it lays an egg five inches long and three inches wide and averaging between eleven and twelve ounces in weight. It has been suggested that prior to laying the hen actually undergoes confinement.

The kakapo, or road-making parrot, finds itself in a peculiar predicament. Its wings are eleven inches long, yet their muscles are so weak that the bird cannot fly. The tracks of this night bird are sometimes more than a foot wide, and in snow they can be followed for miles. It is doubtful if the world has a more economical road maker than the kakapo. This enthusiastic vegetarian eats the greater part of the roots and grass he removes.

A rare bird very much prized by the Maoris is the huia, the long, black tail-feathers of which, tipped with white, are proudly worn by them in their hair and on their hats. The most striking fact about the huia is the difference between the bills of the sexes. The male has a short, straight beak, but that of the female is long and curved. Each bill performs a distinct service. When seeking grubs the male enlarges the grub's hole and the female draws the insect out.

Of New Zealand's singing birds the finest are the tui, or parson bird, the korimako, or bell bird, and the native crow. The parson bird—so named because of the white tuft of feathers under its throat—is truly a wonderful singer. Whenever I heard its marvelous tones—now like a bell, now like an anvil, again like a flute—I was constrained to halt in admiration. So clear are the tui's notes that they have been mistaken for anvil blows.

In strength of wing one of New Zealand's most extraordinary birds is the long-billed godwit. Every year the godwit makes a return journey of about fifteen thousand miles between the North Island and eastern Siberia. Arriving in New Zealand in September and October—spring in the Southern Hemisphere — it remains until autumn, and then takes flight for Asia.

KIWI AND EGG

Two other migrating birds are the shining cuckoo and the long-tailed cuckoo, the first arriving in New Zealand from New Guinea, the other from Polynesia. Considering the cuckoo's small size, this is a wonderful flight.

An astonishing feature of bird life in New Zealand is its great number of shags, or cormorants. That country has fourteen species, or half as many as are found in the entire world. The presence of so many shags there is accounted for by assuming that in ages past, when there was far more land in this part of the world, New Zealand was the meeting-place of two streams of birds, one from the Malay Archipelago and New Caledonia, the other from Antarctica.

The largest sea-bird in New Zealand waters is the albatross. Some of these birds are eighteen inches high, and their wings have a spread of from ten to fourteen feet.

A salt-water bird that is of uncommon interest because of its association with the tuatara lizard is Cook's petrel, a species of the mutton bird. So plentiful is this bird on the east coast of the North Island that cliffs are perforated with its burrows. Frequently it shares its home with the lizard, and the two seem to live peaceably together. The reptile can make its own burrows, and for egg-laying it does; but it prefers basking to burrowing.

For fishermen New Zealand is, like all other good fishing regions of the earth, "a paradise." All around its coasts is a great variety of fish, and in hundreds of lakes and streams trout are found. Altogether New Zealand has about two hundred and thirty kinds of fish, including mackerel, bream, mullet, flounder, barracouta, cod, butter-fish, herring, trumpeter, king-fish, and groper. It also has the very singular frost-fish, which is never taken with hook or net, but swims ashore, especially on frosty mornings; and the peculiar deep-sea ribbon-fish, which loses its swimming power and floats as helplessly as a block of wood when it chances to come near the surface.

Such a fishing country is Aotearoa that English and Scottish sportsmen annually go there to catch trout; and the Liberal Government, seeing another opportunity to distinguish itself, became a fishmonger not long before the Conservatives relieved it of its fishing gear. In the thermal wonderland trout commonly weigh from ten to twenty pounds, and they are so plentiful there that on the shores of Lake Taupo and along the Tongariro River Maoris are said to feed them to pigs.

New Zealand is celebrated not only for its fish resources. It is renowned for one of the biggest fish stories the world has ever heard. Unlike others, this tale has not expanded with repetition; apparently it is big enough to satisfy the most extravagant story-teller. Any fisherman who can make such a catch as did the man this story concerns certainly deserves some free advertising; and that is what the Maori demigod, Maui, has been getting ever since, as tradition records, he fished the North Island, "The Fish of Maui," from the sea with the jawbone of his grandfather, or, as some accounts have it, of his grandmother. This is the same stalwart who previously belabored the sun with this same mighty bone, and, by crippling *te ra*, made the days longer.

Had Maui followed his own inclination he would not have become the central figure of a tale which allegorically describes the discovery of a new land. Maui was not fond of fishing, and only relatives' contemptuous references to his idleness caused him to go to sea on this eventful day. Hidden in his mat he carried the jawbone, which he had fashioned into a hook. Seeing no fishing-tackle in his hands, Maui's brethren laughed at him, and asked him how he expected to catch fish without hook and lines.

Unruffled by their sarcasm, Maui continued to urge his brothers to go seaward until they lost sight of land. Then Maui dropped his tackle into the sea, and the jawbone, descending to the ocean's bottom, became fastened in the house of Tonganui, Tangaroa's son. To the accompaniment of cries of terror from his kindred, Maui pulled until "the turbid ocean boils, the mountain-tops are near, and many a whirling vortex roars." Then "Ha! the fish of Maui rises from the waters—a land fish—a spacious country—Papa-tu-a-nuku!"

After the fish was taken, Maui told his brothers to remain behind while he went a short distance to offer a piece of the catch to the gods, at the same time cautioning them against touching the fish until his return. His caution was wasted; as soon as Maui had disappeared the brothers cut and ate portions of the fish. This sacrilege so angered Tangaroa, the Maoris' Neptune, that he caused the fish to leap about until it was badly deformed. It is thus that this legend accounts for the formation of the mountains of the North Island.

Chapter XIX

At Ngaruawahia, once the capital of the Maori kingdom,—a very limited monarchy confined to the Waikato country,—is held once a year a great Maori carnival. Here, at the junction of the Waikato and Waipa Rivers, from ten thousand to twelve thousand natives and Europeans congregate on St. Patrick's Day to see exciting war canoe races, comic canoe hurdles, stirring hakas, and the graceful poi.

From the north and the south, the east and the west, people travel in long excursion trains to witness the chief Maori festivity of its kind. Especially from Auckland, about seventy-five miles distant, thousands of excursionists journey to Ngaruawahia in passenger coaches and goods trucks.

On the day I left Auckland to see the carnival I reached Ngaruawahia about noon. At that hour the banks of the Waikato were thronged by thousands of people and hundreds more swarmed through the town, and nowhere more so than inside and outside the bars of the two hotels. The whole was a moving panorama of colors, ill matched, many of them, but worn none the less proudly for that by their Maori owners.

Heading for the forty side-shows in the grove, I first passed a stand stacked with bottled mussels and smoked schnapper, the latter one of New Zealand's most popular sea-fish. A white hawker was selling these wares to the Maoris, two of whom stood by eating fish with their fingers. Below this was another schnapper stand, also well patronized by natives. Had there been a shark stand in the neighborhood it likewise would have prospered, for Maoris are fond of shark flesh.

Not all the Maoris about stood eating in the highway. Many were dining in roughly furnished tents. Here also was fish in abundance. And here, too, were table manners in great variety. One of the best examples of table etiquette was provided by a Maori man. He was using a knife and fork, but suddenly tiring of them, he put them down, and seizing a potato in his fingers he ate it in true primordial fashion.

Everywhere I went there were Maoris, many of them being men and women of great girth and weighing two or three hundred pounds and upward. Hundreds of both sexes were smoking pipes or cigarettes. It was a happy Maori crowd. Hand in hand, three girls came hurrying across the green. On the same track followed two youths awkwardly leading a big girl between them. Here and there gossipy mothers carried babies papoose fashion, in shawls on their backs; and here grizzled age made merry and flushed with youth again.

All the Maoris, from babies to grandfathers and grandmothers, were well dressed, though not always with good taste. There were yellow dresses and green, red, white, and blue dresses. There were loose-fitting blouses and diffusive skirts, and as it were a reproach to these, close-fitting gowns on young wahines.

"Did you see that Maori woman in a hobble skirt?" a friend asked me.

"No; where is she?" I inquired.

"She just disappeared in the crowd with a bloke," answered he.

Soon after I heard a voice exclaim: "Get off my dress."

The speaker was a big Maori woman, and as she gave this command she struck a white woman, who accidentally had trod on her skirt.

There were ribbons and sashes of all hues; and the premier color of Ireland was not the least of these. Incongruities of dress were common. Although the day was hot, one woman wore an ostrich boa, with a gayly-colored parasol raised above it, and another woman carried a fur muff. Occasionally there was a flash of the truly picturesque,—one, a girl poi dancer wearing a flax mat, another, a warlike man bared to the waist and kilted with flax. With young men colored waistcoats found favor.

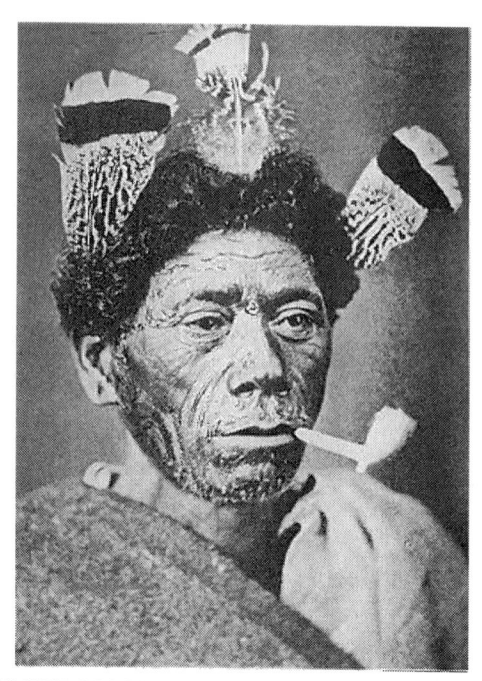

TATTOOED MAORI WITH HUIA FEATHERS IN HAIR

Ornaments were at all places conspicuous, especially large greenstone pendants and greenstone earrings with black ribbons attached. One pendant looked like a papercutter. There also were silver-tipped boar tusks; in large frames photographs of men; cheap, gaudy jewelry; metaled and tinted flower and leaf; and feathers—plumes of the huia, the duck, the pheasant, and the long, slender red tail feather of the amokura. More lasting than all these adornments were the tattooed chins of the women. The decorations of the men also were noticeable, some of the elder ones even wearing earrings; but the women carried enough ornaments to furnish a second- or third-rate jewelry store.

"Let me know as soon as you see a hongi," I said to my friend. "I want to see every kind of hongi there is."

"There they are. Quick! before they've finished," shouted my companion.

"They" were two old Maori women, and they were engaged in the prosaic occupation of rubbing each other's nose. They were squatting on the ground, their hands were clasped, tears rolled down their cheeks, and moans escaped from their slightly moving lips. They had long been separated, and were simply greeting each other in the most approved Maori fashion.

For several minutes this singular greeting lasted, two flat ihus pressing each other all the while. Of the hundreds of people about them these two were apparently unmindful. Finally they arose, and one, immediately grasping the hand of a native man seated near her, started another hongi.

Compared with some nose salutations, the hongi just witnessed was a mild exhibition. One that I saw later between an elderly Maori man and a youth was more energetic. These two fairly howled as they condoled with each other. After a prolonged effort they had an intermission, in which they wiped their tears away. Then they started all over again.

All that day at Ngaruawahia there were hongis, and had we reached the town in the early morning, we should have seen hundreds of such exchanges of affection. At purely Maori meetings there are remarkable nose-rubbing performances. In fact, they are such days for the nose that it is a wonder the rest of the face does not get jealous at this show of esteem. At these huis the hosts, or the inhabitants of the villages where they are held, fall into line after the speeches of welcome and responses, and as the visitors pass by, hosts and guests rub noses. Often one man will rub hundreds of noses in a single day. Necessarily, these fraternal displays are not individually so prolonged as at family reunions or small parties of relations and friends.

A HONGI

There are, I found, several kinds of nose-rubbing, or, rather, preliminaries thereto. After two noses have found a proper setting, perhaps with some skirmishing for position, there is little or no rubbing. Some noses are so expert in their manœuvres that they instantly find a satisfactory resting-place; others, not so experienced, or having only a slight acquaintance with a friendly nose, feel their way or proceed cautiously, like an Indian tracker on a stealthy mission.

Fortunately for the Maori, with few exceptions his nose is flat. Thus it is admirably adapted for hongis, and its owner regards it as the most beautiful nose in the world. All hail, then, to the Maori nose! For it a laurel wreath, a gold medal, or a blue ribbon.

Beyond the nose-rubbing group stretched the tents and booths of the side shows. At the stands we could have bought almost anything from flashy jewelry and alarm clocks to bandanna handkerchiefs and potato-parers. Above one pyramidal booth floated a small American flag. How dignified it looked in that place of noise and jostle!

Here, too, were the "Petrified Lady"; "take-all-comers" wrestlers and boxers; a "professor" wildly proclaiming the "wonders" of a dog show; and, in adjoining tents, a fat man and Darwin's "Missing Link," both from America.

Of course, there were games of chance, and two merry-go-rounds with rumbling music. More than half the passengers on the merry-go-rounds were Maoris. Not all were able to ride the horses. I saw one Maori girl make three unsuccessful attempts to mount a painted steed.

Down by the Waipa stood an old unpainted building which evidently was the headquarters of a watermelon vendor. From it I frequently saw Maoris emerge hugging watermelons. One two-year-old girl, dressed neatly in white, walked about holding half a melon to her breast. She did not care to associate with pakeha children or their parents, and every time one spoke to her, she cried.

It is doubtful if anywhere else in the world there are canoe races superior to those held on the Waikato River, at Mercer and at Ngaruawahia. The canoe contests of Washington and British Columbia are usually exciting enough for anybody, but the crews are limited to about a dozen men. In the long Maori war canoes from thirty to forty men flash paddles as they are urged forward by the rhythmic cries of their captains. In the Society Islands, canoes and crews are about equally large, but I would hesitate to back the Tahitians or Mooreans in a contest with the hardier Maoris.

As is customary, the Ngaruawahia regatta was opened on this day with a canoe parade. The first aquatic event was a canoe hurdle race for men. There were three hurdles, placed several rods apart, and each consisting of a pole raised about a foot above the river. Over these obstacles the contestants had to drive their wakas, and then paddle for a short distance to the winning stake.

Each crew was limited to two men, and as they paddled they sat in the back of their light canoes, thus raising the long bow above the hurdle. As the nose of the canoes glided over the top of the pole the paddlers rushed forward. Those who had selected the psychological moment and were able to maintain their advantages got safely over. Others less fortunate lost their equilibrium or were not active enough, and slid back or were capsized.

When well timed, and movements were not too quick or too slow, the weight of the crews forced the canoes over as smoothly as the passage of logs down a chute. When the calculations were wrong, another start had to be made, and always amidst the laughter and badinage of the multitude. In the first hurdle race the six canoes entered were close at the finish, and but one was capsized.

Following this contest was a mirth-provoking women's hurdle. There were two wahines to each canoe, and at the first pole the canoes pressed each other closely. Pare and Mere, the leaders, wriggled over the hurdle after the other canoes, sliding along the pole, had crowded them to one side and nearly sent them backward. The second crew got over at their second attempt, and found themselves parallel with the pole, with their craft headed shoreward and half full of water. Baling it out, they started again, and reached the barrier with six inches of water in their canoe.

The third crew was fated to be the laughing-stock of the crowded banks. At the first three attempts to get over the first hurdle they were forced back, and on the third failure the forward stroke fell into the river. The fourth effort was as ignoble as its predecessors. The fifth was the worst of all. The canoe capsized, and both women went into the stream. Two canoes manned by native men went to their aid and righted the canoe. Seeing now that they were hopelessly out of the race, the discomfited twain abandoned further trials.

WOMEN'S CANOE HURDLE

The next hurdle was scarcely less amusing. This was an over-and-under hurdle for men, the crews being required to pass under the hurdles and send their canoes over them. One man negotiated the first hurdle successfully, but his opponents were so close together at that point that they piled up in one tangled heap. While they were extricating themselves the first canoe got well away, and won.

There were two war-canoe races, three canoes competing in each. Two of the canoes were eighty feet long, and were advertised to carry thirty-six men. The smallest canoe carried twenty men. The courses were three miles long and both events were handicaps. The first race was the Ngaruawahia Handicap, in which the smallest canoe was given three hundred and fifty yards' start; the Te Waonui a Tane's crew of thirty-two was allowed one hundred and ten yards' start of the Tangitekiwi, the scratch canoe, which carried thirty-six men.

The bows of the canoes were boxed In and when the crews were seated, their gunwales were a very few inches above water. In the centre of the largest canoes stood a feather-bedecked captain, who, from a slightly raised platform, prepared to flourish his arms, to cut the air with his taiaha (sword), and to shout and chant encouragement to the paddlers.

As the canoes started they were followed by a fleet of small steamers and launches loaded to capacity with excursionists. As they moved swiftly down the Waikato, they were hailed by excited Maoris ashore. These vied with the canoe captains in the fervor of their demonstrations,—men, women and children joining in the clamorous chorus.

The large canoes strained hard to overtake the flying Tauanui, yet it was impossible appreciably to diminish the gap. But meanwhile what amazing paddling we witnessed. So rapidly, so rhythmically did the paddles rise and fall that the canoes looked like great marine monsters with long rows of palpitating gills. Through it all the captains balanced themselves on their little elevations, singing and gesticulating. At one moment they were exhorting the forward paddlers; then, turning, they addressed the stalwarts aft. Their bodies swayed in rhythm with the glinting blades; their straining eyes noted every gain and loss, which they emphasized by brandishing taiaha or hand aloft; and as they lunged forward the canoes seemed to respond like trained living creatures.

On the eastern borders of the little-known Urewera country I sought the prophet Rua, the most talked-of Maori of the day. I had heard so many strange stories about him that I resolved to interview him, if possible. Just where I should find him I did not know, but I knew that he could not be more than one or two days' journey into the mountainous regions back of Opotiki, a Bay of Plenty town which Rua often visited. Here, I had heard, he had walked up and down Church Street with a money-box, buying everything he or his wives fancied.

Yes, his wives! For when I saw him he had seven, and no one in Opotiki knew when he would take unto himself another. But most wonderful of all, so exemplary are these seven that they are not jealous of each other! So Rua assured me in a most matter-of-fact way when, after four days of fruitless efforts, I cornered the long-haired predictor.

AT THE FINISH LINE

While, according to Caucasian standards, Rua was morally a bigamist, he was not legally such, having taken his wives according to Maori custom. Doubtless many other Maori women would have been proud to join the prophet's household; but Hurinui Apanui, foremost of living Urewera chiefs, told me Rua would take no more wives. From Hurinui, too, I learned that in his polygamous views Rua was somewhat selfish; his "Follow me" was not all embracing. He would not permit his followers to have more than one wife at a time, although, Hurinui assured me, "he allows them to change their wives when they want to."

I reached Opotiki at an opportune time. The Native Land Court was sitting there adjusting the large transfers of land Rua had made to the State in behalf of his followers. The town was full of Maoris, and on the main streets they were more numerous than Europeans. Half of Urewera appeared to have moved into the town. The hotel bars were thronged with Maoris; they flocked about the shops; and they were scattered about in tents.

The majority of the Maoris were well dressed, though by no means faultlessly. Some of the make-ups were clownish. Many of the women were gorgeous in colors and extravagantly bedecked with greenstone ornaments. Some were barefooted, but a large percentage were shod. Not a few squatted in rows on the sidewalks in front of stores; others walked about and peered into shop windows. Tattooed chins were numerous, and pipes overhung a good number of them. From lobes hung earrings of greenstone decorated with gold and silver, some hanging direct from the ear, others pendent on black ribbons fastened in the ear. One woman had silver-mounted earrings and two gold-mounted brooches.

Among the women were odd inconsistencies of dress. Brilliancy was in close company with sombreness; colors that should have been strangers to each other hobnobbed together on skirt, waist, and hat; slouch hats bordering on the disreputable looked dull beside flaring red or bright green; and flashy neckties were set on gloomy blouses.

Here came one woman with a blue skirt, a red waist, and bright yellow hat trimmings sufficient for at least two hats. Beside her walked a woman carrying a baby on her back in the folds of a big colored shawl, and with a large striped flax kit in one hand. Another woman approached me wearing a boyish-looking green hat, held in place with long brass pins; a red hair-ribbon and a red tie; a brown waist; and black skirt and black shoes, or boots, as they call shoes in New Zealand. The waist had long, flapping lace sleeves, matched in color by the flax kit, or shopping-bag, she carried. She was met by another woman wearing a lavender gown, a big red sash, a red neckcloth, and a straw hat with a liberal amount of white trimming.

Most interesting of all was a row of Rua's wives, brightly arrayed, and occupying the whole width of the walk as they strolled up the street with all eyes on them.

All the native men wore European clothes. Riding habits were common, and a number had feathers in their hat bands. A few followers of Rua had hat-pins thrust through their long hair, and a humpbacked zealot had a back comb. Many men were as incongruous in their attire as the women. There were yellow and orange neckcloths, and green, blue, red and lavender socks over riding-breeches; while garters of various hues encircled thick calves.

Every day for a week there were additions to this exhibition of colors and sartorial absurdities. They entered the town on the gallop. Seeing two wagonloads of men and women dressed in their best driving into Opotiki on the run, I said to my half-caste Maori guide, "Those Maoris drive like Tahitians."

"Oh," replied he with a touch of ennui, "they are just making a show of themselves."

Few of the male visitors failed to patronize a hotel bar soon after reaching the town, but not many were allowed in the other hotel rooms, and as a rule no Maori women. At the hotel where I was staying a Maori man sat down in a wicker chair in the hallway, just as the landlady entered.

"Here, here!" said she, clapping her hands, "these chairs are for the pakeha."

Another Maori man brought in a native woman, and straightway the landlady was upon him.

"You must n't bring her through here," she protested. "You know it is n't allowed."

"All right," grunted the man, and then he passed through despite the order.

At this hotel noisy Maoris were drinking every day, and one of them fought a white man. The Maori is a convivial spirit, and nowhere more so than in a bar. Maoris are always willing to "shout," but after they have treated, some will say, "I shouted for you, now you shout for me."

"Where can I hear Maori singing?" I asked Mokomoko, pilot for a steamship company.

"If you want to get a Maori to sing," he advised, "give him a beer."

Of all these thirsty natives the most frequent visitor to Opotiki's "pubs" was Tamaikoha, an aged ex-cannibal. With pipe in mouth, this wrinkled Polynesian shuffled into the commercial room of the hotel one Sunday. Halting at the door, he looked appealingly at the inmates and passed a forefinger across his throat. Did he mean to convey by pantomime that he intended to commit suicide? No; he was thirsty! and the bar was closed.

"That man is more than ninety years old," said an Opotiki merchant present, "and he has eaten pakeha."

Tamaikoha was not ashamed to acknowledge that he was once a cannibal, and he even joked about that fact. "You are no good for me," said he to a solicitor. "You are too thin and yellow."

When in Opotiki the old man divided his time between two public-houses. To one he always went early in the morning, and I often saw him crouching on the walk outside. Later he would appear at the hotel where I lodged, and frequently squat on the floor before the bar. There I saw him finishing a haka one morning, a sure evidence that he had been given or promised a "beer."

Tamaikoha was a ludicrous mixture of the solemn and the comic. He was never too solemn to become comical, nor too comical to lapse quickly into solemnity. He was a walking caricature. He wore a round slouch hat that meagrely shaded a stubby white beard and side whiskers. Over summer trousers that looked as if they had been thrashed about in a greasy dust heap, and an unbuttoned vest with a liberal exposure of neck above it, he wore a dull-colored overcoat. He was barefooted, and walked slowly, usually with hands behind back; which, with bowed head, clothed him with a judicial, studious air.

I had not been long in Opotiki until I heard of Rua. He had taken a cottage, and four of his wives occupied it with him. He was the busiest man in town. More than a hundred thousand dollars had passed through his hands a short time before, and many thousands more were soon to be paid to him. He had proved himself to be more successful as business agent for the Urewera tribe than as its prophet, and he was regarded by his supporters and clients as a great man. In the Bay of Plenty district he was in truth the man of the hour. Cognizant as he was of his power and prestige, would he be pliable in the hands of one who had come to ask him meddlesome questions? This appeared so doubtful that, to influence Rua, I had solicited an introduction to him from the Native Minister.

Before I called on Rua, I heard astonishing tales about him. I learned that a few years ago he was an obscure laborer, who later professed healing virtues, and cured many Maoris of their ills. Puffed with success, he proclaimed himself a second Christ, and even imagined he had a facial resemblance to the Saviour. Turning to prophecy, he gathered a large following, who believed in him implicitly.

As an instance of his influence, Rua announced that on a certain day he would walk on the river at Whakatane. A great crowd collected to see him. Standing before it, Rua asked:—

"Do you believe I can walk on the water?"

"Yes," shouted a number of natives.

"Well," said Rua, "so long as you believe I can do it, that is all that is necessary."

Rua's predictions were remarkable, but not more so than the blind trust placed in them by his adherents. For a certain date he prophesied an earthquake. Luckily for him there was a shock in the South Island that day. It was far from where it had been promised, but Rua's face wore an I-told-you-so expression despite the miscarriage, and he received wide and loud acclaim from the Maoris.

At another time Rua said that the late King Edward VII was coming to Gisborne to visit him on an appointed day. In this brazen prophecy such trust was placed that a number of natives bet heavily with whites that the King would come. One Maori bet a buggy and two draft-horses against $250;

another native put one horse against $125. When the King did not appear the first Maori wanted his horses back, and even tried to steal them, the winner told me.

RUA AND FOUR OF HIS WIVES

As usual, Rua had an excuse when the monarch failed to arrive. The King was too sick, he explained; later he blamed Halley's comet for the non-arrival; and when the King died, some Maoris declared he had been caught up in the comet's tail!

A prediction that had more effect was that respecting a tidal wave seventy-five feet high, which was to invade the Bay of Plenty. Rua, I was informed by Hurinui Apanui, advised the Maoris of that locality to sell all their possessions before the wave arrived, and many did so. When the natives decided to sell their lands to the State, Rua dreamed, and foresaw for himself wealth and great honor. Beside the picture he drew prophecy was tame. So, acting as his people's agent, he sold thousands of acres of land. With the receipts therefrom in hand the unique village he had established in the far interior lost its magnetic interest, and with many of its inhabitants the seer moved fifty miles nearer civilization and founded Waimana, which, unlike Maungapohatu, could be reached by carriage.

When he first emerged from obscurity, "Rua did not like to be stared at; now he doesn't mind," one who knew him told me. "But if you go to his settlement," this man warned me, "don't stare too long at his wives. Rua is very jealous."

The arrival of the Native Minister's letter of introduction was delayed, and tiring of waiting for it, I determined to face Rua without it.

"How shall I know Rua when I meet him?" I asked a man at the hotel.

"Oh, you will know him easy enough," he replied. "He is wearing red socks."

So out I went to look for a pair of flaming socks. It was not long before I saw a pair sticking out of two brown shoes, and as they were the only red socks on the street, I decided that they were Rua's. The man above these socks was large. He wore riding-breeches, a blue, unbuttoned coat, a colored shirt, and a blue tie. Above his bushy face was a soft straw hat with a white-headed pin stuck through it. This was Rua with his hair "done up," and he was standing on a corner of the main street, talking with Maoris.

I did not know whether he could speak English or not, for my informers were disagreed on this point; therefore I approached him cautiously, and inquired of a Maori more civilized-looking than the others.

"Yes, Rua speaks little English, not very well," he answered me.

I told him what I wanted, and he explained it to the prophet. In reply, Rua said he would meet me at that corner at five o'clock that day. I thought then that I should have no difficulty in persuading him to talk. But I did not know Rua.

At five I was at the corner, but Rua was not there. "Just like a Polynesian," I concluded, thinking of appointments with Tahitians the year before. Presently I spied the red socks at the other end of the street, and with them was a red hair-ribbon. It was Rua with one of his wives—she displaying a long gold chain necklace—walking leisurely up the thoroughfare. At my corner they sauntered into a store.

Apparently the prophet had not seen me, and presuming that the two wished to shop there, I resolved to let them do so before reminding Rua of his appointment. Fifteen minutes' waiting made me impatient and suspicious, and I entered the store to find him doing nothing, so far as I could see.

When Rua saw me, he raised his eyes and asked the storekeeper, who for the moment acted as my interpreter, what I wanted. On this being explained to him, the prophet replied that he was too busy to see me unless I had business to transact with him. There were many land titles to be adjusted, said he, and he could not spare me any of his time unless money were involved. This was discouraging, but there was more to come, and it came bluntly. It was: "What you want is nothing." And this cruel thrust from one claiming resemblance to the Great Teacher!

I had been told that the man had a certain Jewish cast of countenance. If he ever had had such a cast, he certainly had lost a lot of it before I saw him. To me he was just plain Polynesian, with a broad face and a broad, flat nose.

I knew he could afford to give me the time I wanted if he chose to do so, and I declined to cease my importunities. It was then or never. As I continued arguing my case, Rua rose, and throwing out his hands in true oratorical fashion, addressed the storekeeper. He wore a shrewd look, and he had the air of the most independent of men. Probably he regarded my request for a claim on his hours as rash and unwarranted. At first he seemed amused by it, but at last he agreed to meet me two days later, on Sunday afternoon, provided it rained; otherwise he would go to Waimana. If he went to Waimana he would meet me Monday night.

It did not rain, and at six o'clock Monday evening he promised my interpreter to see me at this corner store at eight that same evening. At that hour there was no sign of him, nor half an hour later. By that time it was not hard to conclude that the prophet was long on promises, but short on their fulfillment. Why had he evaded me again? I put this question to a merchant the next day.

"Oh," he explained, "he may have got into an argument with a lot of natives, and forgot. There he is now, in that hotel, having a discussion."

After this failure of Rua to keep his appointment, I almost despaired of interviewing the wily exhorter. Fortunately the next day's mail brought the Native Minister's introductory letter, and with it I prepared for the final attack. Getting a good interpreter, I started for Rua's cottage. In turning off Church Street, I saw him coming round a corner in his shirt-sleeves. He was aflame with a red tie, red suspenders, and red socks, moderated by a bright pink sash.

Giving him the Minister's letter, I explained that I had heard so many conflicting stories about him that I desired to hear his own account of himself. Rua did not so much as open the letter; it was quite enough that it was from the Native Minister. Becoming talkative, he assured me that he was willing to tell me anything I wished to know about himself, his people, and his plans. Yes, he would go with me to my hotel.

En route he stopped several times to speak with Maoris; and just before reaching the hotel he hailed a white man passing on a horse, and from a roll of bank bills which he drew from his pocket as he walked, he gave one note to the horseman. In spite of these interruptions, however, I eventually got him to my room. He was warm, and taking out a long pin, he removed his hat. To my astonishment, a big back comb was in his hair. It looked like part of an encircling crown.

With hands on his knees, Rua informed me that he would start at the beginning to give his history. "No use to start from the limbs of a tree and work down," said he emphatically. "I will start at the roots." The metaphorical tree proved to have tremendous roots; it could n't have been anything less than a *Sequoia gigantea*. Details were one of his specialties, and he all but went back to the days of Adam for some of them. He certainly submitted a good case for himself, and possibly he imagined I believed everything he told me.

"I was born," he began, "in 1868. At twelve years of age I began to ponder on the questions of life. I thought on the Maoris' future, and dwelt on their past. I saw that to do right man must live right; but though I thought much, I was not bold to speak my opinions, fearing the elders among my people would say, 'He is too young for that.'

"In 1906 I could see clearly. God's power came to me, and people who knew me as a boy recalled the sayings of my youth. Then these said, 'Rua talked sense in those days.' I saw there were two laws in the world—one, God's, the other, man's; the law that came from the Spirit, and the law that comes from man's mind. But it is God's law that should direct man. I talked to my people about this. I told them I was not taught in any school, but that my knowledge and inspiration came from God. God was my teacher. God's schooling is everything. He is in all knowledge.

"In 1908 I saw all the faults of the Maoris, and I had more of God's power in me then than in 1906. I was not afraid to say anything to anybody. I saw that the natives were dying out, because they were not using themselves rightly. I believed they should do something to improve their condition.

"I studied the land question. I saw there was little money in New Zealand, and that because of this the country was all the time borrowing. The reason was partly the tying up of so much land. Nobody was working it. If it were opened up for the pakeha, more money would come into the country. So I told the Maoris to sell some of their lands, but not for less than one pound an acre. My people have sold much land to the Government, and they will sell more."

I asked Rua if all the land-sale receipts were paid into his hands.

"No; every man gets his share," replied he. "I get my share and the other Maoris get their shares."

"Do you get a commission?" I suggested.

"No; all I have I earned working for the pakeha, and from my land. I have much land yet, also many cattle."

Detailing his plans for building a village at Waimana, Rua said he would spend $15,000 there in improvements. All this talk about possessions and town building was well enough for commercial history, but I wanted to know what the man's claims as a prophet were.

"There have been many prophets," he reminded me. "I am a general prophet. I know something of everything."

Could it be that Solomon reincarnated was before me! "Do you claim to be a second Christ, Rua?"

"Yes," he instantly assured me.

"Do you maintain that you have the same powers as Christ? Can you heal the sick?"

At the moment I asked these questions there came a knock at the door. A merchant with whom the prophet dealt extensively entered, and told him he was wanted at the wharf, at once. Freight had arrived, and only he knew where to store it. Rua left me with a promise to see me again at seven o'clock that evening, in the back room of that merchant's store.

Shortly after that hour he sauntered past the appointed place, with a wife on each side of him. One wore a sky-blue skirt and a black waist, the other had a pink gown with lace trimmings. Each woman had a gold chain necklace and enormous greenstone ornaments. Their husband seemed to have forgotten me, but at the hail of my interpreter he entered the store and resumed the interview.

Answering my last question, he said he was Christ's successor. I asked for his authority. That started him in earnest. Straightway he made for the roots of his figurative tree, and as he burrowed he waved his hands, pointed with fingers, and thumped his knees. There was no pause in his speech, and he proved to be a master of circumlocution.

I had told the interpreter it would not take me long to complete the interview, but I was not then acquainted with the Maori way of replying to questions. The Maoris are strong on genealogical history, and when opportunity is offered they delight to beat the entire range of their intellect in quest of material, which, when found, is instantly seized, whether closely or remotely related to the issue involved.

Rua was like the rest of his race. With his wives sitting near him he expounded the Scriptures like an old-time revivalist, with himself as the central figure. He talked until he perspired, yet he seemed to be getting farther from the end every minute. Like the Irish seaman's rope, the end appeared to be cut off. It was too much.

"Stop him!" I commanded the interpreter. "We shall be here all night if he is going to continue like this. Won't he answer 'yes' or 'no'?"

"No," replied he. "Rua wants to go far back to give you a good explanation of everything leading up to your questions."

I threw a switch to sidetrack the prophet, for I was feeling musty under this sprinkling of the dusty past. Did he have any rules of moral conduct for his followers? Only advisory, he told me. He had advised the Maoris neither to drink nor smoke, because such indulgence tended to decrease their numbers, but they had not accepted his counsel. Any other result, however, could scarcely have been expected,—at least with regard to drinking intoxicants,—for, I was informed, Rua could at that time "take a long beer with anybody."

As I had heard conflicting stories regarding the number of Rua's wives, I asked him for census returns. "Seven," came his reply. "And none of them is jealous."

I took a deep breath, gripped my chair, and stared at him. Wonderful man! I asked for the formula. It was brief: "My power keeps them from being jealous of each other."

Was not this the first instance of the kind the world had ever known? I asked this model bigamist. No, he modestly disclaimed, there was one other man equally distinguished. He also had seven unjealous wives, and he was an Old Testament prophet named Rameka. That was a Maori name for this seer, so I demanded an English translation. This was about the only point on which Rua apparently was ignorant.

By this time Rua's two wives, who had been acting like bashful children, were so amused by the interview that they could scarcely control their risibility, and fain would have laughed. In truth, the proceedings were equal to a vaudeville sketch.

Rua confidently told me that God approved of his polygamy, but it would be wrong, he maintained, for other men to do likewise.

"It is right for me to have seven wives," declared he, "because the Bible say so. I have more wives than any other man because the law of the Almighty protects me from man's law. Man's law say only one wife. I take more to see if man's law reached me. The law did nothing. God protected me from the Government, and I know he means for me to have seven women."

"Would the Lord allow your followers to have more than one wife?" I finally asked him.

"No," he explained, "because they are not prophets."

To the pakeha Rua would concede nothing. God objected to the white man having more than one wife at a time. When I asked for further particulars, he immediately started on a return to the dawn of history. As it promised to be the dawn of morning before he reached current events again, I hastily fled to the gaslight glare of my hotel.

The next morning I saw him and one of his wives in a trap, bound for Waimana. Preceding them were two wagonettes of color; in these were his other wives.

Weeks later I learned that Rua had been fined five hundred dollars and costs for sly-grog selling in Waimana. As he pulled out a roll of notes representing from two thousand to five thousand dollars, he remarked: "I will see the Governor about this." Had Rua been moved to prophecy at that moment, probably he would have forecasted some dreadful calamity—at least an earthquake, or a tidal wave.

To dog the footsteps of the fanatical warrior-prophet Te Kooti forty years before would have been a risky venture. But one morning, with the cunning seer long in spirit land, with peace restored, and with Tom, the half-caste Opotiki constable, at my side, it was quite safe to go where the doughty Hauhau once had trod. We were bound for Waioaka, a former stronghold of Te Kooti's, and now a shiftless-looking spectacle at the base of foothills, seven miles from Opotiki. It was Saturday, the Hauhaus' Sabbath, and we hoped to reach the pa in time for church.

Many years ago, an old Maori told me, Waioaka was the largest of four pas that then stood in the immediate neighborhood, and had three thousand inhabitants. As Maoris are not noted for accuracy in furnishing census returns, that number of inhabitants probably was an exaggeration. Perhaps it included dogs and cattle; for the Maori loves a joke, and census enumerators not infrequently have learned that heads of native households have represented canines and livestock to be human beings, and they have been so entered. At any rate, the settlement's population was now little more than one hundred persons.

There was nothing formidable in Waioaka's appearance as we drew near it. Only low, grass-grown sections of the demolished ramparts remained. There were no ditches to cross, no closely-set tree-trunks to scale, to reach the group of small one-story houses built around the carved house of worship. Still there was a barrier, a sort of mongrel affair. It was a diversified fence, a fence in evolution. Tree-fern trunks tied with supplejack were succeeded by barbed wire, and that by smooth wire; then came a gate; not a carved portal with hostile form above it, but just a common pasture gate. It was opened to us by a Maori boy.

Scarcely anybody was about. "The people must be in church," said I.

"No, I don't think so," replied Tom. "If they were the church door would be open."

Near us stood a group of boys and girls with uncombed hair and loose-fitting clothes. Was it a Sunday-School class? No; these youths and maidens were merely waiting for dinner. As we drove toward the village square, an old man waved his hand to Tom, and came to meet us. He was clad in new overalls, a torn gray coat, and a vest; a cap crowned his head and unlaced shoes protected his feet. He shook hands with us. Following him came a large, barefooted man wearing a dark suit. Both were prominent men of Waioaka. Then we were called upon to shake hands with a woman in black. We accepted their invitation to sit down on the village green, and there told this volunteer entertainment committee why we had come.

Alas! we were too late. Church was dismissed. The benediction or its equivalent had been pronounced at 10.30, and there would not be another service that day until seven, and again on Monday. On Monday!

"Yes, and on every other day of the week, before breakfast and after supper," I was informed.

"But," explained a committeeman, "they don't all go to church every time. If they pray in their own homes, it is all right if they don't attend service. If they don't go to church or don't pray at home, they are not doing right."

A great many pray at home in Hauhau land, and on this day Waioaka could not be excepted. Where were the villagers? There were so few the place was lonely. Some had gone to town.

"But this is their Sunday," I said to Tom.

"Well," explained he, "they like to see what's going on in Opotiki. Even Mary Hira, the chief woman of Waioaka, has gone to town to-day."

We were late for church services, but could we not do the next best thing, and see the church's interior? Yes, said the man in overalls, as he turned to lead the way to the wharepuni, which stood inside a fenced area, and had a flower garden in front. At one corner hung a little bell. The building was old, with the exception of the roof, the outside carvings being decayed with age and dull with faded paint. Outside the inclosure was a meeting house of more modern appearance. Indeed, it was so modern that the carved figure at the front gable peak looked more like a Beau Brummel than a Maori warrior, although a mere held in one hand indicated warlike propensities.

Passing under two long gable boards bearing carved representations of three noted Maori ancestors coming to New Zealand astride a great fish, our village guide opened a large wooden sliding window and threw back the heavy sliding door. Just prior to this Tom warned me, "You must not take food, pipe, or matches into this house. To do so would be a desecration."

Suiting action to words, he placed his pipe and matches on the ground outside.

The wharepuni's interior was gloomy. It was a good place for solemnity. On the bare floor of the one large room there was not a single bench or chair. All around the room were carved wood panels, thick, and of various widths. Each of them, said my guide, represented a dead great man or woman. I wished to know why some panels were so much wider than others.

"Because," elucidated Tom, "some persons were greater than others."

So, after death, a Maori's greatness was measurable by the width of his memorial panel! Simplicity, like consistency, thou art a jewel! Why should not the memorial tablets of the Caucasian be modeled likewise?

Each panel bore a different design, and between the panels, likewise differing from each other in pattern, were combinations of strips of wood tied to toitoi with narrow strips of flax and the tough creeper kiekie. The wood and flax were dyed red and black, and the kiekie's bleach furnished white.

At the bases of the posts supporting the roof were carved figures. One was an incongruous production, being such a mixture of ancient and modern styles that one would be justified in presuming that the finishing touches were made by a humorous great-grandson of the artist who began it. The head was carved in ancient fashion, the face being elaborately tattooed. The remainder of the figure was painted, showing a black tie, a low black waistcoat, and black trousers and shoes. It looked as if the upper part had come from a Maori battlefield and the lower from a ballroom or a banquet hall of the twentieth century.

As it was with this carved and painted pedestal, so differences distinguish the Hauhaus of to-day from their warring forefathers. The Hauhau faith was established in 1864 at the base of Mount Egmont by the mild-mannered Te Ua. About the same time its believers started a war against the colonials, and for seven years their war-cry of "Father, Good and Gracious," accompanied by right-hand passes and the cry "hau," was heard from Taranaki to the Bay of Plenty. When they marched to battle a sacred party of twelve warriors preceded the army; and when in action bullets were rendered harmless, they professed to believe, by mystic hand and barking "hau." When a warrior fell, loss of faith was given as the cause. Chief of all the Hauhaus was Te Kooti. By his followers he was regarded as a demigod, and by the troopers, who were three years effecting his capture, he was admitted to be an accomplished Artful Dodger.

Not many religious sects, if any, are more tolerant than the Hauhaus of today. Where, for example, has there occurred an instance of one Caucasian religious denomination giving one of its important yearly meetings into the hands of widely differing believers? The Hauhaus have done so. A Mormon missionary told me that he reached a Maori village soon after the Hauhaus had opened an annual conference. He entered the Hauhaus' wharepuni, and as soon as his presence was known the meeting was placed in his hands, and he conducted it two days. As soon as he was gone, the Hauhaus reconvened. After all, was this liberality undisguised politeness, or a disguised desire to get rid of the missionary in a diplomatic way?

TE KOOTI'S HOUSE

Following our inspection of Waioaka's house of worship, Tom and I strolled about the village, entering smoke-stained kitchens, mat-carpeted sleeping-houses, and mouldy sweet potato pits. In the native-built houses warmth seemed to be the main consideration. That is why, looking into a sleeping-house large enough for two or three families, I saw that the interior resembled a smokehouse. The walls and ceiling were as brown as a cured side of bacon, and there was no apparent outlet for smoke excepting through open door and sliding window. When these were closed, the room was a capital place for coughs and inflamed eyes, as was many another Maori house of olden days, when a hole in the roof was commonly a substitute for a chimney. Some of the sleeping-houses of Waioaka contained mattresses, but the majority had only flax and kiekie mats, under which bulrush was sometimes spread.

Excepting one place, we were welcome in all parts of the village. The exception was the little cemetery on the hill. In their graveyards the Maoris do not, as a rule, want white visitors, I was told. Fear of desecration is given as one reason for this attitude; another reason is fear of the theft of ornaments from the bodies. If these are stolen, say superstitious natives, the spirit of one whose body is thus dishonored cannot abide in Heaven.

As we neared the close of our village sight-seeing an odor of cooking was wafted to us. Waioaka was preparing its noonday meal. Most of the cooking was done outdoors, in pots and on heated stones. When the stones were sufficiently heated by the fire built around them all the ashes and unconsumed wood were raked away, whereupon vegetables and meat or fish were placed on the stones, and over all water was poured. The whole was then covered with sacks, and in the smothered steam the food was soon and wholesomely cooked.

Unknown to me, I had been invited to dine while I was inspecting Waioaka. Tom told me about it after we had departed.

"I did n't accept the invitation for you," he laughingly explained. "I said, 'No, we will go home to dine.' They were eating rotten corn. It had a terrible smell. It must have been in water twelve months."

Not often does one hear of a king in the rôle of a real estate agent. In Mahuta, third of Maori kings. New Zealand had such a potentate when I was in the Dominion. When he was not in his royal city of Waahi, beside the broad Waikato River, this king, since dead, was usually at the offices of Messrs. Mahuta and Kaihau, Queen Street, Auckland. About the first intimation Auckland had that there was a king in the ranks of its land and estate agents was a newspaper item detailing the flight of Mahuta's partner from a wrathful wahine, who vigorously scratched and kicked the big Maori Member of Parliament for alleged unfair dealings.

Desiring to see the monarch in his new character, I resolved to call on him. But first I went to the public library to read up on his majesty. I thought I should find all I required in "Who's Who in New Zealand." Diligently I searched between its red covers, but vainly. Other Maoris were recorded in this book of greatness, but of Mahuta, King of all the Waikatos, there was not one word!

I called on Messrs. Mahuta and Kaihau one afternoon. Through an open door I saw a Maori of large size seated in an equally ample leather-bottomed chair. It was Henare Kaihau, for fifteen years a Member of Parliament, so he told me. On the opposite side of his desk was a chair similar to his own, empty. Intuitively I felt that the King was out. He was, and would not return until the following morning. At the appointed hour I was there, but the King was still out.

"Gone home to-day," said Kaihau. "Won't be in till next week,"

That would not do, as I should not then be in Auckland. "I shall have to see Mahuta at his home," I told Kaihau.

"What you want to see him for?" asked he. "I can speak for him. Mahuta leave me to do the business. I am just the same as King. I can answer all your questions."

"Oh, you are the King's prime minister?"

"Just the same."

"What does Mahuta do?" I interrogated.

"He does nothing," came the astonishing reply. "He leave me to do the business here."

"The King is merely a drawing card, then?" I asked; but Kaihau evaded the query, or preferred not to view his association with Mahuta in that light.

"I have the King come here, and Maoris come here and see him. They ask him if they should do this or do that. The

King may be say, 'Yes, do that,' and sends them to me. I do everything."

"How old is Mahuta; Mr. Kaihau?"

"Same age as me."

"How old are you?"

"About fifty-four."

"What is the name of the King's wife?"

"She has two names. You have a pencil? I show you."

Then the M.P. quaintly wrote:—

Nganeko Mahuta

Mara Mahuta

I was not satisfied with the interview, and I told the "prime minister" I intended to visit his royal partner at Waahi. Would I find anyone in the royal household able to speak English? Yes, a woman.

The next day I took train for Huntly, a coal-mining town sixty-five miles south of Auckland, opposite to which the Maori sovereign dwelt. Crossing the Waikato River in a rowboat, and walking up its left bank three quarters of a mile, I reached the outskirts of Mahuta's capital. It looked like a village in a cornfield. Half encircling it were little patches of ripened maize, and high in willow trees that lined the river bank hung bunches of husked yellow corn. Near the corn sweet potatoes grew and pumpkins yellowed.

On a near approach no imposing architecture such as befits the resident city of a king was revealed. In what might well be termed a suburb of the village stood a Mormon church, the only European church in sight. Close at hand were small houses of wood and of wood and tree-fern trunks combined. Some of these huts brushed sides with large galvanized-iron chimneys; all were humble. Within the pa proper a tall, unpainted flagstaff cast a crooked shadow on a long carved meeting-house, which had on the apex of its front gable boards a wooden effigy with protruding tongue. Nearer the road stood a longer one-story building used as an eating-house at large meetings.

I looked for the village gate. I had thought I should find a carved door, perhaps with a wooden Colossus of ferocious mien bestride it. Instead I saw only a barbed-wire fence, which my eyes followed until they encountered a gap, such as one sees on a farm when bars are down. This was the village entrance. There was no barrier of any kind, nor any ornamentation.

Through the gap I saw fern-trunk fencing on one side of the village, and houses partly built of the same material. Most of the houses here were more substantial and respectable-looking than in the outskirts, and nearly all were on the right-hand side of the road, which corresponded to the main street.

As it was noon few of Waahi's inhabitants were astir. Some were squatting on floors eating, others were walking lazily about.

Hailing a Maori, I asked, "Where is Mahuta?"

"Somewhere up there," he answered carelessly.

In that vague precinct I paused at a picket fence surrounding a European cottage of more pretentious appearance than any other dwelling of the village. Under an awning raised on the front lawn a group of natives lay on mats and shawls. All were women excepting one, a contented-looking man. I surmised that I stood before Mahuta's "palace," and that this man was the King.

I made inquiry, but smiles of the "don't-understand" sort were the only responses. Where was that English-speaking woman Kaihau had told me I should find? I needed her badly now. Perhaps she was in that smiling group. At my query the man slightly inclined his head, but not enough to convince me that he intended to convey a meaning.

Feeling that I was leaving the King behind me, but determined to skirmish through the entire village in my quest, I continued up the "street." A youth vouchsafed me, "There his house," pointing to a small house adjoining the one I had just left. "He is not here," he added; "he is in Auckland."

"I was told he is here," I rejoined; and believing, from what Kaihau had told me, that the King had a native house, I asked the lad to point it out.

"Big house over there," said he.

"KING" MAHUTA

The big house proved to be the meeting-house behind the crooked flagstaff. I now wondered if I were not being trifled with, Baffled and puzzled, and thinking the journey possibly would be fruitless, I was retracing my steps, when I saw a smiling man approaching me. He was well built and of medium size. His gray hair was closely cut, and he wore only a shirt, open at the throat, a black neckcloth, and a shawl, which served as a kilt. He was smoking a pipe. One hand held the shawl, the other was given me in greeting. I was in the strong grasp of the Waikato King, but it was a hospitable grasp.

I handed Mahuta a letter of introduction from the Native Minister, and he was nearly five minutes reading the two paragraphs, though they were typewritten in his own tongue. Supplementing it, I tried to engage Mahuta in conversation, and it was then I learned I had selected an unfortunate time for my visit.

"I have no time to-day," said the King. "My missus is sick. You see Kaihau in Auckland. He speak for me. What he say all right."

This was not encouraging, but finding that the King could speak more English than I had supposed, I did not want to leave him long enough to get an interpreter, fearing that if I did I should not get near him again. Telling him I had seen Kaihau, I asked, "How do you like the real estate business?"

His Majesty did not evade the question. It was plain he was not dodging the issue when he replied: "Me don't like it. Me rather be in Waahi. In Auckland too much tired. Too much walk around. Me like bed."

O ingenuous king!

Mahuta, I learned, was a popular ruler. "Do many people come to see you?" I asked him. Throwing up his hands, he replied: "Yes, many people. Sometimes big meetings in Waahi. Then all houses full and tents all around. Two thousand hundred men come."

As the King and I conversed, we were standing near a large fern-trunk building. To the immediate right was the village bell, hanging in a dead forked tree and overhung in turn by a cluster of corn. Toward this building the King moved, saying "Come have tea." Stepping across the threshold, we entered a large smoke-blackened room with a rough earth floor. In the centre a fire burned, and around it was a collection of pots and kettles. We were in the royal kitchen.

Four or five native women were present, some of whom were smoking pipes, and I observed a boy five or six years of age wearing only an undershirt. First giving the women some orders, Mahuta motioned me to follow him into a roughly boarded room at the other end of the building. This was the dining-room, furnished with ordinary tables, benches, and chairs. Here Mahuta tendered me an apology. "No meat," said he. Evidently it was not his customary lunch hour.

For his unexpected guest the King poured tea and cut thick slices of bread. Although Mahuta was reputed to be partial to strong drink, he was in a temperate mood this day. For him, as with Count Fosco on a plotting night, it was "the cold water with pleasure, a spoon, and the basin of sugar." He drank but one cup of cold, sweetened water. At the table Mahuta told me that one of his sons was a lawyer in Auckland, and his eager words and sparkling eyes proved that he was proud of his tama's achievement.

Rising at the close of the lunch, Mahuta, saying something I did not hear, crossed the road to the house that had been pointed out to me as his own. As the King mounted the steps several Maori youths were sitting on the veranda. These at once respectfully walked away. Through a window I saw my host searching a room. Presently he returned, holding an object in his hand. It was a piece of greenstone for me, a specimen that caused my ruddy, take-life-easy ferryman to ask, "What's your line?" when he saw the gift.

"Good-bye," said Mahuta, as he held out his hand to me. At the gate of his son's home he echoed my "Kia ora," and, trudging very slowly, went in to see his sick "missus."